STAYING

new poems for *Staying Alive*

'I love *Staying Alive* and keep going back to it. *Being Alive* is just as vivid, strongly present and equally beautifully organised. But this new book feels even more alive – I think it has a heartbeat, or maybe that's my own thrum humming along with the music of these poets. Sitting alone in a room with these poems is to be assured that you are not alone, you are not crazy (or if you are, you're not the only one who thinks this way!) I run home to this book to argue with it, find solace in it, to locate myself in the world again' – MERYL STREEP

RESPONSES TO *STAYING ALIVE*:

'*Staying Alive* is a magnificent anthology. The last time I was so excited, engaged and enthralled by a collection of poems was when I first encountered *The Rattle Bag*. I can't think of any other anthology that casts its net so widely, or one that has introduced me to so many vivid and memorable poems' – PHILIP PULLMAN

'Usually if you say a book is "inspirational" that means it's New Agey and soft at the center. This astonishingly rich anthology, by contrast, shows that what is edgy, authentic and provocative can also awaken the spirit and make its readers quick with consciousness. In these pages I discovered many new writers, and I've decided I'm now in love with our troublesome epoch if it can produce poems of such genius' – EDMUND WHITE

'A vibrant, brilliantly diverse anthology of poems to delight the mind, heart and soul. A book for people who know they love poetry, and for people who think they don't' – HELEN DUNMORE

'*Staying Alive* is a wonderful testament to Neil Astley's lifetime in poetry, and to the range and courage of his taste. It's also, of course, a testament to poetry itself: to its powers to engross and move us, to its ability to challenge and brace us, and to its exultation. Everyone who cares about poetry should own this book' – ANDREW MOTION

'This is a book to make you fall in love with poetry…Go out and buy it for everyone you love' – CHRISTINA PATTERSON, *Independent*

'I don't often read poetry, so *Staying Alive* was a revelation' – IAN RANKIN, *Sunday Telegraph (Books of the Year)*

NEIL ASTLEY is editor of Bloodaxe Books which he founded in 1978. His books include many anthologies, most notably those in the *Staying Alive* series: *Staying Alive* (2002), *Being Alive* (2004), *Being Human* (2011) and *Staying Human* (2020), along with three collaborations with Pamela Robertson-Pearce, *Soul Food* and the DVD-books *In Person: 30 Poets* and *In Person: World Poets*. He received an Eric Gregory Award for his poetry, and has published two poetry collections, *Darwin Survivor* and *Biting My Tongue*, as well as two novels, *The End of My Tether* (shortlisted for the Whitbread First Novel Award), and *The Sheep Who Changed the World*.

CONTENTS

2 Ten Zillion Things

3 Innocence and experience

7 Interesting times

8 Roots and routes

9 Empathy and conflict

10 The future?

EDITORIAL NOTE: An ellipsis in square brackets […] in this anthology denotes an editorial cut to the text. An ellipsis without square brackets is part of the original text. American spellings are retained in work by American authors, except for *-ize* suffixes, which are modernised to *-ise*. Punctuation follows Bloodaxe house style (single inverted commas for quotation, double for qualified expressions).

ABBREVIATIONS: SA: *Staying Alive*   BA: *Being Alive*   BH: *Being Human*

INTRODUCTION

Staying Human is the latest addition to Bloodaxe's *Staying Alive* series of world poetry anthologies which have introduced many thousands of new readers to contemporary poetry.

It is both a sequel and companion volume to the earlier books in the series, but the wide and inclusive range of its selections are such that it can be read just as fruitfully on its own. The first anthology, *Staying Alive: real poems for unreal times*, came out in 2002, with an American edition published by Miramax in 2003. It was so popular that I decided to compile a sequel, *Being Alive*, published in 2004. Readers kept asking for a further compilation, and *Being Human* followed in 2011 as the third part of what had then become the *Staying Alive* trilogy. *Essential poems from the Staying Alive trilogy* (2012) was a pocketbook selection of 100 poems with commentaries, a third drawn from each of the three anthologies.

The range of poetry here complements that of the first three anthologies, with sequences of poems relating to the traditional subjects of poetry, such as love, relationships, birth, family, growing up, ageing, illness, loss, mental health and bereavement, as well as our relationship with time and nature, and the challenges of living in our own times. There are sections covering all of these themes, but also amplified here to highlight areas not commonly represented in anthologies of this kind. Thus the 'Innocence and experience' section includes not just the joy of having children but also the trauma experienced by many over child loss; poems about growing up and family include painful accounts of difficult areas such as sexual, physical and psychological abuse. On the positive side, poems about love in the 'Harmony and discord' section include affirmations of love in old age, while love, music and art come together in many of the poems in that section and elsewhere in the book. 'Interesting times' has poems on how our lives have been massively changed over the past thirty years.

There's a strong focus on the human side of living in the 21st century in poems from the past two decades relating to home and migration, political oppression and the permeation of racism into everyday life. Many of these poems are by British and American poets from diverse backgrounds first published since 2000.

There are also poems by 20th-century poets whose work been especially influential for new generations of poets, continuing to resonate with today's readers, none more so than America's Frank O'Hara, the quintessential poet of living life to the full – living for the moment – who has his own section in the anthology. 'After Frank O'Hara' includes poems by later writers extending conversations O'Hara started over 50 years ago in his *Lunch Poems* (1964). Conversations between poets from past and present have continued throughout the literary tradition, most notably in the Renaissance period when English and European poets engaged with Greek and Roman poets through translation, imitation and recapitulation.

This is something I have tried to reflect in all the anthologies in this series, pairing poems by different writers which address each other either directly or by picking up a theme or phrase, as composers do in music, and "orchestrating" the selections in such a way as to bring these conversations alive for the reader, so that poems will seem to talk to one another, with themes picked up and developed across a whole series of poems, and not just by writers known to one another. Each poem has its own voice while at the same time speaking from a broad chorus of poems with shared concerns. In this way *Staying Human* serves, I hope, as a vocal testament to both the individual and the universal power and relevance of contemporary poetry.

When I started working on *Staying Human*, the major challenges of our time were political polarisation, populism, war, terrorism, racial violence, civil unrest, and the global threat to the environment. The coronavirus pandemic of 2020 has led to a complete re-set in everyone's priorities, with many people turning to literature, poetry in particular, to help make sense of our changed world in human terms. This upturned world is something I felt I had to respond in this book, despite it being ready to go to press. So at a very late stage I took the decision to extend 'The future?' – the book's final section relating to the environmental crisis – to add a selection of powerfully evocative poems written during the first three months of 2020 about our shared, worldwide experience of the pandemic, which I'm convinced will resonate with readers for years to come.

NEIL ASTLEY

1
Staying human

Whose life? you asked
And I answered
my life, and yours
There are no other lives [...]
There's nothing but
you, and you [...]

GÖRAN SONNEVI

GÖRAN SONNEVI's poem 'Whose life? you asked...' (23) shows how 'language is
the life we lead together', according to his translator Rika Lesser: 'Throughout
the Swedish original, the "you" is *du*, singular and familiar; the mode of
address is therefore individual and intimate. In my experience, Sonnevi's
poems simultaneously go straight to one's heart and head. What Sonnevi tells
us in this poem, and in many others, is that a large part of what it means to
be "human" is to participate in each other's lives, and this necessarily begins
in dialogue.'

The opening poems in this selection – by Göran Sonnevi (23) and Tom
Leonard (22) – set up this anthology's key themes. They ask us to examine
who we are and how we relate to each other as human beings. In a number
of the poems the mirror or self-portrait becomes a metaphor for questioning
the self and asserting our sense of identity, embracing both our individuality
and our care and responsibility to others. Many show the need for community
not conformity, for diversity not isolationism, asserting that only by trying to
lead a full life connected with others and kind to each other can we truly know
our common humanity. This involves celebrating what Louis MacNeice called
'the drunkenness of things being various' in his poem 'Snow' (SA 74), the kind
of variety which acknowledges men and women alike, pluralism and imperfec-
tion. In another poem, 'Entirely' (SA 60), written over half a century ago when
the threat was from fascism or communism, MacNeice opposes the fundament-
alist view of the world as 'black or white entirely', seeing life as 'a mad weir of
tigerish waters / A prism of delight and pain'. The poems of *Staying Human*
are reflections of that prism in all its multicoloured glory.

Being a Human Being
(for Mordechai Vanunu)

not to be complicit
not to accept everyone else is silent it must be alright

not to keep one's mouth shut to hold onto one's job
not to accept public language as cover and decoy

not to put friends and family before the rest of the world
not to say I am wrong when you know the government is wrong

not to be just a bought behaviour pattern
to accept the moment and fact of choice

I am a human being
and I exist

a human being
and a citizen of the world

responsible to that world
– and responsible for that world

TOM LEONARD

'Here I am, I do my bit...'

Here I am, I do my bit,
though I don't know what that may be.
If I did I could at least let go of it
and free of it be free of being me.

PATRIZIA CAVALLI
translated from the Italian by Gina Alhadeff

'Whose life? you asked'

Whose life? you asked
And I answered
my life, and yours
There are no other lives
But aren't all people
different?
There's nothing
but difference
It makes no difference!
People live in different conditions:
internal, external
I can hold no one
in contempt, for then
you have the instrument
What about those
who don't want to change their conditions,
those who believe
change
is impossible?
It makes no difference
There's nothing but
you, and you
Only when you become explicit,
when you
question me, and I
answer, when there's
an exchange   Only then is there language
only then are we human
And this doesn't happen
very often?
No, most everything
remains difference, without seeing
the difference
Will we talk again some time?
Yes

Do you believe change is possible?
Yes, that too

GÖRAN SONNEVI
translated from the Swedish by Rika Lesser

They Spoke to Me of People, and of Humanity

They spoke to me of people, and of humanity.
But I've never seen people, or humanity.
I've seen various people, astonishingly dissimilar,
Each separated from the next by an unpeopled space.

FERNANDO PESSOA
translated from the Portuguese by Richard Zenith

Bonsai Master

The trick is not to neglect it just enough
but to deny it just enough.
Decades of managing the stresses
of survival – the exacting balance
of staying alive but only just;
the importance of suffering
to the sublime, against
the inevitable grounds for remorse.

JOHN BARR

A Litany for Survival

For those of us who live at the shoreline
standing upon the constant edges of decision
crucial and alone
for those of us who cannot indulge
the passing dreams of choice
who love in doorways coming and going
in the hours between dawns
looking inward and outward
at once before and after
seeking a now that can breed
futures
like bread in our children's mouths
so their dreams will not reflect
the death of ours;

For those of us
who were imprinted with fear
like a faint line in the center of our foreheads
learning to be afraid with our mother's milk
for by this weapon
this illusion of some safety to be found
the heavy-footed hoped to silence us
For all of us
this instant and this triumph
We were never meant to survive.

And when the sun rises we are afraid
it might not remain
when the sun sets we are afraid
it might not rise in the morning
when our stomachs are full we are afraid
of indigestion
when our stomachs are empty we are afraid
we may never eat again
when we are loved we are afraid
love will vanish

when we are alone we are afraid
love will never return
and when we speak we are afraid
our words will not be heard
nor welcomed
but when we are silent
we are still afraid.

So it is better to speak
remembering
we were never meant to survive.

AUDRE LORDE

Samurai Song

When I had no roof I made
Audacity my roof. When I had
No supper my eyes dined.

When I had no eyes I listened.
When I had no ears I thought.
When I had no thought I waited.

When I had no father I made
Care my father. When I had
No mother I embraced order.

When I had no friend I made
Quiet my friend. When I had no
Enemy I opposed my body.

When I had no temple I made
My voice my temple. I have
No priest, my tongue is my choir.

When I have no means fortune
Is my means. When I have
Nothing, death will be my fortune.

Need is my tactic, detachment
Is my strategy. When I had
No lover I courted my sleep.

ROBERT PINSKY

You Fixed It

And if the compass broke you fixed it, fastened
the pencil to it with a rubber band,
and if there was no hot water you fixed it, learnt
to sit on that plastic stool in the bathroom
and count, and if it was too cold outside
you fixed it, and there was the smell of burnt
lemon on the brazier, or the *click*
click click of the gas heater.
And if you were bored you fixed it, learnt how to cut
paper and color the scraps, learned to write
on the walls, and if you wrote on the walls you
fixed it, scrubbed them with your mom who yelled
at your big brother who what on earth
was he doing just watching? And if the TV blurred
you fixed it, adjusted the antenna to catch
those Japanese cartoons translated into Arabic
on the Syrian channel, and if the cartoons
hadn't begun you fixed it, danced
to those nationalistic Syrian songs about Hafiz, repeated
ya hala ya hala ya hala heh. And if you didn't have enough
books you fixed it, read that French-Arabic dictionary the size
of your torso, stared at the words *crépuscule* and شفق.
And if you tripped on the missing tile you fixed it,
learnt to count your steps in the dark

27

afternoon without electricity, gauged
how dark it was by whether or not you could see
your thumb, and if you couldn't see your thumb
you fixed it, got the candle from under the sink,
and if the sink was leaking you fixed it, tied
a cloth to the pipe, and if the pipe burst
you fixed it, pressed your palms
against the hole in the wall until
Mom called the grocer to call the butcher to call
the plumber next to him, and if there was a hole
in your sock you fixed it, learnt to fold it
under your big toe. And if your window shattered
you fixed it, taped cardboard to the frame,
and if someone died you fixed it by telling stories
about how crusty their *lahm bi 'ajeen* was,
and if the *lahm bi 'ajeen* was too crusty
you fixed it by dipping it in the tahini,
and if your sorrow hardened you fixed it
by dipping it in sea water, and if your country
hardened, if your country hardened you fixed it
by dipping it in song.

ZEINA HASHEM BECK

Life and Other Terms

I split autumn perennials,
layer rhododendrons for spring,
lashed by winds,
lacking even good bones
against the virtues of age.

With full hands
I pull at heels of rosemary,
lad's love sweet and sad,
bitter rue and yarrow.

Geraniums on the patio
turned out like children to get the sun;
the faint green of old bottles
wait for something to be done with them,

and I see living's a job like any other,
that there are no true and perfect implements
to trim the edges, only working usages, like knives.

JANET FISHER

Excuse Me

At odds from the start – it always was my flipside
Hand that waved the celluloid rattle
And banged my pudding spoon against the plate.

Miss Mullen in Infants spotted the flaw at once
And cheerfully shifted the chalk from left to right,
Over and over. I developed a slight stutter.

Later, in Needlework, Miss MacDonald said no,
It wouldn't do, sewing wrong way round like that.
Her thin sharp scissors nipped every stitch.

Crumpled, smudged, and dotted with pinpricks
Of blood, it took ages to finish, the lap-bag
With my name crawling slowly across the front

And the whipstitched monkey in the corner.
But they finally did it: got me to write and sew
And think like all the rest – or near enough.

It's second nature now, this fake dexterity,
But who's deceived? I stumble, maladroit, undeft,
A non-conformer still – with two left hands.

VINCENZA HOLLAND

A Minor Role

I'm best observed on stage,
Propping a spear, or making endless
Exits and entrances with my servant's patter,
Yes, sir. O no, sir. If I get
These midget moments wrong, the monstrous fabric
Shrinks to unwanted sniggers.

But my heart's in the unobtrusive,
The waiting-room roles: driving to hospitals,
Parking at hospitals. Holding hands under
Veteran magazines; making sense
Of consultants' monologues; asking pointed
Questions politely; checking dosages,
Dates; getting on terms with receptionists;
Sustaining the background music of civility.

At home in the street you may see me
Walking fast in case anyone stops:
O, getting on, getting better my formula
For well-meant intrusiveness.
                                    At home,
Thinking ahead: *Bed? A good idea!*
(Bed solves a lot); answer the phone,
Be wary what I say to it, but grateful always;
Contrive meals for hunger-striker; track down
Whimsical soft-centred happy-all-the-way-through novels;
Find the cat (mysteriously reassuring);
Cancel things; tidy things; pretend all's well,
Admit it's not.

Learn to conjugate all the genres of misery:
Tears, torpor, boredom, lassitude, yearnings
For a simpler illness, like a broken leg.

Enduring ceremonial delays. Being referred
Somewhere else. Consultant's holiday. Saying *Thank you*,
For anything to everyone.
                                    Not the star part.

And who would want it? I jettison the spear,
The servant's try, the terrible drone of Chorus:
Yet to my thinking this act was ill advised
*It would have been better to die.** No, it wouldn't!

I am here to make you believe in life.

U.A. FANTHORPE

* Chorus: from *Oedipus Rex* (trans. E.F. Watling)

Against Hate

Sole passenger on an early morning tram
I'm half asleep when the driver brakes,
dashes past me, dives into a copse of trees,
gone for so long I almost get out to walk.
Then he's back, his face alight,
I saw the wren! explaining
how he feeds her when he can
and her restless, secretive waiting.
We talk of things we love until the station.

I tell him of the Budapest to Moscow train
brought to a halt in the middle of nowhere,
everyone leaning out expecting calamity
but not the engine driver, an old man,
kneeling to gather armfuls of wild lilies,
orchids. He carried them back
as you would a newborn, top-heavy, gangly,
supporting the frail stems in his big, shovel hands.
These are small things, but I pass them on

because today is bloody, inexplicable
and this is my act, to write,
to feel the light against my back.

PIPPA LITTLE

The Woman at the Till

She had a plain, hard face,
a head thrust forward like a hawk's.
Impossible brass triangles
dangled from pierced ears,
improbable steel manacles
cluttered her thin arms.
Clearly, she had little love for the world:
she had learned, though,
that she would not win,
so she did not throw your change at you,
nor did she press it in your palm,
but placed it, sullenly,
on the counter in between.
She would wrap your purchase languidly,
yet fast enough to cut off a complaint,
and when she had her punch-up with the till,
it was an exercise in ferocity,
delicately restrained.
She was what we call 'maboer',
a low white trash,
AWB most probably,
slouching barefoot in Boksburg or Mayfair West.
I did not feel any particular hate for her,
perhaps because I was what
she would call a low black trash,
which made us quits.

And then I noticed that
she did not look at or thank
anyone, black or white,
and such an undiscriminating unsociability
won for her my respect!
But then one day a brazen clash
of colours drew my eyes
from their customary casting down,
the ritual bartering of cash for cloth,
the careful I-do-not-see-you stale pretence –

She had bought herself a brand-new blouse,
a rioting of palms and psychedelic birds,
a raw, extravagant, revolutionary thing,
as African as I.
I exclaimed in wonderment I could not hold in –
'What?' she barked,
looking at my hands.
'I said your blouse is beautiful.'
For the first time ever she looked into
my eyes, and time stood still:
her universe turned on an axis thin as a pin.
Then a strange and lovely tenderness touched her mouth,
a faint blush tinged her dead-white skin:
'Thank you,' she said, and smiled.

TATAMKHULU AFRIKA

AWB: *Afrikaner Weerstandsbeweging*, a South African neo-Nazi separatist political and paramilitary organisation. [Ed.]

The Word That Is a Prayer

One thing you know when you say it:
all over the earth people are saying it with you;
a child blurting it out as the seizures take her,
a woman reciting it on a cot in a hospital.
What if you take a cab through the Tenderloin:
at a street light, a man in a wool cap,
yarn unraveling across his face, knocks at the window;
he says, *Please.*
By the time you hear what he's saying,
the light changes, the cab pulls away,
and you don't go back, though you know
someone just prayed to you the way you pray.
Please: a word so short
it could get lost in the air
as it floats up to God like the feather it is,

knocking and knocking, and finally
falling back to earth as rain,
as pellets of ice, soaking a black branch,
collecting in drains, leaching into the ground,
and you walk in that weather every day.

ELLERY AKERS

Insha'Allah

I don't know when it slipped into my speech
that soft word meaning, 'if God wills it'.
Insha'Allah I will see you next summer.
The baby will come in spring, insha'Allah.
Insha'Allah this year we will have enough rain.

So many plans I've laid have unraveled
easily as braids beneath my mother's quick fingers.

Every language must have a word for this. A word
our grandmothers uttered under their breath
as they pinned the whites, soaked in lemon,
hung them to dry in the sun, or peeled potatoes,
dropping the discarded skins into a bowl.

Our sons will return next month, insha'Allah.
Insha'Allah this war will end, soon. Insha'Allah
the rice will be enough to last through winter.

How lightly we learn to hold hope,
as if it were an animal that could turn around
and bite your hand. And still we carry it
the way a mother would, carefully,
from one day to the next.

DANUSHA LAMÉRIS

Blind man

Each month I walk deftly to the Standard Bank
My ears dazzled by the colours of suburban streets
I speak to anyone who speaks to me
Am patient in the nudging queue
While the teller and computer trade their secrets
I depart unguarded a wealthy man again
A block from home
I hear the bus stop approaching on my right
Where people we call blacks
Are always waiting
As I pass they croon and murmur their concern
An impulse urges me to scatter bank-notes at their feet
But I never do
At the curb a black man takes my arm to help me cross
Can't you see I am a white man
With money in my hand to feed your family?
But he only sees my white cane searching
And the blood colour of my need
We cross the street
And go our separate ways.

DAVID FRIEDLAND

Small Kindnesses

I've been thinking about the way, when you walk
down a crowded aisle, people pull in their legs
to let you by. Or how strangers still say 'bless you'
when someone sneezes, a leftover
from the Bubonic plague. 'Don't die,' we are saying.
And sometimes, when you spill lemons
from your grocery bag, someone else will help you
pick them up. Mostly, we don't want to harm each other.

We want to be handed our cup of coffee hot,
and to say thank you to the person handing it. To smile
at them and for them to smile back. For the waitress
to call us honey when she sets down the bowl of clam chowder,
and for the driver in the red pick-up truck to let us pass.
We have so little of each other, now. So far
from tribe and fire. Only these brief moments of exchange.
What if they are the true dwelling of the holy, these
fleeting temples we make together when we say, 'Here,
have my seat,' 'Go ahead – you first,' 'I like your hat.'

DANUSHA LAMÉRIS

Smiles

These little smiles that fill my eyes with tears
mean nothing really, signals between women
who pass each other on the street as strangers,
as casual friends whose names are now forgotten

or local friends who stop to say hello
at bus stops, coughing little coughs like Lily,
Chinese Lily from Rouge, her shop, but also
English Lily who used to welcome me

by name and I'd respond in rhyme, whose sweet
presence stood at odds with her black Goth gear.
She's gone to art school now and down the street

Bake Street café isn't the same without her.
Why tears though? I don't know – the loneliness
of women's lives, perhaps, that smiles express.

MIMI KHALVATI

The Brag

I am known by sight in the neighbourhood
to shopkeepers, baristas, cab drivers.
There I go, there I come, in likelihood
alone, up and down the road, in all weathers.

I am on smiling terms with hosts of people.
There she blows with her silver hair, they grin,
staking out a beanrow, spouting the Bible.
Roadsweepers chat, guards greet me at the station.

Some call me lady, auntie, mammie – ask me
how I'm doing, endorse me with endearments,
watch my footing for me, rescue my bag.

Caregivers all! Small wonder if I brag
a little, graced with such acknowledgements
and such a large extended family.

MIMI KHALVATI

When Someone Goes Away Everything That's Been Done Comes Back

In the embrace on the corner you will recognise
someone's going away somewhere. It's always so.
I live between two truths
like a neon light trembling in
an empty hall. My heart collects
more and more people, since they're not here anymore.
It's always so. One fourth of our waking hours
are spent in blinking. We forget
things even before we lose them –
the calligraphy notebook, for instance.

Nothing's ever new. The bus
seat is always warm.
Last words are carried over
like oblique buckets to an ordinary summer fire.
The same will happen all over again tomorrow –
the face, before it vanishes from the photo,
will lose the wrinkles. When someone goes away
everything that's been done comes back.

NIKOLA MADZIROV

*translated from the Macedonian by Peggy Reid, Graham W. Reid,
Magdalena Horvat and Adam Reed*

Gate C22

At gate C22 in the Portland airport
a man in a broad-band leather hat kissed
a woman arriving from Orange County.
They kissed and kissed and kissed. Long after
the other passengers clicked the handles of their carry-ons
and wheeled briskly toward short-term parking,
the couple stood there, arms wrapped around each other
like he'd just staggered off the boat at Ellis Island,
like she'd been released at last from ICU, snapped
out of a coma, survived bone cancer, made it down
from Annapurna in only the clothes she was wearing.

Neither of them was young. His beard was gray.
She carried a few extra pounds you could imagine
her saying she had to lose. But they kissed lavish
kisses like the ocean in the early morning,
the way it gathers and swells, sucking
each rock under, swallowing it
again and again. We were all watching –
passengers waiting for the delayed flight
to San Jose, the stewardesses, the pilots,

the aproned woman icing Cinnabons, the man selling
sunglasses. We couldn't look away. We could
taste the kisses crushed in our mouths.

But the best part was his face. When he drew back
and looked at her, his smile soft with wonder, almost
as though he were a mother still open from giving birth,
as your mother must have looked at you, no matter
what happened after – if she beat you or left you or
you're lonely now – you once lay there, the vernix
not yet wiped off, and someone gazed at you
as if you were the first sunrise seen from the Earth.
The whole wing of the airport hushed,
all of us trying to slip into that woman's middle-aged body,
her plaid Bermuda shorts, sleeveless blouse, glasses,
little gold hoop earrings, tilting our heads up.

ELLEN BASS

Gate A-4

Wandering around the Albuquerque Airport Terminal, after learn-
ing my flight had been detained four hours, I heard an announce-
ment: 'If anyone in the vicinity of Gate A-4 understands any Arabic,
please come to the gate immediately.' Well – one pauses these days.
Gate A-4 was my own gate. I went there.

An older woman in full traditional Palestinian embroidered dress,
just like my grandma wore, was crumpled to the floor, wailing
loudly. 'Help,' said the Flight Agent. 'Talk to her. What is her
problem? We told her the flight was going to be late and she did
this.' I stooped to put my arm around the woman and spoke
haltingly. *'Shu dow-a, Shu-bid-uck Habibti? Stani schway, Min
fadlick, Shu-bit-se-wee?'* The minute she heard any words she
knew, however poorly used, she stopped crying. She thought the

flight had been cancelled entirely. She needed to be in El Paso for major medical treatment the next day. I said, 'You're fine, you'll get there, who's picking you up? Let's call him.' We called her son, I spoke with him in English, saying I would stay with his mother till we got on the plane.

She talked to him. Then we called her other sons just for fun. Then we called my dad and he and she spoke for a while in Arabic and found out of course they had ten shared friends. Then I thought just for the heck of it why not call some Palestinian poets I know and let them chat with her?

This all took up two hours. She was laughing a lot by then. Telling about her life, patting my knee, answering questions. She had pulled a sack of homemade *mamool* cookies – little powdered sugar crumbly mounds stuffed with dates and nuts – from her bag – and was offering them to all the women at the gate. To my amazement, not a single woman declined one. It was like a sacrament. The traveler from Argentina, the mom from California, the lovely woman from Laredo – we were all covered with the same powdered sugar. And smiling. There is no better cookie.

And then the airline broke out free apple juice from huge coolers and two little girls from our flight ran around serving it and they were covered with powdered sugar too. And I noticed my new best friend – by now we were holding hands – had a potted plant poking out of her bag, some medicinal thing, with green furry leaves. Such an old country traveling tradition. Always carry a plant. Always stay rooted to somewhere. And I looked around that gate of late and weary ones and thought, this is the world I want to live in. The shared world. Not a single person in that gate – once the crying of confusion stopped – seemed apprehensive about any other person. They took the cookies. I wanted to hug all those other women too. This can still happen anywhere. Not everything is lost.

NAOMI SHIHAB NYE

Excise

Each year I travel, my passport photo
looks less like me. Two of us
trick our way through customs.

My heart dances and I tell myself,
Don't breathe so shallow,
when I face a uniform block

my path, unlike my laminated
photo tucked in my breast pocket,
locked in amber and oblivious.

I age for both of us at double speed.
My silent partner keeps his poker face,
I do the talking for the two of us.

Nights, I dream this face but not my life,
leaving me with a sour taste and smell,
longing for a country not on any map:

to be the man who crosses borders
without a passport; whose face matches
curved lines that spell my name.

The official behind Plexiglass
takes her time, looks me up and down.
I speak as she scans my passport

and watches for what the screen brings
up about me. I've no idea what she sees
that makes her ask about my line of work.

I answer with a face
that's stranger to my passport every day,
telling lies about a life not lived, not his.

FRED D'AGUIAR

41

Mirror in February

The day dawns with scent of must and rain,
Of opened soil, dark trees, dry bedroom air.
Under the fading lamp, half dressed – my brain
Idling on some compulsive fantasy –
I towel my shaven jaw and stop, and stare,
Riveted by a dark exhausted eye,
A dry downturning mouth.

It seems again that it is time to learn,
In this untiring, crumbling place of growth
To which, for the time being, I return.
Now plainly in the mirror of my soul
I read that I have looked my last on youth
And little more; for they are not made whole
That reach the age of Christ.

Below my window the awakening trees,
Hacked clean for better bearing, stand defaced
Suffering their brute necessities,
And how should the flesh not quail that span for span
Is mutilated more? In slow distaste
I fold my towel with what grace I can,
Not young and not renewable, but man.

THOMAS KINSELLA

Mirrors at 4 a.m.

You must come to them sideways
In rooms webbed in shadow,
Sneak a view of their emptiness
Without them catching
A glimpse of you in return.

The secret is,
Even the empty bed is a burden to them,
A pretense.
They are more themselves keeping
The company of a blank wall,
The company of time and eternity

Which, begging your pardon,
Cast no image
As they admire themselves in the mirror,
While you stand to the side
Pulling a hanky out
To wipe your brow surreptitiously.

CHARLES SIMIC

Mirror

Once regrets come to mind
plum blossoms fall
Like watching her swim to the other shore
Like climbing a pine ladder
There is beauty in danger
Why not watch her return on horseback
cheeks warm
with shame. Head bowed, she answers the Emperor
A mirror awaits her forever
Let her take her usual place in the mirror
looking out the window, once regrets come to mind
plum blossoms fall over the southern mountain

ZHANG ZAO

translated from the Chinese by Fiona Sze-Lorrain

Desperate Meetings of Hermaphrodites

In the hotel on the other side of the mirror
the chaise longue dictates the poem of the film
can only be a snapshot, seeing as the film

is a book – and as it snaps shut it opens
again on a random page at any moment
of a keyhole or doorframe through which

you look for an unabridged view of whoever
has left their black brogue and white stiletto
in the corridor exchanged for a halo of the five

points of a star becoming the snap of a finger until
you're falling back through the smashed mirror
into the room – or so it looked – seeing as the mirror

is a poem, which, in any case, is made of water –
finding the dripping statue, from whose mouth
all this had come, is dressing up as you.

RACHAEL BOAST

You and I and the World

Don't ask who *you* are or who *I* am
and *why* what is, is.
Let the professors sort it out,
it's their job.
Place the scale on the kitchen table
and let reality weigh itself.
Put your coat on.
Turn the light off in the hallway.
Close the door.
Let the dead embalm the dead.

Here we walk now.
The one wearing white rubber boots
is you.
The one wearing black rubber boots
is me.
And the rain falling on both of us
is the rain.

WERNER ASPENSTRÖM
translated from the Swedish by Malena Morling & Jonas Ellerström

What Use Is Knowing Anything If No One Is Around

What use is knowing anything if no one is around
to watch you know it? Plants reinvent sugar daily
and hardly anyone applauds. Once as a boy I sat
in a corner covering my ears, singing Qur'anic verse

after Qur'anic verse. Each syllable was perfect, but only
the lonely rumble in my head gave praise. This is why
we put mirrors in birdcages, why we turn on lamps

to double our shadows. I love my body more
than other bodies. When I sleep next to a man, he becomes
an extension of my own brilliance. Or rather, he becomes
an echo of my own anticlimax. I was delivered

from dying like a gift card sent in lieu of a pound
of flesh. My escape was mundane, voidable. Now
I feed faith to faith, suffer human noise, complain
about this or that heartache. The spirit lives in between

the parts of a name. It is vulnerable only to silence
and forgetting. I am vulnerable to hammers, fire,
and any number of poisons. The dream, then: to erupt
into a sturdier form, like a wild lotus bursting into

its tantrum of blades. There has always been a swarm
of hungry ghosts orbiting my body – even now,
I can feel them plotting in their luminous diamonds

of fog, each eyeing a rib or a thighbone. They are
arranging their plans like worms preparing
to rise through the soil. They are ready to die
with their kind, dry and stiff above the wet earth.

KAVEH AKBAR

Self-Portrait with Aquarium Octopus Flashing a Mirror

Where water, glass and light cut through each other, where one side
of the glass is underwater and the other is not, one cosmos

seems first to bisect, then kiss, another. Up against the steamy divide
the octopus explodes and collapses, explodes and collapses

in its soft hysteria of saying: it is compelled by will or ennui to be
wholly on display, compelled, like any extraterrestrial, to show itself –

This is what I've got, it says with every lunge, I'll show you all I've got
which you don't have, this head, for example, clumsily bashing glass

like a blunt-nosed angel's, a throb of plasma. Though many limbs flower
crazily from this eye-lens, it says, I don't know what it is I've got

but here's the centre, the centre where it is. And you a man, a woman,
it says, and you neither or nothing at all – a smudge in need of an apogee.

You don't know what I am or what it is you are, you do not know,
whatever you are, whatever you are, whatever you are.

TIM LIARDET

The IJsselmeer Dam

The bus drives through the darkness like a room,
the narrow road is straight, the dam is endless,
the sea is on the left, subdued but restless,
we look out, a smallish moon relieves the gloom.

In front of me, the freshly-shaven necks
of two young sailors, who smother one yawn, then another
and later, after a quick and limber stretch,
sleep innocently leaning on each other.

Then all at once, as if it's a dream, I see in the glass
the thin, transparent gleam of a bus that's wed to ours,
sometimes as clear as us, then underwater, drowned;
the clumps of roadside grass
cut through the sleeping seamen.
I see myself as well, my features
floating over the surface
of the sea, an astonished mermaid;
lips move as if to say,
There is no tomorrow, no yesterday,
no start or end to this long trip,
just one extended present – strangely split.

M. VASALIS
translated from the Dutch by David Colmer

Conundrum

You'd think there would be a neat equation for how
when travelling by train the view from the window
and in the mirror opposite make clear we are hurtling
away from the past, and into our future, at precisely

the same speed. Simple you say, stating the obvious.
But it doesn't explain how images, as they recede,
may enlarge in the memory; tunnels ahead shorten
or lengthen in accordance with changes of mood.

Even more how an intrusive cell or invisible speck
between sets of nerves can have an impact more
catastrophic than a rock fissure in a mountain ravine;
the tremor of an eyelid, cataclysmic as any fault-line.

STEWART CONN

Vanishing Point

Which is the left-hand side of the word?
How does it move about in space?
Where does it throw its shadow
(and can a word cast shadow)?
How can it be observed from behind
or set against the recession of space?
I should like to render in poetry
the equivalent of perspective in painting.
To give a poem the depth of a rabbit
escaping through fields and make it
distant whilst already
it speeds away from the one who's watching
and veers towards the frame
becoming smaller all the time
and never moving an inch.
The countryside observes
and disposes itself around the creature,
around a point that's vanishing.

VALERIO MAGRELLI
translated from the Italian by Jamie McKendrick

Landscape with Fruit Rot and Millipede

I cut off my head and threw it in the sky. It turned
into birds. I called it thinking. The view from above –
untethered scrutiny. It helps to have an anchor
but your head is going somewhere anyway. It's a matter
of willpower. O little birds, you flap around and

make a mess of the milk-blue sky – all these ghosts
come streaming down and sometimes I wish I had
something else. A redemptive imagination, for
example. The life of the mind is a disappointment,
but remember what stands for what. We deduce

backward into first causes – stone in the pond of things,
splash splash – or we throw ourselves into the future.
We all move forward anyway. Ripples in all directions.
What is a ghost? Something dead that seems to be
alive. Something dead that doesn't know it's dead.

A painting, for instance. An abstraction. *Cut off your*
head, kid. For all the good it'll do ya. I glued my head back
on. All thoughts finish themselves eventually. I wish
it were true. Paint all the men you want but sooner or
later they go to ground and rot. The mind fights the

body and the body fights the land. It wants our bodies,
the landscape does, and everyone runs the risk of
being swallowed up. Can we love nature for what it
really is: predatory? We do not walk through a passive
landscape. The paint dries eventually. The bodies

decompose eventually. We collide with place, which
is another name for God, and limp away with a
permanent injury. Ask for a blessing? You can try,
but we will not remain unscathed. Flex your will
or abandon your will and let the world have its way

with you, or disappear and save everyone the bother
of a dark suit. Why live a life? Well, why are you
asking? I put on my best shirt because the painting
looked so bad. Color bleeds, so make it work for you.
Gravity pulls, so make it work for you. Rubbing

your feet at night or clutching your stomach in the
morning. It was illegible – no single line of sight,
rno many angles of approach, smoke in the distance.
It made no sense. When you have nothing to say,
set something on fire. A blurry landscape is useless.

RICHARD SIKEN

Gift

> – my Muslim grandmother's words when giving
> a crucifix to my Methodist mother in Tehran

It doesn't matter that she's blonde,
doesn't know a single word of Farsi,
or how to *taarof*, always refuse first,
before accepting a gift.

what you believe is your own trouble;
not one of us understands all the words
of our mother tongue. Look at the eye,
my father told me, watch it speak.

as long as you are here, I will be shelter.

believe in something: your hands pressed
together, palm to palm, are my body folded
into the *namaz*; each of us maps ourselves
in the mirror, measures what we already know.

MARJORIE LOTFI GILL

'It's pretty clear, I'm dying...'

It's pretty clear, I'm dying
I'm about to die, in a matter of days
or years, I'm about to die,
I'm dying. Everyone does it,
I'll have to do it, too. Yes, I must conform
to that humdrum law. But in the meantime,
between one sleep and another as long as there is sleep
(only the living can enjoy sleep)
looking at the sky, rolling my eyes
in those uncertain moments
I am most certainly immortal.

PATRIZIA CAVALLI
translated from the Italian by Gina Alhadeff

Recognition

Once, I thought
nothing could be sadder
than to spend a lifetime
paddling at the brink
of your real self

Now, I think
that saddest of all
is not to recognise
that figure stumbling
along the shore

LAWRENCE SAIL

Nanluoguxiang Alley

(from 'Eternity')

Every chance I get, every face I see, I find myself
Searching for a glimpse of myself, my daughter and sons.

More often, I find there former students, old lovers,
Friends I knew once and had until now forgotten. My

Sisters, a Russian neighbor, a red-haired American actor.
And on and on, uncannily, as though all of us must be

Buried deep within each other.

TRACY K. SMITH

Self Portrait as a Creature of Numbers

I shifted into this human life from the spirit world,
the fusion of 1 egg and 1 sperm at 8.42 pm, where
Latitude 51° 31′ 0 N straddles Longitude 0°– 6′ E.
London, N19 to be exact.

At 8 days my mother out-doored me, crossed
the threshold back and forth 7 times, whispered
a prayer over 3 glasses, dabbed my tongue,
one drop from each – water, honey, salt.
She showed my face to the 4 elements each in turn,
punched 2 holes in my earlobes. To bind mind, body
and spirit to a destiny of life path 1, she took 3
new laid eggs cracked them open over my head.

1st daughter of a 4th son of Ghana, my soul surges
8° 00′ north of the equator 2°00′ west of the prime meridian.
I march to a 4 beat over 50,000,000 knots
on this ocean called forever knowing that bigger, better
numbers can be reached by always adding just 1 more.

Sketched from 300 moons minus 3
plus 25 valentine cards I never received, I am ruled
by lustre bouncing off the Evening Star, second planet in,
108,000,000 kilometres from the sun.

If you encounter me in the underground standing
1.66 metres tall on the escalator going up or going down,
know that I own 1001 options raised to the power
of infinity plus 1 – dreamer, sinner, interloper.
Always climbing 1 more number. At the very least 1.

DZIFA BENSON

A Contribution to Statistics

Out of a hundred people

those who always know better
– fifty-two

doubting every step
– nearly all the rest,

glad to lend a hand
if it doesn't take too long
– as high as forty-nine,

always good
because they can't be otherwise
– four, well, maybe five,

able to admire without envy
– eighteen,

living in constant fear
of someone or something
– seventy-seven,

capable of happiness
– twenty-something tops,

harmless singly,
savage in crowds
– half at least,

cruel
when forced by circumstances
– better not to know
even ballpark figures,

wise after the fact
– just a couple more
than wise before it,

taking only things from life
– forty
(I wish I were wrong),

hunched in pain,
no flashlight in the dark
– eighty-three
sooner or later,

worthy of compassion
– ninety-nine,

mortal
– a hundred out of a hundred.
Thus far this figure still remains unchanged.

WISŁAWA SZYMBORSKA

translated from the Polish by Stanisław Barańczak & Clare Cavanagh

People

So many nights
the lines of chairs, frames and bureaus,
I have have seen off with movements
of my arms and shoulders
on their regular

and unknown paths.

I didn't notice
how this happens too with people.
I must admit: when I talk to them,
I imagine my finger measuring

the lines of their eyebrows.

And they were everywhere,
so that I did not forget
about life in the form of people,

and there were weeks and years
to say goodbye to them,

and there was the idea of thinking
so that I knew
the patches of light on their pianos
had relatives

in hospitals and prisons.

GENNADY AYGI
translated from the Russian by Sarah Valentine

Sanctuary

For terrible minutes I searched for the word, like a country
that's missing; thought of the bird flying into the arms
of the figure my father had sketched in a notebook.

This is what matters, he said, grief-struck, unsteady,
grounding himself by holding his pencil up to the light
to measure the distance. A room is a place a story

might begin or end, where doors can open paths
to dreaming. I hear a man's voice over the radio
proclaiming desperate measures in Calais, in Budapest,

in Sofia, in Zagreb. I cannot imagine it: a train station;
a wire fence; the overflowing latrine; children playing
on a stony road. The cold distance between there and here.

My pen scratches paper. Words hinged with cries fly off,
come home to roost. I cannot not imagine it.

LINDA ANDERSON

The Way

The way you sometimes get to a room, not knowing why,
and then have to figure out what you were after,
the way you take something out of a closet
without feeling around for it and only after you hold it
know what you were looking for,
the way you bring a package somewhere
and when you leave are startled, feeling too light,
the way you wait for someone, fall madly in love
for a second with anyone passing, and still go on waiting.
The way you know I've been here once, what was it about,

until a smell comes back to tell you what,
the way you know whom to be careful with
and whom not, whom you can lie down with –
that's the way animals think, I think,
the way animals know the way.

JUDITH HERZBERG
translated from the Dutch by Shirley Kaufman with Judith Herzberg

The Same Inside

Walking to your place for a love feast
I saw at a street corner
an old beggar woman.

I took her hand,
kissed her delicate cheek,
we talked, she was
the same inside as I am,
from the same kind,
I sensed this instantly
as a dog knows by scent
another dog.

I gave her money.
I could not part from her.
After all, one needs
someone who is close.

And then I no longer knew
why I was walking to your place.

ANNA SWIR
translated from the Polish by Czesław Miłosz & Leonard Nathan

Rednecks

At Scot Gas, Darnestown Road,
the high school boys pumping gas
would snicker at the rednecks.
Every Saturday night there was Earl,
puckering his liquor-smashed face
to announce that he was driving
across the bridge, a bridge spanning
only the whiskey river
that bubbled in his stomach.
Earl's car, one side crumpled like his nose,
would circle slowly around the pumps,
turn signal winking relentlessly.

Another pickup truck morning,
and rednecks. Loitering
in our red uniforms, we watched
as a pickup rumbled through.
We expected: Fill it with no-lead, boy,
and gimme a cash ticket.
We expected the farmer with sideburns
and a pompadour.
We, with new diplomas framed
at home, never expected the woman.
Her face was a purple rubber mask
melting off her head, scars rippling down
where the fire seared her freak face,
leaving her a carnival where high school boys
paid a quarter to look, and look away.

No one took the pump. The farmer saw us standing
in our red uniforms, a regiment of illiterate conscripts.
Still watching us, he leaned across the seat of the truck
and kissed her. He kissed her
all over her happy ruined face, kissed her
as I pumped the gas and scraped the windshield
and measured the oil, he kept kissing her.

MARTÍN ESPADA

The Beauty of a Busted Fruit

When we were children, we traced our knees,
shins, and elbows for the slightest hint of wound,
searched them for any sad red-blue scab marking us
both victim and survivor.

All this before we knew that some wounds can't heal,
before we knew the jagged scars of Great-Grandmother's
amputated legs, the way a rock can split a man's head
open to its red syrup, like a watermelon, the way a brother
can pick at his skin for snakes and spiders only he can see.

Maybe you have grown out of yours –
maybe you no longer haul those wounds with you
onto every bus, through the side streets of a new town,
maybe you have never set them rocking in the lamplight
on a nightstand beside a stranger's bed, carrying your hurts
like two cracked pomegranates, because you haven't learned
to see the beauty of a busted fruit, the bright stain it will leave
on your lips, the way it will make people want to kiss you.

NATALIE DIAZ

Monologue for an Onion

I don't mean to make you cry.
I mean nothing, but this has not kept you
From peeling away my body, layer by layer,

The tears clouding your eyes as the table fills
With husks, cut flesh, all the debris of pursuit.
Poor deluded human: you seek my heart.

Hunt all you want. Beneath each skin of mine
Lies another skin: I am pure onion – pure union
Of outside and in, surface and secret core.

Look at you, chopping and weeping. Idiot.
Is this the way you go through life, your mind
A stopless knife, driven by your fantasy of truth,

Of lasting union – slashing away skin after skin
From things, ruin and tears your only signs
Of progress? Enough is enough.

You must not grieve that the world is glimpsed
Through veils. How else can it be seen?
How will you rip away the veil of the eye, the veil

That you are, you who want to grasp the heart
Of things, hungry to know where meaning
Lies. Taste what you hold in your hands: onion juice,

Yellow peels, my stinging shreds. You are the one
In pieces. Whatever you meant to love, in meaning to
You changed yourself: you are not who you are,

Your soul cut moment to moment by a blade
Of fresh desire, the ground sown with abandoned skins.
And at your inmost circle, what? A core that is

Not one. Poor fool, you are divided at the heart,
Lost in its maze of chambers, blood, and love,
A heart that will one day beat you to death.

SUJI KWOCK KIM

The Years

It was six years after the fact
that I became I
perhaps again, perhaps for the first time.

There was the suggestion
that I should mark each passage

with a commemoration
to what had been lost,
or survived,
words like redemption
but that was never I,
for I have nothing to apologise for
and I'll take my time.

Simply put,
the days followed the days
and the weeks followed the weeks
and the months the months
and the years the years
until I became I
until I became I.

NADINE AISHA JASSAT

Let Me Tell You

Let me tell you this:
I did not always look this way
and there were times
when you would not have recognised me.
I recognise you now.
I see you.

This road has been hard
and for you I won't lie
about the times of struggling –
suspicious of the walls
and wearing 'I'm fine' like a badge,
all the while hiding that beat beat beat in my chest,
I confess, I never felt less sane
than when his hand was clawing through my brain
and every man seemed to wear his face

and I thought, I might die tonight,
truly die tonight,
no one can sustain this.

So, you see,
it's hard to imagine one day you'll be living
when you're trying to survive.

Yet here I am.
And there you are.

I can't make any promises
or take it all away,
but, if you would like me to,
I can tell you, some things which I have learned:

That beat,
when you're terrified,
when it hurts,
when you think it can't get worse, *that* beat,
is a fight – but it's not the knife –
it's you.

It's you staying alive.

NADINE AISHA JASSAT

In Praise of Fixer Women

So many corners in this world just waiting to knock out your teeth,
how many times can that broken nose knit itself up like new?

You're a punch-bag, a suit stuffed with duck-down, a helium balloon in a
    furnace,
but still you trip about forgetting your vitamins (a pint is not a meal!)

and between your whimsical pratfalls (the missed appointment, the lost job,
the unpaid loan) there are those tar-pits we all tiptoe around,

the abandoned wives, the child that no one mentions –
because tar sticks and we don't like the look of your filthy shoes.

You're a laugh riot! An ice-cube on a stove! An unattended chip pan
spitting your gold into our faces and oh how it burns our eyes,

but we hide it in the tiny pockets of silence that line our clothes
that keep us afloat in the dark water when we drag you, yet again, towards
    the shore.

And though your warehouse is bare, they are out there waiting,
those women fixers-of-men, ready to pull the stones from your pockets,

replace them with cups of tea that scald your balls as they spill
and to stop your mouth with slices of cake as they wrap a hundred scarves

round your neck and wind and wind until you find you're choking –
and isn't it only what's best for you. And doesn't it serve you right.

JESSICA TRAYNOR

Magdalene Afterwards

Remember the woman in the blue burka forced to kneel in the stadium
then shot in the head? That was me.
And I was the woman who secretly filmed it.

I was hung as a witch by the people in my own town
I was sent to the asylum at sixteen.
I was walking with my younger sister looking for firewood
when we saw the group of men approaching.

I'm the woman so in love with my husband
sometimes I wait in the kitchen chair and stare at the door.

I'm bored at the business meeting,
impatient with the Do Not Walk sign.

I'm parked in my wheelchair with the others in the hallway
in the home – three hours till lunch, I don't remember who it is
who leans down to kiss me.

I've forgotten my keys, dropped the dish, fallen down
the icy stoop.

I'm sitting on the bench with my bags, waiting for the bus.
I'm the woman in the black suit and heels hailing a taxi.
I'm in prayer, in meditation, I've shaved my head, I wear robes
now instead of dresses.

When I enter the classroom, all the children call out my name at once.

I'm talking on my cellphone while driving.
I'm walking the goats out to the far field, gazing at the mountain
I've looked at every day of my life

I never had children,
I bore nine living children and two dead ones
I adopted a girl in my late middle age
I'm cooking rice and beans
cooking dal
cooking lamb
reheating pizza
lighting the candles on the birthday cake
standing quietly by the window
still hungry for I don't know what.

Often I'm lonely.
Sometimes a joy pours through me so immense.

I want to see through the red bricks of the building across the street,
into the something else that almost gleams through the day.

MARIE HOWE

One day

One day the patterned carpet, the folding chairs,
the woman in the blue suit by the door examining her split ends,

all of it will go on without me. I'll have disappeared,
as easily as a coin under lake water, and few to notice the difference

– a coin dropping into the darkening –
and West 4th Street, the sesame noodles that taste like too much peanut
          butter

lowered into the small white paper carton – all of it will go on and on –
and the I that caused me so much trouble? Nowhere

or grit thrown into the garden
or into the sticky bodies of several worms,

or just gone, stopped – like the Middle Ages,
like the coin Whitman carried in his pocket all the way to that basement

bar on Broadway that isn't there anymore.
Oh to be in Whitman's pocket, on a cold winter day,

to feel his large warm hand slide in and out, and in again.
To be taken hold of by Walt Whitman! To be exchanged!

To be spent for something somebody wanted and drank and found delicious.

MARIE HOWE

Girls Are Coming Out of the Woods

Girls are coming out of the woods,
wrapped in cloaks and hoods,
carrying iron bars and candles
and a multitude of scars, collected

on acres of premature grass and city
buses, in temples and bars. Girls
are coming out of the woods
with panties tied around their lips,
making such a noise, it's impossible
to hear. Is the world speaking too?
Is it really asking, *What does it mean
to give someone a proper resting?* Girls are
coming out of the woods, lifting
their broken legs high, leaking secrets
from unfastened thighs, all the lies
whispered by strangers and swimming
coaches, and uncles, especially uncles,
who said spreading would be light
and easy, who put bullets in their chests
and fed their pretty faces to fire,
who sucked the mud clean
　　　　　off their ribs, and decorated
their coffins with briar. Girls are coming
out of the woods, clearing the ground
to scatter their stories. Even those girls
found naked in ditches and wells,
those forgotten in neglected attics,
and buried in river beds like sediments
from a different century. They've crawled
their way out from behind curtains
of childhood, the silver-pink weight
of their bodies pushing against water,
against the sad, feathered tarnish
of remembrance. Girls are coming out
of the woods the way birds arrive
at morning windows – pecking
and humming, until all you can hear
is the smash of their minuscule hearts
against glass, the bright desperation
of sound – bashing, disappearing.
Girls are coming out of the woods.
They're coming. They're coming.

TISHANI DOSHI

2

Ten zillion things

Poetry, in its seeking and questing, in its notice and naming, is one
means of giving praise.

PATTIANN ROGERS

The poet is like a mouse in an enormous cheese excited by how much
cheese there is to eat.

CZESŁAW MIŁOSZ

These are poems of the senses, of praise and wonder. In Matthew Dickman's
poem 'The World is Too Huge to Grasp' (101), he writes 'I like the world in
all its incredible forms' and 'It's not the world / with its ten-zillion things
we should be grasping, / but the sincerity of penguins, the mess we made of
the roses.' The poems in this section have it both ways, praising 'ten-zillion
things we should be grasping' as well as everything else on offer, mistakes
included, living for the moment as well as for all time: winter, snow, mornings,
a change in the weather, springtime, the thaw, sunlight, water, birds, olives,
marmalade, jam and every kind of food. All of these are both themselves in
life while also resonating with so many other meanings in the poems, like
John F. Deane's enigmatic red gate in 'The Red Gate' (75) and 'The World is
Charged' (78), which also appears in other poems of his, including 'Canticle'
(BH 233), where the dead are out there celebrating 'the fact of a red gate and a
yellow moon / that tunes their instruments with you to the symphony', as the
red gate somehow becomes his means of tuning into the music of the universe.

Craig Arnold (1967-2009), author of 'Meditation on a Grapefruit' (95),
vanished while hiking on a remote volcano in Japan on the very day that the
editors of the journal *Poetry* sent him an email he would never receive
accepting the poem for publication. The poem ends with the lines 'each year
harder to live within / each year harder to live without'.

Poems celebrating the other essentials of life – love, art and music – are
to be found in sections 4 and 5 of this anthology.

This section ends with a series of poems on our relationship with time,
picking up a key preoccupation of poets in *Being Human* (4: 'About time',
161-44), but where those poems related to generations, memory, mortality and
second chances in life, the poems in this selection are more quizzical, focussing
on eternity and lost time, regret and choices, and the reconciliation of opposites.

Lines for Winter

(for Ros Kraus)

Tell yourself
as it gets cold and gray falls from the air
that you will go on
walking, hearing
the same tune no matter where
you find yourself –
inside the dome of dark
or under the cracking white
of the moon's gaze in a valley of snow.
Tonight as it gets cold
tell yourself
what you know which is nothing
but the tune your bones play
as you keep going. And you will be able
for once to lie down under the small fire
of winter stars.
And if it happens that you cannot
go on or turn back
and you find yourself
where you will be at the end,
tell yourself
in that final flowing of cold through your limbs
that you love what you are.

MARK STRAND

Imaginary Conversation

You tell me to live each day
as if it were my last. This is in the kitchen
where before coffee I complain
of the day ahead – that obstacle race

of minutes and hours,
grocery stores and doctors.

But why the last? I ask. Why not
live each day as if it were the first –
all raw astonishment, Eve rubbing
her eyes awake that first morning,
the sun coming up
like an ingénue in the east?

You grind the coffee
with the small roar of a mind
trying to clear itself. I set
the table, glance out the window
where dew has baptised every
living surface.

LINDA PASTAN

Failing and Flying

Everyone forgets that Icarus also flew.
It's the same when love comes to an end,
or the marriage fails and people say
they knew it was a mistake, that everybody
said it would never work. That she was
old enough to know better. But anything
worth doing is worth doing badly.
Like being there by that summer ocean
on the other side of the island while
love was fading out of her, the stars
burning so extravagantly those nights that
anyone could tell you they would never last.
Every morning she was asleep in my bed
like a visitation, the gentleness in her
like antelope standing in the dawn mist.

Each afternoon I watched her coming back
through the hot stony field after swimming,
the sea light behind her and the huge sky
on the other side of that. Listened to her
while we ate lunch. How can they say
the marriage failed? Like the people who
came back from Provence (when it was Provence)
and said it was pretty but the food was greasy.
I believe Icarus was not failing as he fell,
but just coming to the end of his triumph.

JACK GILBERT

Snow

We're brought to our senses, awake
to the black and whiteness of world.
Snow's sensational. It tastes
of ice and fire. Hold a handful of cold.

Ball it between your palms
to throw at the moon. Relish its plushy creak.
Shake blossoms from chestnut and beech,
gather its laundered linen in your arms.

A twig of witch hazel from the ghost-garden
burns like myrrh in this room. Listen!
Ice is whispering. Night darkens,
the mercury falls in the glass, glistening.

Motorways muffled in silence, lorries stranded
like dead birds, airports closed, trains trackless.
White paws lope the river on plates of ice
in the city's bewildered wilderness.

GILLIAN CLARKE

Snow

The snow began to fall at midnight. And it's true
that the best place to sit is in the kitchen,
even if it's the kitchen of insomnia.
It's warm there, you fix some food, drink wine
and look out the window into the familiar eternity.
Why should you worry whether birth and death are only two points,
when life is not a straight line after all.
Why should you torture yourself staring at the calendar
and wondering how much is at stake.
And why should you admit you have no money
to buy Saskia a pair of slippers?
And why should you boast
that you suffer more than others.

Even if there were no silence on earth,
that snow would have dreamed it up.
You're alone. As few gestures as possible. Nothing for show.

VLADIMÍR HOLAN
translated from the Czech by C.G. Hanzlicek & Dana Hábová

Breakfrost

The frost is touching everything before the sun:
each blade has a pencil nudity that makes
the yolk-like orange seem already old,
each flatness reached, brick-like,
as though all cold was urban.
Sheep crunch its windscreen splinters,
horses' heads are glued to it down the blue
flanks of shade. Each leaf is a sucrose flake.
Its intimacy is more exhausting than light.

Morning's sepia, like medieval photographs,
has to fight its way through every scattered grain.
And hollows will persist, like patches left
by the Dark Age bulks of giant sleeping saints,
since Christianity was like a glacier.

Each shadow stuck to it like a tongue
is long and brittle. Everything is biscuit,
feather, spit, viscous, barbed, as though
the land was bait for light, hooking it
and holding it close, gutting the photons
for their kernels of warmth.

W.N. HERBERT

Rising Late

Sun on the eyes, clear voices, open window,
birdsong; ponies clop by on the road below.
Whine of a chainsaw, the recurrent roar
of power tools from a building site next door
with crashing, rumbling, safety beep and buzz.
A seagull shadow flickers; harbour noise;
a honking coaster backs out from the quay.
Enter a fly, the vast breath of the sea.

Waking mid-morning to a springlike new year
and a new age of unbeauty, rage and fear
much like the previous one, I wonder if
a time could ever come when human life,
relieved of ego and finance, might thrive
on the mere fact of existence. A naive
hope, but naive hopes are what unchain
the doors when January comes round again.

Such tiny houses, such enormous skies!
The vast sea-breath reminds us, even these days
as even more oil and junk slosh in the waves,
the future remains open to alternatives.
A stretch in the evenings as returning light
slowly expands. Crocuses, yellow and white,
have sprung up overnight under the pines.
It just keeps happening; life always finds

somewhere to whisper, thought a place to grow
even while the poets fade, as now they do
this winter, taking with them when they die
their quotient of soul, song and singularity,
their fierce resistance to the philistinism;
those acute angles, inspired algorithms,
that first-day-of-creation point of view
old Hugo in his Guernsey exile knew.

Best skies at first light, but I don't do dawn
no more. The enchantment has already gone
when I rise, creaking, to the noise outside,
phenomenal moment of cup, pine and cloud,
the things themselves and the idea of them
embodied there. Plato (*Timaeus*): 'Time
is the moving picture of eternity' –
in love, the pair of them, or said to be.

Salvation lies in love of the simple thing
such as our complex poets used to sing:
a rose, a table with its magic glow,
the ideal forms they body forth also.
I would become, in the time left to me,
the servant of a restored reality –
chalks and ochres, birdsong, harbour lights,
the longer days and the short summer nights.

DEREK MAHON

73

What Was Mistook

The road that kept close to the coast.
The field that kept from the road.
The weighted length of spring.

The stream that opened a hand.
The hill that opened to a shoulder.
The drunk-remorse of summer.

The sun that packed in its fairground.
The woodland that packed copper with gold.
The hound at the heel of autumn.

The wind that looked to recede.
The hoar that looked only hale.
The studded mouth of winter.

MICHELLE O'SULLIVAN

Lines

Words never came. Only silence, exact
and searching with that black-eyed stare.
Winters returned, as they do, and new
snow covered the ground.

I remember how I tried to tinder the light,
flesh-warm snags that felt human
between my hands.

And I remember the dark, a taut flat
line that stiffened the fields and quelled
the dog's bark.

I tell myself that something was said.
That someone was heard.
I tell myself these things
knowing words couldn't cross this threshold.

MICHELLE O'SULLIVAN

The Red Gate

Mornings, when you swing open the red gate –
admitting the world again with its creeds and wars –
the hinges sing their three sharp notes of protest;
you hear the poplars in their murmurings and sifflings
while the labouring high caravans of the rain
pass slowly by; it will seem as if the old
certainties of the moon and stars, mingled
with the turnings and returnings of your dreams, mist
to unreality, although there rise about you
matins and lauds of the meadowsweet and rowan; the first
truck goes ruttling down the wet road and the raw
arguments, the self-betrayed economies of governments
assault you so you may miss the clear-souled drops
on the topmost bar that would whisper you peace.

JOHN F. DEANE

So

This is the trouble with spring. The snow comes down,
and it is all gone, under drift, dune, powder,
cats must be tunnelled for, dogs retrieved,
while milk is a dream, down the next street.

The cars stall on the hill.
Their wheels spin, then scream. The migrant jay
flashes for food. Blue is the wing
of the truant sky, soared Swiss, and pitiless.

How sudden the thaw is. Out of its burrow
the lawn creeps, tired but safe. The streets run smooth once more.
The cold no longer aches. At the end of a war,
your life limps home. And you are not sure that you want it.

ALISON BRACKENBURY

Any Common Desolation

can be enough to make you look up
at the yellowed leaves of the apple tree, the few
that survived the rains and frost, shot
with late afternoon sun. They glow a deep
orange-gold against a blue so sheer, a single bird
would rip it like silk. You may have to break
your heart, but it isn't nothing
to know even one moment alive. The sound
of an oar in an oarlock or a ruminant
animal tearing grass. The smell of grated ginger.
The ruby neon of the liquor store sign.
Warm socks. You remember your mother,
her precision a ceremony, as she gathered
the white cotton, slipped it over your toes,
drew up the heel, turned the cuff. A breath
can uncoil as you walk across your own muddy yard,
the big dipper pouring night down over you, and everything
you dread, all you can't bear, dissolves
and, like a needle slipped into your vein –
that sudden rush of the world.

ELLEN BASS

In Passing

How swiftly the strained honey
of afternoon light
flows into darkness

and the closed bud shrugs off
its special mystery
in order to break into blossom:

as if what exists, exists
so that it can be lost
and become precious

LISEL MUELLER

A Healing

That first day of springtime thaw when the ice
began to melt and pour down the mountains,
I walked to the top of the old mining road
to hear all the slow loosening and letting go;
the kick-back of copper and clay from my heels,
the steady blasts following like the sound
of another person's footfall on the shale,
spirited behind me; the streams that thundered
down to disappear again underground
so the whole place was all tremble and go,
lightening into a stiller and clearer air.
I loved the copper-lit, the downhill skid and slack,
the water roaring out of time, turning back
with so much sound and rush that it seemed
to be gathering strength from ore and dust and clay,
under the shade of that green and beaten ground.

LEANNE O'SULLIVAN

'It's terrible...'

It's terrible.
Everything starts afresh
as if nothing
happened.

In thorny branches
the racket of birds.
Squeaking and screeching,
spring sets in. The wind
plucks untuned chords
of hope and delusion.

Nothing
happened. Everything
starts afresh. It's
terrible.

HANNY MICHAELIS
translated from the Dutch by Judith Wilkinson

The World Is Charged

I was startled by the squawk, the simultaneous
long-tailed and spread-winged half-spectacular half-dive

of the cock-pheasant, his wattles, his bronzed body
up over the hedge; and see! there! the Japanese anemone,

pea-green heart within a scatter-ring of gold; and here –
humbler still, and local – see the mare's-tail weed

and the quick reaching of the briars, note, too, how the tiny
pimpernel persist along the driveway, from the red gate

to the front door. Astonishment, from heart to eye to ragwort,
from there to woodlouse, eucalyptus, owl, and on to Sirius

and the Plough... And we have been, years, she and I,
walking by fields where generations lived and loved,

have laboured and have disappeared – with their sheds
and implements and cattle – into the deep, where they stay

resonant in their silence, their poorer cottages crumbled
into liqueur of rose hip, dust of nettle, knowing that we too

will be with them, alive and loving in the warm light
that still persists, hereabouts, and everywhere, and forever.

JOHN F. DEANE

And Then the Sun Broke Through

A sea of jade and muscatel; the sky, gun-metal.
Landward, the storm-portending birds, white-lit,
Riding wild contours of wind, uplift
To tilt at the raucous crows. This
Is how it is to live, the ticker tells,
Looping the floor of the newsfeed.
Somewhere, an outrage; an airstrike;
Somewhere, a politic withdrawal. This
Is how it is to live: the wind blowing
The charcoal of crows' feathers;
The rent in the clouds; oblique tines beating
Sudden ochre out of a sullen ocean.

DAVID BUTLER

You Reading This, Be Ready

Starting here, what do you want to remember?
How sunlight creeps along a shining floor?
What scent of old wood hovers, what softened
sound from outside fills the air?

Will you ever bring a better gift for the world
than the breathing respect that you carry
wherever you go right now? Are you waiting
for time to show you some better thoughts?

When you turn around, starting here, lift this
new glimpse that you found; carry into evening
all that you want from this day. This interval you spent
reading or hearing this, keep it for life –

What can anyone give you greater than now,
starting here, right in this room, when you turn around?

WILLIAM STAFFORD

'Over the years...'

Over the years
a great deal has to be thrown out.
The notion, for instance,
that happiness is mild and enduring,
something like a southern climate
instead of a bolt of lightning
that leaves scars
cherished a lifetime.

HANNY MICHAELIS
translated from the Dutch by Judith Wilkinson

Meteor

And this is how everything vanishes,
how everything that vanishes begins,
the hinged moment looking forwards and back.
Like that night when we sat with the back door open,
the summer distilled to the scent of jasmine,
the scrape of cutlery, the chink of glass.
A robin stirred in the dusty hedgerow.
Clothes held our bodies as a mouth might a kiss.
Then the meteor brought us to our feet:
a stripped atom, trapping electrons
to excite the darkness with its violet light.
I remember how it disturbed the heavens,
burned against the air to leave no trace.

DERYN REES-JONES

Wonder

If after everything that has happened
you can still hear the blackbird,
the tufted lark at dawn, the bulbul and the honey-bird –
don't be surprised that happiness is watching the clouds being
    wind-carried away,
is drinking morning coffee, being able to execute all the body's needs
is walking along the paths without a cane
and seeing the burning colours of sunset.

A human being can bear almost everything
and no one knows when and where
happiness will overcome him.

TUVIA RUEBNER
translated from the Hebrew by Rachel Tzvia Back

Happiness

...but the occasional episode in a general drama of pain
THOMAS HARDY

Cloudless skies, old roses coming into flower,
a breeze flicking through *The Mayor of Casterbridge*.

Toasted granary bread with damson jam,
a pair of goldfinches on the bird-feeder.

The whiff of fennel and rosemary,
the farmer's quad bike leaving the field.

Two deckchairs in the shade of a weeping birch.
Everyone you love still alive, last time you heard.

BLAKE MORRISON

Happiness

Yesterday it appeared to me in the form of two purple
elastic bands round a bunch of asparagus, which was
a very small happiness, a garden variety, nothing like
the hulking conversation cross-legged on a bed we had
ten years ago, or when I saw it as a thin space in a mouth
that was open slightly listening to a friend pinning them
with an almost-cruel accuracy; the sense of being *known*
making a space in their mouth that was happiness.
There was the happiness of my mother as we sat on
a London bus, her having travelled alone to visit her son,
and she seemed more present which might have been
the luggage I was carrying for her that weighed heavy
as her happiness, or was her happiness. It is rare you see
a happiness so nut-like as that which we permit my
father to pass around when he is talking sentimentally,

embarrassing us all. And of course, the goofy ten gallon
hats of happiness that children plant on us everytime
they impersonate knowledge. Or when I am standing on
a step breathing it in and out, staying death and the deadness
that comes after dying, sighing like a song about it. Or
privately with you, when we're watching television and
everyone else can be depressed as rotten logs for all we care,
because various and by degrees as it is, we know happiness
because it is not always usual, and does not wait to leave.

JACK UNDERWOOD

Wanting

Wanting and dissatisfaction
are the main ingredients
of happiness.
To want is to believe
there is something worth getting.
Whereas getting only shows
how worthless the thing is.
And this is why destruction
is so useful.
It gets rid of what was wanted
and so makes room
for more to be wanted.
How valueless is the orderly.
It cries out for disorder.
And life that thinks it fears death,
spends all of its time
courting death.
To violate beauty
is the essence of sexual desire.
To procreate is the essence of decay.

RUTH STONE

Sentiments

In the autumnal town
sentiments are strewn here and there
to bruise you without warning.
Made sad in return,
sentiment sometimes
turns into a metal spoon
and mutely rests on a wooden table.
Yesterday he was sulking at the side of a porcelain plate,
today taken out of a kitchen drawer
he is breaking the half-boiled eggshell in good humour,
now I am leaving for a picnic
and have no time for grieving.
Inside a caged-up heart
look, the little birds are fluttering.
Sentiments are strewn around every town
stark naked till they sing out.

MIKIRO SASAKI
translated from the Japanese by Mitsuko Ohno,
Beverley Curran & Nobuaki Tochigi

Lake Water

It is a summer afternoon in October.
I am sitting on a wooden bench, looking out
At the lake through a tall screen of evergreens,
Or rather, looking out across the plane of the lake,
Seeing the light shaking upon the water
As if it were a shimmering of heat.
Yesterday, when I sat here, it was the same,
The same displaced out-of-season effect.
Seen twice it seemed a truth was being told.
Some of the trees I can see across the lake

Have begun to change, but it is as if the air
Had entirely given itself over to summer,
With the intention of denying its own proper nature.
There is a breeze perfectly steady and persistent
Blowing in toward shore from the other side
Or from the world beyond the other side.
The mild sound of the little tapping waves
The breeze has caused – there's something infantile
About it, a baby at the breast. The light
Is moving and not moving upon the water.

The breeze picks up slightly but still steadily,
The increase in the breeze becomes the mild
Dominant event, compelling with sweet oblivious
Authority alterations in light and shadow,
Alterations in the light of the sun on the water,
Which becomes at once denser and more quietly
Excited, like a concentration of emotions
That had been dispersed and scattered and now were not.
Then there's the mitigation of a cloud,
And the light subsides a little, as if into itself.
Although this is a lake it is as if
A tide were running mildly into shore.
The sound of the water so softly battering
Against the shore is decidedly sexual,
In its liquidity, its regularity,
Its persistence, its infantile obliviousness.
It is as if it had come back to being
A beginning, an origination of life.

The plane of the water is like a page on which
Phrases and even sentences are written,
But because of the breeze, and the turning of the year,
And the sense that this lake water, as it is being
Experienced on a particular day, comes from
Some source somewhere, beneath, within, itself,
Or from somewhere else, nearby, a spring, a brook,
Its pure origination somewhere else,
It is like an idea for a poem not yet written

And maybe never to be completed, because
The surface of the page is like lake water,
That takes back what is written on its surface,
And all my language about the lake and its
Emotions or its sweet obliviousness,
Or even its being like an origination,
Is all erased with the changing of the breeze
Or because of the heedless passing of a cloud.

When, moments after she died, I looked into her face,
It was as untelling as something natural,
A lake, say, the surface of it unreadable,
Its sources of meaning unfindable anymore.
Her mouth was open as if she had something to say;
But maybe my saying so is a figure of speech.

DAVID FERRY

Well Water

What a girl called 'the dailiness of life'
(Adding an errand to your errand. Saying,
'Since you're up...' Making you a means to
A means to a means to) is well water
Pumped from an old well at the bottom of the world.
The pump you pump the water from is rusty
And hard to move and absurd, a squirrel-wheel
A sick squirrel turns slowly, through the sunny
Inexorable hours. And yet sometimes
The wheel turns of its own weight, the rusty
Pump pumps over your sweating face the clear
Water, cold, so cold! you cup your hands
And gulp from them the dailiness of life.

RANDALL JARRELL

A Drink of Water

She came every morning to draw water
Like an old bat staggering up the field:
The pump's whooping cough, the bucket's clatter
And slow diminuendo as it filled,
Announced her. I recall
Her grey apron, the pocked white enamel
Of the brimming bucket, and the treble
Creak of her voice like the pump's handle.
Nights when a full moon lifted past her gable
It fell back through her window and would lie
Into the water set out on the table.
Where I have dipped to drink again, to be
Faithful to the admonishment on her cup,
Remember the Giver, fading off the lip.

SEAMUS HEANEY

Going to the Well

Three wells,
as in a fairytale:
the first well is dry,
the second well is dry,
the third well is dry.

A woman asks if there is a well committee
someone to tell us where the water went.

We are thirsty then, desperate for a drink.

A woman climbs down into the well
begins to dig with an old tin cup.

We wait for a trickle,
some hint of moisture to wet our lips
with whatever cure is there.

She holds it up,
we lean forward to see,
but in the cup there's only money.

LANI O'HANLON

The Fountain

Don't say, don't say there is no water
to solace the dryness at our hearts.
I have seen

the fountain springing out of the rock wall
and you drinking there. And I too
before your eyes

found footholds and climbed
to drink the cool water.

The woman of that place, shading her eyes,
frowned as she watched – but not because
she grudged the water,

only because she was waiting
to see we drank our fill and were
refreshed.

Don't say, don't say there is no water.
That fountain is there among its scalloped
green and gray stones,

it is still there and always there
with its quiet song and strange power
to spring in us,
up and out through the rock.

DENISE LEVERTOV

The Miraculous Issue

Up from the dark strata
pulsing out through moss
centuries of downpour,
an ever-unfurling spring
alive against the heather,
a bull-nosed sinuous thing
of sunlit question and answer
greening its way downhill
to feed the house clear water.

The faithful on their knees
think it miraculous,
beyond common reason,
in winter warm in summer cool,
quick to bless the season;
when I kneel
wrist-deep in its thrust and passion
my fingers feel
that truth of imagination.

Yet a thermometer
there through the year
reads four degrees always;
regardless where truth lies.
I set my measure,
my sweat, my shiver,

beside that halt of quicksilver,
its fix of realities,
its scale before my eyes.

For the water about my hand
answers to life;
and the living imagination
pulses that mercury column
degrees of belief I mark up as truth
to stand by my mind; when little seems true
but to kneel on steep ground
and grasp at a flow
ceaseless and vanishing as faith.

G.F. DUTTON

Water

The hard beautiful rules of water are these:
That it shall rise with displacement as a man
does not, nor his family. That it shall have no plan
or subterfuge. That in the cold, it shall freeze;
in the heat, turn to steam. That it shall carry disease
and bright brilliant fish in river and ocean.
That it shall roar or meander through metropolitan
districts whilst reflecting skies, buildings and trees.

And it shall clean and refresh us even as we slave
over stone tubs or cower in a shelter or run
into the arms of a loved one in some desperate quarter
where the rats too are running. That it shall have
dominion. That it shall arch its back in the sun
only according to the hard rules of water.

GEORGE SZIRTES

Introductions

Some of what we love
we stumble upon –
a purse of gold thrown on the road,
a poem, a friend, a great song.

And more
discloses itself to us –
a well among green hazels,
a nut thicket –
when we are worn out searching
for something quite different.

And more
comes to us, carried
as carefully
as a bright cup of water,
as new bread.

MOYA CANNON

Olives

Sometimes a craving comes for salt, not sweet,
For fruits that you can eat
Only if pickled in a vat of tears –
A rich and dark and indehiscent meat
Clinging tightly to the pit – on spears

Of toothpicks maybe, drowned beneath a tide
Of vodka and vermouth,
Rocking at the bottom of a wide,
Shallow, long-stemmed glass, and gentrified,
Or rustic, on a plate cracked like a tooth,

A miscellany of the humble hues
Eponymously drab –
Brown greens and purple browns, the blacks and blues
That chart the slow chromatics of a bruise –
Washed down with swigs of barrel wine that stab

The palate with pine-sharpness. They recall
The harvest and its toil,
The nets spread under silver trees that foil
The blue glass of the heavens in the fall –
Daylight packed in treasuries of oil,

Paradigmatic summers that decline
Like singular archaic nouns, the troops
Of hours in retreat. These fruits are mine –
Small bitter drupes
Full of the golden past and cured in brine.

A.E. STALLINGS

quince jelly

when october hung them among the leaves, those
bulging lanterns, then it was time: we picked ripe
quinces, lugged the baskets of yellow bounty
      into the kitchen,

soused the fruits in water. the pears and apples
grew towards their names, to a simple sweetness –
unlike quinces, clinging to branches in some
      shadowy border's

alphabet, obscure in our garden's latin,
tough and foreign in their aroma. we cut,
quartered, cored the flesh (we were four adult hands,
      two somewhat smaller),

veiled by clouds of steam from the blender, poured in
sugar, heat and effort to something that – raw –
made our palates baulk. but then who could, who would
       hope to explain them:

quinces, jellied, lined up in bellied jars on
shelves and set aside for the darkness, stored for
harsher days, a cellar of days, in which they
       shone, are still shining.

JAN WAGNER
translated from the German by Iain Galbraith

Marmalade

I open the jar
of marmalade

and morning fills
with the bitter

(no, sweet) taste
of Algiers, Morocco, Seville,

where fragrant bombs hang
from tree branches.

When they burst
on the bare ground

(I like the ones
with blood in them best)

the air is scorched all around
with the noise of revolution

and street markets
in places I've never been

but still my nose
remembers

their bitter
(no, sweet) smell.

When I return
to the kitchen,

worn out from wandering
beyond the borders of the senses,

get real, you say,
frowning,

I bought those oranges
yesterday, in the butcher's

and it was I who made
your marmalade,

bittersweet,
the way you like it.

Exactly, I say,
as your body's fragrance

detonates, burning
the air all around me.

The riot has already started
in the street market

of my heart, just there
beside the stall of oranges.

LOUIS DE PAOR

*translated from the Irish by Louis de Paor with
Kevin Anderson, Biddy Jenkinson & Mary O'Donoghue*

If God Made Jam

If God made jam the jars wouldn't necessarily glow
like Christmas lights or the new home of seventy fireflies,
the berries wouldn't have to be so divine
they dribbled rainbows and healed the sick,
each pip released a *Gloria* when it
cracked between your teeth,
and God's jam would never refuse to touch earthly bread –

Aunt Lydia has worked out this much
since Cousin Bobby told her about a comma
he skipped long ago while learning his catechism.
Now, on a rainy morning, spared the news
that lay in her grass and is too wet to read,
she's flexed her stiff hands and found them able
to slice the bread baked by a friend
and twist the lid from a royal-red jar,
and with the first crusty, raspberry bite
she's ready to affirm God does make jam.
It still counts if people figure among
the instruments that have been put to use,
and Bobby catechised wasn't wrong
when he pictured a deity, willing to work in the kitchen,
who made preserves and redeemed us.

SARAH LINDSAY

Meditation on a Grapefruit

To wake when all is possible
before the agitations of the day
have gripped you
            To come to the kitchen
and peel a little basketball
for breakfast

To tear the husk
like cotton padding   a cloud of oil
misting out of its pinprick pores
clean and sharp as pepper
                To ease
each pale pink section out of its case
so carefully   without breaking
a single pearly cell
                To slide each piece
into a cold blue china bowl
the juice pooling   until the whole
fruit is divided from its skin
and only then to eat
                so sweet
                        a discipline
precisely pointless   a devout
involvement of the hands and senses
a pause   a little emptiness

each year harder to live within
each year harder to live without

CRAIG ARNOLD

Chocolate

He died in order to be the bar of chocolate in front of you.
He wishes that you too would consume the anguish of his death.

Limitlessly. That fear and deliverance would melt in your mouth.
His sweet entrails, the bitter curves of his concoctions.

He asks you to unwrap him, to reveal yourself in the proper light.
Beyond kindness. Beyond mercy and forgiveness.

The two of you touch wordlessly, in the tongue of mute gifts.
What you break and eat, breaks and feeds on you.

Your saliva, the secret feeling of an empty mouth is his.
Your fingers, which search for him in drawers. But not the reverse.

You must remain hungry so that god can still give.
And what your god once gave, he endlessly takes.

ALEŠ ŠTEGER
translated from the Slovenian by Brian Henry

Egg

When you kill it at the edge of the pan, you don't notice
That the egg grows an eye in death.

It is so small, it doesn't satisfy
Even the most modest morning appetite.

But it already watches, already stares at your world.
What are its horizons, whose glassy-eyed perspectives?

Does it see time, which moves carelessly through space?
Eyeballs, eyeballs, cracked shells, chaos or order?

Big questions for such a little eye at such an early hour.
And you – do you really want an answer?

When you sit down, eye to eye, behind a table,
You blind it soon enough with a crust of bread.

ALEŠ ŠTEGER
translated from the Slovenian by Brian Henry

Refrigerator, 1957

More like a vault – you pull the handle out
and on the shelves: not a lot,
and what there is (a boiled potato
in a bag, a chicken carcass
under foil) looking dispirited,
drained, mugged. This is not
a place to go in hope or hunger.
But, just to the right of the middle
of the middle door shelf, on fire, a lit-from-within red,
heart red, sexual red, wet neon red,
shining red in their liquid, exotic,
aloof, slumming
in such company: a jar
of maraschino cherries. Three-quarters
full, fiery globes, like strippers
at a church social. Maraschino cherries, maraschino,
the only foreign word I knew. Not once
did I see these cherries employed: not
in a drink, nor on top
of a glob of ice cream,
or just pop one in your mouth. Not once.
The same jar there through an entire
childhood of dull dinners – bald meat,
pocked peas and, see above,
boiled potatoes. Maybe
they came over from the old country,
family heirlooms, or were status symbols
bought with a piece of the first paycheck
from a sweatshop,
which beat the pig farm in Bohemia,
handed down from my grandparents
to my parents
to be someday mine,
then my child's?
They were beautiful
and, if I never ate one,

it was because I knew it might be missed
or because I knew it would not be replaced
and because you do not eat
that which rips your heart with joy.

THOMAS LUX

Cookery

Strange how the heat both softens and hardens:
Turning sinews to gelatine
And liquid batters into crispness and substance
Or cricket-bat solidity.

Soon, I will take you and feed you
My stew. It will be thick, reddish brown,
And rich as the beginning of the world.
In it will be dark mouthfuls engorged with wine,
Crusted and melded with gold and amber tenderness.

Rumour of it will reach you from the kitchen,
Embarrassing you with saliva –
But when you eat, I shall leave the room,
For you must be alone to commune
With this dark tide, which will flood,
Like evangelism, through the blood
Under your pale accountant's skin.

Later, I will sit with you over crumbly meringues
And you will smile, under the pearls on your moustache.

Such goodness. I know it is right.
You will soften and harden for me.

CONNIE BENSLEY

Timberland

Paul's Fish Fry in Bennington, Vermont, is no longer
Closed For The Season Reason Freezin. The umbrellas
have opened over the picnic tables and the bees are
beginning to annoy the french fries, the thick shakes
and real malts of my past.

I am thirteen thousand miles removed, on the delta
of the Pearl River, eating a litchi. Its translucent flesh just
burst in my mouth; shreds of it glitter between my teeth.
I smile but the fruit seller is sour. In fact, he is so sour
the only man on earth he resembles is Paul. But the litchi...

Actually none of this has happened yet. I am nineteen
years old. I am riding in the boxcar of a freight train
hurtling toward Pocatello, Idaho. In a very dangerous move
I maneuver my way back to the car behind me, an open gondola
carrying two tons of timberland eastward out of Oregon:

it is here I will lie all night, my head against the logs,
watching the stars. No one knows where I am. My mother thinks
I am asleep in my bed. My friends, having heard of a derailment
at ninety miles an hour on the eastbound freight, think I am
dead. But I'm *here*, hurtling across the continent with un-

believable speed. We are red-hot and we go, the steel track
with its imperceptible bounce allows us to go, our circuitous
silhouette against the great Blue Mountains and my head in a
thrill watching the stars: I am not yet at a point in my life
where I am able to name them, but there are so many and they are

so white! I'm hurtling toward work at Paul's, toward the litchi-
bite in Guangzhou, toward the day of my death all right, but all
I can say is I am *happyhappyhappy* to be here with the stars and
the logs, with my head thrown back and then pitched forward
in tears. And the litchi! it's like swallowing a pearl.

MARY RUEFLE

100

The World is Too Huge to Grasp

Still, tiger, there's no reason
not to tie your wife up
if that's what she's been dreaming about
in traffic. No reason not to
go out and eat twenty doughnuts
if that's what you want instead of granola
because, whether you like it or not,
it's a skeleton you're wearing
under those Italian jeans. For my part
I'm going to watch hours of television
wearing nothing but a pair of running shoes.
I'm going to walk out
into the yard and begin courting
the rosebushes. I'm not going to
let a little thing like the world stand in my way.
Why should I? I understand it
as much as I understand penguins
and I still go to the zoo. I still watch them
swimming underwater.
It's like watching really beautiful gods
moving within a universe
that other, taller gods built for them
out of compassion and ingenuity.
It would be easy to sit at the bar smoking,
drinking, ruminating about the why of penguins,
pulling our hair out, crying into our gin
about how the penguins have forsaken us,
how nature is having another party
and we're not invited.
I like the world in all its incredible forms.
When I've had the shit beat out of me, my friends
who have died their violent and accidental
deaths, falling from windows, swerving
into the lights of traffic, my suffering,
my unearned joy, my hand reaching up
through the yards of fabric that made your dress,

the midnight movies, all the kids huffing
all the paint thinners, the comedy
of the poor and the ruthlessness
of the rich, how we're too hungry to fight,
too crushed by debt and the psycho
promise of there's-always-tomorrow,
of rent-to-own, the smell
of carrots, the smell of gasoline, the mysteries
of bread and wine, the sky
in Montana with Laura beneath it,
the sky in Portland when my brother was buried
in his little tin of ash, the happiness
of love and the pity of sex, the bathroom stalls,
the fruit markets, Rob proposing on one knee
wearing a panda costume, sweating inside
the fake fur, his bride in love,
the quarterback's son
paralysed from the neck down
and then gone, the fear and fetish
of genitals, the way
we beat our selves into our suits and high heels.
I see how we are with each other.
I see how we act. It's not the world
with its ten-zillion things we should be grasping,
but the sincerity of penguins, the mess we made of the roses.

MATTHEW DICKMAN

Let Birds

Eight deer on the slope
in the summer morning mist.
The night sky blue.
Me like a mare let out to pasture.
The Tao does not console me.
I was given the Way

in the milk of childhood.
Breathing it waking and sleeping.
But now there is no amazing smell
of sperm on my thighs,
no spreading it on my stomach
to show pleasure.
I will never give up longing.
I will let my hair stay long.
The rain proclaims these trees,
the trees tell of the sun.
Let birds, let birds.
Let leaf be passion.
Let jaw, let teeth, let tongue be
between us. Let joy.
Let entering. Let rage and calm join.
Let quail come.
Let winter impress you. Let spring.
Allow the ocean to wake in you.
Let the mare in the field
in the summer morning mist
make you whinny. Make you come
to the fence and whinny. Let birds.

LINDA GREGG

Carving

Others can carve out
their space
in tombs and pyramids.
Our time cannot be trapped
in cages.
Nor hope, nor laughter.
We let the moment rise
like birds and planes and angels
to the sky.

Eternity is this.
Your breath on the window-pane,
living walls with shining eyes.
The surprise of spires,
uncompromising verticals. Knowing
we have been spared
to lift our faces up
for one more day,
into one more sunrise.

IMTIAZ DHARKER

A Short Story of Falling

It is the story of the falling rain
to turn into a leaf and fall again

it is the secret of a summer shower
to steal the light and hide it in a flower

and every flower a tiny tributary
that from the ground flows green and momentary

is one of water's wishes and this tale
hangs in a seed-head smaller than my thumbnail

if only I a passerby could pass
as clear as water through a plume of grass

to find the sunlight hidden at the tip
turning to seed a kind of lifting rain drip

then I might know like water how to balance
the weight of hope against the light of patience

water which is so raw so earthy-strong
and lurks in cast-iron tanks and leaks along

drawn under gravity towards my tongue
to cool and fill the pipe-work of this song

which is the story of the falling rain
that rises to the light and falls again

ALICE OSWALD

Ars Poetica

May the poems be
the little snail's trail.

Everywhere I go,
every inch: quiet record

of the foot's silver prayer.
> *I lived once.*
> *Thank you.*
> *It was here.*

ARACELIS GIRMAY

Fragments

So, where does time go?
All the days of our lives,
the hours we've spent waiting
for buses, or rehearsing
conversations round and round
in our heads? Isn't it there still,
imprinted on brain cells,

each moment freighted
with every moment gone
before, the memory of people,
places, things? Fragments
reach us now and then
from those distant galaxies –
tiny, random and bright,
like that moment in the garden
when we stood watching
a trail of mercury in sunlight,
so far away we couldn't be sure
if they were geese or swans.

RUTH SHARMAN

The House of Lost Time

I knocked on the doors of lost time. No one answered.
I knocked a second time, a third, a fourth.
No answer.
The house of lost time is half covered
with ivy; the other half is ashes.

A house where no one lives, and me knocking and calling out
because it hurts to call and not be heard.
Knocking, knocking. The echo returns
my desperate longing to open, at least a little, this frozen palace.
Night and day become the same haze in my waiting,
in my knocking and knocking.

Lost time surely doesn't exist.
The imposing house is vacant and condemned.

CARLOS DRUMMOND DE ANDRADE
translated from the Portuguese by Richard Zenith

'If there is something to desire...'

If there is something to desire,
there will be something to regret.
If there is something to regret,
there will be something to recall.
If there is something to recall,
there was nothing to regret.
If there was nothing to regret,
there was nothing to desire.

VERA PAVLOVA
translated from the Russian by Steven Seymour

Leave Poetry

For subtracting while you add.
For filling your table with birds.
For taking you to a place you don't know how to leave.
For punishing you without speaking.
For telling you: you are alone.
For preferring that you carry the burden
of its centuries-long pain
when you feel new.
For its preposterous magnet.
For the thirst it produces
when it pretends to be water.
For its parallel life.
For speaking to you
when you want to sleep.
For its pride of a misguided beast.
Because it looks at death
out of the corner of its eye
when it sings oh beauty.
For not giving explanations.

For being self-sufficient.
For being insufficient.
For drinking the shadow of tomorrow.

LUIS MUÑOZ
translated from the Spanish by Curtis Bauer

Decisions: 11

Between two words
choose the quieter one.

Between word and silence
choose listening.

Between two books
choose the dustier one.

Between the earth and the sky
choose a bird.

Between two animals
choose the one who needs you more.

Between two children
choose both.

Between the lesser and the bigger evil
choose neither.

Between hope and despair
choose hope:
it will be harder to bear.

BORIS A. NOVAK
translated from the Slovenian by Mia Dintinjana

Absence

I used to consider absence a lack.
And I ignorantly regretted that lack.
Today I have nothing to regret.
There is no lack in absence.
Absence is a presence in me.
And I feel it, a perfect whiteness, so close and cosy in my arms
that I laugh, dance, and invent glad exclamations,
since absence, this embodied absence,
can't be taken away from me.

CARLOS DRUMMOND DE ANDRADE
translated from the Portuguese by Richard Zenith

Facing the Music

It's not frost; it's snow
It's not backfire; it's gun-fire
It's not fun; it's alcoholism
It's not a tantrum; it's violence
It's not witty; it's abuse
It's not marriage; it's divorce
It's not anger; it's rage
It's not nothing; it's a lump
It's not fear; it's reality
It's not sleep; it's death
It's not *au revoir*; it's the end

MAIRÉAD BYRNE

Hilltop

You see it sometimes:
the way the light strikes
a distant hill, singling out
that space between trees

like a sudden bolt
of memory, or an answer
coming through
from the other side.

RUTH SHARMAN

Nocturne

Time for sleep. Time for a nightcap of grave music,
a dark nocturne, a late quartet, a parting song,
bequeathed by the great dead in perpetuity.

I catch a glance sometimes of my own dead at the window,
those whose traits I share: thin as moths, as matchsticks,
they stare into the haven of the warm room, eyes ablaze.

It is Sunday a lifetime ago. A woman in a now-demolished house
sings *Michael, Row the Boat Ashore* as she sets down the bucket
with its smooth folds of drinking water...

The steadfast harvest moon out there, entangled in the willow's
stringy hair, directs me home like T'ao Ch'ien: *A caged bird
pines for its first forest, a salmon thirsts for its stream.*

DENNIS O'DRISCOLL

3

Innocence and experience

Pregnancy and motherhood is like *being* the poem,
like the word made flesh.

CAROL ANN DUFFY

THE POEMS IN THIS SECTION offer contrasting perspectives on family life and childhood; on being as well as having daughters and sons; on both motherhood and fatherhood, the latter most notably in Niall Campbell's poems (137-38) from his collection *Noctuary* (2019). The selection complements those in *Staying Alive* (7: 'Growing up', 171-216), *Being Alive* (3: 'Family', 107-78), and *Being Human* (3: 'Life history', 95-160), but also highlights areas not commonly represented in anthologies of this kind, such as Hannah Sullivan on giving birth by caesarean section (128). There are poems on the joys of having children but also the pain experienced by many over child loss, including miscarriage, still birth, abortion and the deaths of young children.

In her essay (2018) on her poem 'An uncommon language' (122-24), Sandeep Parmar identifies 'a minor note in the canon of women's writing': 'It is said that one in four women miscarry at some point in their lives. Yet why are there so few poems about miscarriage, something that many women evidently experience? Why is this private and unseen loss near invisible or taboo, to speak or write about? [...] There has been, of late increasingly so, what seems like a flowering of poems and whole collections about motherhood. But how might poems about miscarriage, its silence, broaden our picture of maternity, a range of experiences, too often co-opted by the logic and language of productivity? Where is the special language of grief given to women who miscarry?'

That 'special language of grief' is voiced here in several poems, as well as in Jane Duran's poem 'Miscarriage' (SA 180). This is by no means a 'minor note' in women's *lives*: in breaking this 'taboo' these poets are giving permission for others to write out of their own experiences, speaking to women everywhere, just as that flowering of collections about motherhood was encouraged by brave first steps taken by poets including Gillian K. Ferguson in *Baby: poems on pregnancy, birth and babies* (2001), and by Kate Clanchy (BA 118, 123, 128; BH 100) whose collection *Newborn* (2004) was savaged by reactionary male critics.

Other themes of poems in this section include sexual and physical abuse, survival and fighting back. In her unnerving sequences on family abuse and mental illness, Selima Hill been breaking taboos for three decades, as in the extracts here (182-86) selected from *Fruitcake* (2009) and *Jutland* (2015).

Some readers may find a number of the poems in this section quite disturbing, particularly if they've had personal experience of some of the difficult areas mentioned above, or if finding these issues addressed unexpectedly in emotionally direct poems is itself upsetting, as when a title like 'Hide and Seek' (135) masks a darker narrative.

111

Cement

Last week my tears were sucked out
with our aborted child. Yesterday
in the shower, pain contorted me,
I squatted, expelled a souvenir:

red, liver-textured, squeezed out.
I scooped it up and flushed it away.
You were not there. Your absence
no longer makes me cry.

My tears are gone, so I plaster my heart
against every grit-worried wound.
Now I understand older black women
like my aunts, their hard posture,

why I never saw them cry.
My father made my mother stony,
a martyr for her kids, brittle and bitter,
till my stepdad unbricked her wall;

layer by layer I watched it crumble.
My aunt, shattered by fists, blocked her heart;
stone cold, her tears dried up.
All my life, I never saw her cry, until, foetal

in a hospital bed, wrapped in my mother's arms,
facing death, tears tracking her face,
she whispered, *I am scared.*
Crying for all her tear-barren years.

Washing water-diluted blood down the drain,
bleaching the bath tiles white, I want to bawl
my eyes out, but I have learnt my lesson well.
Each passing day hardens my voice.

MALIKA BOOKER

Erasure

This is no elegy; no one can write elegies
for such as you. There are no scuff marks here
for your erasure. No etches on a strong barked tree.

There was no grief. You are my silence.
Why do you choose to rise now like shifting sand
blown by a slight breeze?

You were my simple crime against humanity,
and, like a criminal, I claim no regrets.
I buried you too deep to call you a name;

you are my trail of invisible lines
like the stretch marks that did not have time to form.
No guilt resides in my house.

I did what we women have always done.
I froze the tears into a block of ice
buried so deep that the guilt is a cold in me,

a thing that will not melt.
What can I say to you who never breathed, you callous dust?
I can talk of sacrifices, broken lives.

I can talk of Abraham almost slashing Isaac's life.
But this was no holy decision.
I cannot tell you why I said no to you.

I am a white dress all ash and grey.
You unspeakable requiem, do not rise now.
Do not ask me the worth.

Who can measure the weight of ambition
against what could have been?

MALIKA BOOKER

Happy Birthday

It would have been your birthday today.
The Furies found me and brought me
a cake and lit the candles with their fiery
breath. The heat is intolerable. Perhaps
this is what it is like to be in Hell.
You'll never blow them out. I didn't
allow you even one breath. Their eyes
are dripping blood as I did. The nurses
told me to keep my eyes shut. Well,
you were just a random selection of cells,
nothing like me at all. I still wanted
to see you, my little bloody paperweight.
Could I have counted your toes and fingers,
seen ancestors in your tiny face? The drugs
made me float like a sunset above my aching
body. *By the 22nd week the eyes have formed*
but the irises still lack pigment and are shut.

Every month, I lie like a broken mannequin
on the bed. There is a fist or a heart
in my stomach and the furies are here
to remind me I am empty, although
there's no need. I know why I bleed.
You were scraped away like unwanted food.
Look at you lying there in your little glass coffin,
or is it a snow globe? Were you terribly cold?
Will I sprinkle your cradle with snow? Will
you wake in one hundred years and see
my face in the mirror and shudder?
Will the trees have grown up to the skies,
the briars and roses climbing your stone wall,
the Prince circling on his white horse,
the rope pulling tighter? He will never
have any intention of rescuing you,
in your bloody shift with your blind eyes.

TRACEY HERD

114

Fairground Music

The fair had come. It must have been Whitsun.
They'd camp every year at the end of our yard –
you could hear the screams and the grinding of the rides
and a noise like whizz-bangs from the house.
Tom had taken Hazel off to get lost in it
so I had the kitchen to myself. Which was larger,
somehow, and scented, and lonely. I was baking scones.

It was Esther gave me the shock – *hello Doris* –
standing in the door-frame like a ghost.
She's been riding all afternoon: the dipper,
the dodgems, the giant wheel. You could tell
she was five months gone just by looking at her.
She needed the privy – *it would save me the walk* –
and I said all right because she was family.

She was out there an age. I had the scones in the oven
and the table scrubbed and the dishes washed
and draining on the rack and was wondering
if she'd stumbled on the garden path
when she came back, grey as a newspaper.
She put a hand to her hair and straightened her frock.
See you at church, then. Give Tom my best –

And then she left. I waited till the scones were finished,
dried my hands on a tea-towel, slipped my rings
from the windowsill, and made my way
past the rain barrel and the rabbit hutch to the door
of the outhouse, which was shut. Spiders' webs,
threaded like a lattice, covered the blistering paint.
I lifted the latch.

Inside, blood was everywhere: on the floor, on the walls.
You could tell where Esther had walked
by a set of white shadows. And then I saw her child –
bigger than the span of my hand and furred,
its fingers were curled near its ears and its eyelids were closed.

Its back was to the bowl. It was a girl.
I couldn't take my eyes off it, until I remembered

where I was and what had happened,
and stepped out onto the path and went back to the kitchen.
The sounds from the fair seemed louder
after that: hurdy gurdy music and the cries of the ticket sellers
ratcheting up for the evening...
I sat at the table, waiting for Tom to come in.
The ceiling caught the colours of the machines.

SINÉAD MORRISSEY

To Our Miscarried One, Age Thirty Now

Though I never saw you, only your clouds,
I was afraid of you, of how you differed
from what we had wanted you to be. And it's as if
you waited, then, where such waiting is done,
for when I would look beside me – and here
you are, in the world of forms, where my wifehood
is now, and every action with him,
as if a thousand years from now
you and I are in some antechamber
where the difference between us is of little matter,
you with perhaps not much of a head yet,
dear garden one, you among the shovels
and spades and wafts of beekeeper's shroud
and sky-blue kidskin gloves.
That he left me is not much, compared
to your leaving the earth – you shifting places
on it, and shifting shapes – you threw off your
working clothes of arms and legs,
and moved house, from uterus
to toilet bowl and jointed stem
and sewer out to float the rivers and

bays in painless pieces. And yet
the idea of you has come back to where
I could see you today as a small, impromptu
god of the partial. When I leave for good,
would you hold me in your blue mitt
for the departure hence. I never thought
to see you again, I never thought to seek you.

SHARON OLDS

The Miscarriage

The doctor says it's an empty room in there

And it is

A pale sack with no visitors
I have made it and surrounded it with my skin
To invite the baby in

But he did not enter
And dissolved himself into the sea so many moons ago

I wait to see
Will the giant bean be in there another day

The women of the world say
Work harder!

The men in the world say
Work harder!

I work and work but I am an empty sack
Until I bleed the food all over the floor

Then I am once again with everything
Until the gods say, you've done well, good sir
You may die now

And the people who were asking me for favors all along
Knock on the coffin door
But I am gone, gone

DOROTHEA LASKY

Sheep

She's lying under a low wind
bedded in mud and afterbirth
her three dead lambs

knotted in a plastic bag.
Crows have pecked out her arse
and now the hen

that's been circling all morning
tugs at a string of birth-meat
like she's pulling a worm in the yard.

I can't not watch.
I too lay stunned
in my own dirt,

the miscarried child
guttering out,
soaking the mattress in blood.

I was afraid to look down
for what I might see –
a human face, a fist.

Yet once it was done I got up,
gathered my bedding
and walked.

FIONA BENSON

Stillborn 1943: Calling Limbo

You were born dead
and your blue limbs were folded
on the living bier of your mother
the umbilical cord unbroken between you
like an out-of-service phone line.
The priest said it was too late
for the blessed baptismal water
that arose from Lough Bofinne
and cleansed the elect of Bantry.
So you were cut from her
and wrapped, unwashed,
in a copy of *The Southern Star*,
a headline about the War across your mouth.
An orange box would serve as coffin
and, as requiem, your mother listened
to hammering out in the hallway,
and the nurse saying to her
that you'd make Limbo without any trouble.
Out of the Mercy Hospital
the gardener carried you under his arm
with barking of dogs for a funeral oration
to a nettle-covered field
that they still call the little churchyard.

You were buried there
without cross or prayer
your grave a shallow hole;
one of a thousand without names
with only the hungry dogs for visitors.
Today, forty years on
I read in *The Southern Star* –
theologians have stopped believing
in Limbo.

But I'm telling you, little brother
whose eyes never opened
that I've stopped believing in them.

For Limbo is as real as Lough Bofinne:
Limbo is the place your mother never left,
where her thoughts lash her like nettles
and *The Southern Star* in her lap is an unread breviary;
where she strains to hear the names of nameless children
in the barking of dogs, each and every afternoon.

DERRY O'SULLIVAN
translated from the Irish by Kaarina Hollo

Born dead

Restless, scalded, all spring
Not wanting to miss any quickening of yours
I burgeoned in time with bulbs and buds
Sap rising giddily in me
Your pulse echoed through
All my nooks and crannies
I couldn't wait
To have you in my arms.

I wondered how you were
So grounded, earthed
In everything,
Your face filling every puddle on the road,
Hair woven in bright trailing clouds
Eyes staring at me from the hearts of daisies,
Your life running fire
In the veins of stone and leaf.

Had I been chanting quietly
Or singing you to sleep,
Not belting out a happy song,
I'd have felt you slip away from me,
Fluttering like a robin
Against the ribs of a bird trap.

Too late I heard your death cry in my guts,
In every scrap of marrow in my bones.

They told me to take a picture of you,
To look at you when I didn't want to
Look at you; to talk to you
When you couldn't answer back.
They told me to dress you in a white babygrow
When I had always intended to dress you
In purple or in crocus-saffron.

These days, the things that interest me
Are things unseen,
The wren's nest in a dark black yew,
The cartography of roots that clamp
Stone and clay under the sod,
The tug of underground rivers,
Treacherous undertow of my own body
That took you when I wasn't looking.

DEIRDRE BRENNAN
translated from the Irish by Biddy Jenkinson

Still Born

She whispers my name often,
the one she gave me after.

No one hears but the worn Jesus
on the swinging crucifix of
her fingered beads.

Fingers that wound the wool
one plain, one purl
for the promise of me.

She stitched my shape into cardigans
I'd never wear,
buttonholes my eyes peeped through
in her nightly dreams.

I never was. Just
slipped into her waiting arms
with the cold absence of sound.

In some deep recess of her loss,
her name for me nestles in her throat.

Shadows play games with her.
Sometimes I skip like a dropped stitch
across the flapping screen
of her washed-out bloody sheets,

loss her repeating pattern:
each cycle, each moon,
each year.

Her cry, the only cry.
Born still but still born,

an almost.

NOELLE LYNSKEY

An uncommon language

A world gone quiet must be this fact.
For which there is no precise language.
The monitor goes off and you are led
past a succession of mothers to a room marked 'empty'.
Taxonomies of grief elude the non-mother,
the un-mothered, the anything-but-this-fact.

No face no teeth no eyes or balled-up fists.
To light the dark with a particular breathing.
A black lamp beats its wings ashore.

In the dark there is breathing.
After five visits to the hospital, the bruising
of inner elbows stitching themselves to themselves
in obsolescence, the nurses stop saying: *sorry for your loss.*
I may come to miss these laminated hallways.
I know my way there, to the artefact of losing.

Loosened from the factual world into a silence
where there is no grave but your own self stumbling
from floor to ceiling without an inch of your life.
Or mine. Or this particular absence.

The Lancastrian nurse is matter-of-fact.
Her metaphors are agrarian; the language of slaughter.
If you start bleeding like a stuck pig.
Under those thick white fingers an ancestry
of collapsing valves and bleating
transfigure into notes. You look familiar.
Why have you come here, again,
to my door with your metaphors of slaughter.

A folder, yellow, the word *baby*
on its cover, refiled as miscellaneous.
What grew in you is not you but a shroud
and any idiot knows a shroud.
A ghost who wakes you up five times a night
stands undecided between rooms
shivering in its thin shadow.
I know my way here, to the language of loss.

My grandmother, who died giving birth,
explains what makes carnelian so red.
I assumed it was the iron in its veins
that made the Romans stamp their profiles
onto its brittle clots. Pulse of empire.

Don't say that / I never visited you.
A ghost is as good a family / as you may get.
Va, itni der baad thusi aaye hai?
After all this time, you've finally come?
The child that clawed you towards death is my kin.
His bones are a line pressed into the earth
you never wanted to cross, transfigured on the back
of a convoy somewhere else. It must be this fact.

A village and its farms and its wells
on an ordinary day in August
smell of blood and panic
carrying a child from this and that
disease, whose death is on your hands.
You look familiar. Why have you come here.

Blighted or to *blight*. What gives up gives over
is absorbed back into itself like a harp gone quiet
imperceptibly in the night.

SANDEEP PARMAR

Sounds of that day
(after Norman MacCaig)

When a silence came,
it was your heart not beating.
When the door hushed, it was
the shuffle of a midwife leaving
us alone in our private grief. A muffled clanging
ten yards down the corridor was the news breaking and
unbreaking in the filing cabinet.
When the black biro rolled, it was me
falling and falling into myself.

When the door
clicked shut behind us, it was the end
of all the silences there were.

They left us
in the busiest corridor in the hospital.

I thought I was hurt in my body only
not knowing that
when your body sleeps
your mind feels all those kicks
in your round stomach before you wake
and the whole world goes numb.

AOIFE LYALL

Ubi Sunt

Where are the sleepsuits, the scratch mitts, and the car seat?
Where are the bassinet, the basket, and the bag?
Where are the bath, the playmat, and the pillow?

Is this the right corridor? Is this the right room?

Where are the smiling faces and the nodding heads?
Where are the screenshots and the photographs?
Where are your heartbeats and your small breaths?

Is this all there is? Is this all I get?

Where are the smiles, the cards, and well-wishes?
Where are the midnight feeds and midday naps?
Where are the songs? Where are the words?

AOIFE LYALL

Her Body

(i.m. Emily Elise Wilson, born 8th June 2002, died 4th May 2013)

I've barely begun to touch this,
yet have done so intimately:

I have lain down beside her
and cradled her heavy head,
cupping the curve of her cold shoulder
in the palm of my hand.

When her arm began to stiffen
in its place across her front,
I've helped strip and re-dress her
in newly-bought things.

I've turned her fair head towards me
so the fluids in her lungs
might spill less copiously,
then let them soak me through.

I have held her body.
I have kept a living lock of her hair.

CATRIONA CLUTTERBUCK

The Lights

Pausing in traffic, I'm miles away
when a file of children forces me
to focus. School now behind them,
they cross in a bustle of coats and bags –
their ages vague to me, but their limbs
bold and flailing, affirming themselves

with shoves and pushes. I marvel
this mass of certainty. Even the loners

get to the other side, lights turning green
as they dawdle. I'm beginning to realise
most children make it. It's rare to see
your child being fought for in intensive care;
to stay with her afterwards, saying her name.
It's unusual, at the undertakers, to finalise
arrangements then fumble for a photograph,
so they could know her when she was warm.

REBECCA GOSS

'That's quite a trick if you can pull it off'

said the boss, breathing heavily down the phone.
He meant Statutory Maternity Pay –
any money a trick, with the company
heading down the tubes, for Christ's sake.

It was months since we last saw him:
taxi-dependent, staggering, a bandaged hand.
Google me a monastery in Spain
he begged. *It's my last chance.*

It was *Google* who finally told me he'd escaped jail
for a fourth drink driving offence.
He'd lost his hair, didn't look like Bill Clinton any more
and died a month later.

I remember those final office days, invoices unpaid,
my pregnant belly snug against the desk.
The phone stayed silent, autumn fell outside.
Inside: regular kicks and a desperate sense of possibility.

CIARA MacLAVERTY

Prayer

I saw you like a hare, stripped and jugged
in your own blood, your tail a rudder
steering you through burgundy and juniper,
your eyes gummed shut. Tadpole,

stripling, elver, don't let the dragtides
pull you under, but root in, bed down,
tucked behind my pelvic bone,
rocked in the emptying stoup of my womb.

FIONA BENSON

from The Sandpit after Rain

Once they began, I was calmer,
I enjoyed the gush of the knife, and the sound of the scissors,
The slop of my bowel being set to one side,
The look on the surgeon's face, his attentiveness and shock,
'Can someone pass me the forceps please?'
And then almost too soon, he was looking away
At the ascension of the 'enormous baby boy',
Rising over the curtain, into the neon ceiling.
And the glowing plinth of green, twitching,
Hacked about...

The fish thrashing on the hook that happened to it.
Well, of course: who wants to be born?

And to be hauled out, in a windowless room
Somewhere near Paddington to Radio 5 Live?

To be born purple, your hair scrambled like eggs?
I have never heard a person so incredulous with rage.

And then they couldn't stop the bleeding.
Everything was larger than they thought, they said.
The baby, the placenta, the vessels, even the womb.
So I lay on the table, haemorrhaging,
And the alarm bell rang and the consultant asked
'What uterine tonics have been administered?'
'Oxytocin, ergometrine…'

It sounded like a restaurant kitchen.
Someone was washing up the fish knives,
And my husband had a face in his hands,
Grave despite the monkey hat,
Benignant, black-eyed, magnanimous.

HANNAH SULLIVAN

Delivery Room

Having you nearly killed me. The problem
with active veins is that I bruise like a peach.
My womb is shaking. I croak out some intensifiers
very   absolutely   utterly   totally   like
I am ready to push now. The doctor asks:
'Do you prefer the geometric or lyrical approach –
I am open to ideas?' 'Neither' I say. His paisley tie
swings like a pendulum over my belly.
When pain strikes it is lilac
against the colour of the walls, which are the colour
of Nice biscuits. In the milk of my mind I draw
a diagonal line and a perfect horizon –
'Have you ever ridden a penny farthing?'
'Is that important? Will I still get the morphine?'
'You are presenting very very posterior,' I hear the rest
of his team concur. One of them doses out the syringe,
the other one is crushing sugared almonds in her teeth.

MONA ARSHI

Inventory: Recovery Room

A thin yellow curtain shivers around my bed.
The IV stand bows its metal head
and a clipboard displays falling numbers.

On the windowsill, empty-eyed bottles stare at rain.
A plastic plug lies on the tile, severing TV from socket.
The screen is black now and shows only my reflection:

pale face, blue gown, surgical socks stretched up to the crotch.
My breasts are funnelled into plastic cups. The machine
whine-whirrs, stretches my flesh, lets go again;

the feeling as strange as a pinned and needled leg.
Still, nothing happens
until I think of milk, of beestings squeezed from a cow's udders,

of my fingers between a calf's gums: the fierce suck of a new mouth,
and the echo of a mother's angry bellows from the field.
Within my chest, an itch begins to stir. The machine's slow suck

and release yields a single drop of yellow liquid.
A second slow drop forms and falls... Another.
Another. I sit and feed the machine, politely, quietly.

Electricity pulls milk from me as I continue my inventory –
by the wall, an empty cot, a hand-knit blanket,
a small white hat and an unused nappy, flat.

DOIREANN NÍ GHRÍOFA

Different rose

I gave birth to an incredibly beautiful daughter, her teeth,
her hair as though from the Song of Songs. And I
felt beautiful myself, thank you. Whereas she –

that's a completely different beauty,
that's beauty I want to protect.
If I had some sort of beauty I'd blush,
anyhow I probably do have some, guys
wouldn't chase after me as much if I didn't,
but I don't like my beauty because guys
chase after it. My daughter's beauty
is something else. My daughter's beauty, I believe,
is the only hope
for this world.

JUSTYNA BARGIELSKA
translated from the Polish by Maria Jastrzębska

Star / Sun / Snow

I *Star*

You were the second. Small in the womb,
kept alive on whispers and songs, nights
spent rocking in the chair, days at the doctor's
listening to your heart beating. You were born
in the Fall. I lay awake through the wee hours
as you spasmed inside. Your father drove us
to the hospital, and it was all
red: sky, leaves, and pavement: your
head a pointed star trapped
by my pelvic bone, but they trimmed, sliced,
opened me up, and out you came screaming,
slippery with my blood. No apology,
but a pause as you laid your head
on my stomach, craned your neck, and
with livid black eyes, you saw
me at last.

II *Sun*

You were the third, big and radiant
in my stomach, but you made me
nauseous at the smell of grilled cheese,
always sick from too much food,
or too little, too much sleep or not
enough. Your growing singed the edges
of my day. You were a hot thing
in snow. On the day of your birth,
I walked to the operating theatre with a cold
spine. Many hands pushed down to wrestle you out
of the abdomen. Then the nurse held you up
in the green light of the surgery. They brought
you close to my face to kiss your wet
head. I couldn't rest until the warm clutch
of you was tucked beneath
my breast.

III *Snow*

You were the first, the one not
born, seen once onscreen shivering with excitement, or
pain. After you died, they scraped
you out of me. But I don't know what they did
with what remained. Knotted in blue plastic, or combusting
from the basement incinerator, smoke hung with the first
unseasonal snow that year? Now, flakes spin,
melt on the warm earth. If you had lived, we would
have opened the door today, and I
would have said: *Look, the snowflakes are*
trying to come in, and you might have crouched
on the wooden boards, your small, round cheek almost
touching the floor, your eye so close to the snowflake, the tiny
perfection of its sharp, white symmetry. Gone by the time
I ask *Can you*
see it?

ZOË BRIGLEY

Jigsaw Puzzle

For a long time
I only had flashes of you:
a shadow spreading
under tightened skin;
my great belly
punctuated with your jumps –
shifting of knee or elbow,
leg, hip or knucklebone
in the mystery mix I carried.

At break of day you burst
out of that dark world
and I spent honeyed months
sorting the bits of your puzzle,
assembling, stroking them:
sole of a foot in the palm of my hand,
curved crown in the hollow of my neck.

Slowly I made your acquaintance, little stranger.

DOIREANN NÍ GHRÍOFA
translated from the Irish by Eiléan Ní Chuilleanáin

William
at four days old

When the lock chucks familiar,
or a cat follows its name from a room,
when silence is strung, or rain
holds back the trees, I thought
I had the lever of these.
But weighing your fine melon head,
your innocent daring to be,

and mouth-first searching,
your tiny fist is allowed absolutely
and I am uncooked
– I can feel my socks being on –
utter, precious apple,
churchyards flatten in my heart,
I've never been brilliant so scared.

JACK UNDERWOOD

Last Poem

So extraordinary was your sister's
short life, it's hard for me to see

a future for you. I know it's there,
your horizon of adulthood,

reachable across a stretch
of ordinary days, yet I can't believe

my fortune – to have a healthy child
with all that waits: the bike, school,

mild and curable diseases.
So we potter through the weeks

and you relax your simian cling,
take exploratory steps, language

budding at your lips. I log the daily
change, another day lived

with every kiss goodnight; wake
relieved by your murmurs at dawn.

Come and hold my hand, little one,
stand beside me in your small shoes,

let's head for your undiscovered life,
your mother's ready now, let's run.

REBECCA GOSS

Hide and Seek

After her swim I wrap my child warm
and take her to the changing room
and lay her down to dry. She holds the corners
of the towel up over her face
like a soft, turquoise tent and yells
'Hide and seek! Hide and seek!'
I lift an edge and shout 'Boo!'
and she shrieks with laughter –
I can feel the heat rising from her body
and smell the chlorine – she hides again,
and again I peek under and she's beside herself
with happiness – she's at an age where she thinks
that if she just stands still in the middle of the lawn
I will not see her, that somehow she is gone –
but always, in the pockets behind this game,
there is this residue, this constriction,
families squeezed behind false walls
or hidden under the floor. I think of the soldier
sensing the hollow under his sole
and prying up the board on all those cramped
and flinching humans; but mostly I think
of the mothers, their hearts jumping out of their mouths
trying to shush their children – my first-born now,
who's never been able to do as she's told,
how she'd have writhed and screamed and bitten like a cat
if I'd tried to hold her quiet, how I'd have hurt her,

clamping her mouth, trying to keep her still.
The trapdoor is always opening, the women and children
are herded into the yard – and I ask myself if,
when my daughters were pulled from me,
I would fight and scream to keep them,
or let them go gently, knowing
there was nothing to be done?
If we were pushed into the showers
would I pretend it was only time to get them clean?
We are not meant to write of the Sho'ah,
we who were not there, but on bad days it's all I can think of,
the mothers trying to shield their children with their bodies
under the showers, screaming for mercy, begging for rain.
And it's never over – here are the children
riding to the border in fridges as the air becomes hot and thin,
their tiny bodies glowing like bright sardines
on the custom officer's hand-held scan;
and here is the tribesman carrying your husband's genitals
and a bloody machete, and you are a mother
running for your life with a baby tied to your back
and two children by the hand
but one small son is falling behind;
Jesus fucking Christ, I don't know who
I'm teaching you to hide from, but look
how eagerly you learn.

FIONA BENSON

Blasket Sound

You're hugged to my chest in a buoyancy aid
called *this is not a Life-jacket*, comfortable
in your skin, in the small, Aran woollen
which still holds the animal smell of sodden sheep.
A crop of them prop up the hill, not judging.

The boat of ourselves rises and falls.
Troughs tower like something out of Exodus.
In the pit of the wave, weighted dark,
from which we're delivered each time to a glimpse
of the Great Blasket, its cataclysm of gulls.

The dark sky's split, but in the boat, storm-engendered
calm; your heart-beat steady, head let fall,
body's profligate heat. Your eyelids close
on eyes whose changing grey this sea trusts,
its moods implicit in their clear transitions.

The child hugs my chest like the island its Atlantic.
My back's bent to the boat's curve, cradled, rocked,
a nautical lullaby, echo of arcs,
like you'd cup the hand to hear the better;
water, listening, like wood, like skin.

ELLEN CRANITCH

Night Watch

It's 1 a.m. and someone's knocking
at sleep's old, battered door – and who
could it be but this boy I love,
calling for me to come out, into
the buckthorn field of being awake –

and so I go, finding him there
no longer talking – but now crying
and crying, wanting to be held;
but *shhh*, what did you want to show
that couldn't wait until the morning?

Was it the moon – because I see it:
the first good bead on a one-bead string;
was it the quiet – because I owned it,
once – but found I wanted more.

NIALL CAMPBELL

February Morning

The winter light was still to hit the window,
and all my other selves were still asleep,
when, standing with this child in all our bareness,
I found that I was a ruined bridge, or one
that stood so long half-built and incomplete;

at other times I'd been a swinging gate,
a freed skiff – then his head dropped in the groove
of my neck, true as a keystone, and I fixed:
all stone and good use, two shores with one crossing.
The morning broke, I kissed his head, and stood.

NIALL CAMPBELL

The Republic of Motherhood

I crossed the border into the Republic of Motherhood
and found it a queendom, a wild queendom.
I handed over my clothes and took its uniform,
its dressing gown and undergarments, a cardigan
soft as a creature, smelling of birth and milk,
and I lay down in Motherhood's bed, the bed I had made
but could not sleep in, for I was called at once to work

in the factory of Motherhood. The owl shift,
the graveyard shift. Feedingcleaninglovingfeeding.
I walked home, heartsore, through pale streets,
the coins of Motherhood singing in my pockets.
Then I soaked my spindled bones
in the chill municipal baths of Motherhood,
watching strands of my hair float from my fingers.
Each day I pushed my pram through freeze and blossom
down the wide boulevards of Motherhood
where poplars bent their branches to stroke my brow.
I stood with my sisters in the queues of Motherhood –
the weighing clinic, the supermarket – waiting
for its bureaucracies to open their doors.
As required, I stood beneath the flag of Motherhood
and opened my mouth although I did not know the anthem.
When darkness fell I pushed my pram home again,
and by lamplight wrote urgent letters of complaint
to the Department of Motherhood but received no response.
I grew sick and was healed in the hospitals of Motherhood
with their long-closed isolation wards
and narrow beds watched over by a fat moon.
The doctors were slender and efficient
and when I was well they gave me my pram again
so I could stare at the daffodils in the parks of Motherhood
while winds pierced my breasts like silver arrows.
In snowfall, I haunted Motherhood's cemeteries,
the sweet fallen beneath my feet –
Our Lady of the Birth Trauma, Our Lady of Psychosis.
I wanted to speak to them, tell them I understood,
but the words came out scrambled, so I knelt instead
and prayed in the chapel of Motherhood, prayed
for that whole wild fucking queendom,
its sorrow, its unbearable skinless beauty,
and all the souls that were in it. I prayed and prayed
until my voice was a nightcry,
sunlight pixellating my face like a kaleidoscope.

LIZ BERRY

My Animal

Amphibian, how you swam
to get here. Left the pond
of your gestation in a rush

of slime. Not quite the blind worm
you were, squirming in light; now
the greedy chick mouthing

for my breast. I clasp you there,
feel your piglet's suck. The skin
on your back velvet as mole

as your nails claw for more.
I turn you upright, pat you
till you purr. It's visceral this love.

REBECCA GOSS

Ruins

Here's my body
in the bath, all the skin's
inflamed trenches
and lost dominions,

my belly's fallen keystone
its slackened tilt –
for all the Aztec gold
I'd not give up

this room where you slept,
your spine to my right,
your head
stoppered in my pelvis

like a good amen –
amen I say
to my own damn bulk,
my milk-stretched breasts –

amen I say to all of this
if I have you –
your screwball smile
at every dawn,

your half-pitched, milk-wild smile
at every waking call,
my loved-beyond-all-reason
darling, dark-eyed girl.

FIONA BENSON

Milk

Could he have known
that any stranger's baby
crying out loud in a street
can start the flow?
A stain that spreads
on fustian
or denim.

This is kindness
which in all our human time
has refused to learn propriety,
which still knows nothing
but the depth of kinship,
the depth of thirst.

MOYA CANNON

Latch

I'd assumed it would be effortless –
mid-morning in a park in spring
love laid against me, lightly veiled
with a square of white muslin

not that shove of mouth
to flesh at some ungodly hour
as you struggled to draw milk
threaded red from your ashen mother.

Three weeks and we were done,
my body flowing back into itself
as I waited for the formula to warm
to the same sluggish temperature as blood

the fear revolving in the darkened kitchen
that I would one day fail again
to give you what you needed,
so preoccupied I almost didn't notice

how, ounce by ounce, you put on life
fingers gripping the bottle tightly
while something – rusted shut inside me –
clicked and lifted.

ESTHER MORGAN

After my son was born

I'd a snip cut in his tongue.
Blood scissored down his chin.
At every squall I'd been unsnibbing
myself and starving him. He knocked

me so my nose coughed blood,
punched a finger through my cornea.
Blood blubbed on my nipple
where his gums met. On the radio
somebody was saying something about Syria.
My son jerked knots of hair from my head,
tears dashed off his fontanelle. He'd fixed
my hips so my clothes didn't fit. I blundered
him once against the door-jamb:
blood. I'd bit his father
when we were younger, drinking harder,
made blood come then. Twice I tried to leave
him screaming, twenty minutes at a time,
but couldn't keep schtum.
One breakfast I broke the mug that insisted
'Don't Mess With Texas.'
Smashed it. And all the time
I smiled so much my teeth dried.
He made everything heavy.
Like they say the bomb did for a while,
so that Americans swam
through their homes, eyes peeled,
picking up everyday things and dropping them
as though they were violated with light and pain.
As though blood hadn't always been there, waiting.

AILBHE DARCY

Embarrassed

I thought it was OK
I could understand the reasons
There might young children, or a nervous man seeing
This small piece of flesh that they weren't quite expecting
So I whispered and tiptoed with nervous discretion
But after six months of her life spent sitting on lids

As she sips on her milk, nostrils sniffing up shift,
Banging her head on toilet-roll dispensers,
I wonder whether these public-loo feeds offend her
'Cos I'm getting tired of discretion and being polite
As my baby's first sips are drowned drenched in shite
I spent the first feeding months of her beautiful life
Feeling nervous and awkward and wanting everything right.
Surrounded by family till I stepped outside the house
It took me eight weeks to get the confidence to go into town
Now the comments around me cut like a knife
as I rush into toilet cubicles feeling nothing like nice
Because I'm giving her milk that's not in a bottle
Wishing the cocaine-generation white powder would topple
I see pyramid-sales pitches across our green globe
and female breasts banned
unless they're out just for show.
And the more I go out, the more I can't stand it
I walk into town, feel surrounded by bandits,
'Cos in this country of billboards covered in tits
And family newsagents' magazines full of it
WH Smith top shelves out for men
– Why don't you complain about them?
'Cos in this country of billboards covered in tits
And family newsagents' magazines full of it
WH Smith top shelves out for men
I'm getting embarrassed
in case a small flash of flesh might offend.

And I don't want to parade this, I'm not trying to make a show
But when I'm told I'd be better just staying at home
And when another mum I know is thrown off a bus
And another one told to get out of the pub
Even my grandma said that maybe I was sexing it up.
I'm sure the milk-makers love all the fuss
All the cussing and worry and looks of disgust
As another mother turns from nipples to powder
Ashamed or embarrassed by comments around her
And as I hold her head up and pull my cardie across
And she sips on that liquor made by everyone's God

I think, for God's Sake, Jesus drank it
So did Siddhartha
Muhammad
and Moses
and both of their fathers
Ganesh, and Shiva and Brighid and Buddha
And I'm sure they weren't doing it sniffing on piss
As their mothers sat embarrassed on cold toilet lids
In a country of billboards covered in tits
In a country of low-cut tops, cleavage and skin
In a country of cloth bags and recycling bins.
And as I desperately try to take all of this in
I hold up her head, I can't get my head round
The anger towards us and not to the sounds
Of lorries off-loading formula milk
Into countries where water runs dripping in filth,
In towns where breasts are oases of life
now dried up in two-for-one offers, enticed
by labels and logos and gold standard rights
claiming breast milk is healthier
powdered and white
packaged and branded and sold at a price
so that nothing is free in this money-fuelled life
which is fine
if you need it or prefer to use bottles
where water is clean and bacteria boiled
but in towns where they drown in pollution and sewage
bottled kids die and they knew that they'd do it;
In towns where pennies are savoured like sweets
We're now paying for one thing that's *always* been free,
In towns empty of hospital beds
Babies die, diarrhoea-fuelled – all that, breastmilk would end.
So no more will I sit on these cold toilet lids
No matter how embarrassed I feel as she sips
'Cos in this country of billboards covered in tits
I think
I should try to get used to this.

HOLLIE McNISH

Miracle

In supermarkets, strapped
in a trolley,

on the motorway,
belted in the back of a car,

under the foundered houses,
open mouthed and fed by drips,

in a box drilled with holes,
in the hold of a boat,

in fish crates and on cardboard,
on pallets and straw,

on a bed of needles
on the forest floor,

in the curve of a rosy scarf
tied to a woman's back,

in a line of walkers
along railway tracks,

under a tarpaulin
on mud and sand,

a child is sleeping,
a child is sleeping.

STEPHANIE NORGATE

Late song

It's a still morning, quiet and cloudy
the kind of grey day I like best;
they'll be here soon, the little kids first,
creeping up to try and frighten me,
then the tall young men, the slim boy
with the marvellous smile, the dark girl
subtle and secret; and the others,
the parents, my children, my friends –

and I think: these truly are my weather
my grey mornings and my rain at night,
my sparkling afternoons and my birdcall at daylight;
they are my game of hide and seek, my song
that flies from a high window. They are
my dragonflies dancing on silver water.

Without them I cannot move forward, I am
a broken signpost, a train fetched up on
a small siding, a dry voice buzzing in the ears;
for they are also my blunders
and my forgiveness for blundering,
my road to the stars and my seagrass chair
in the sun. They fly where I cannot follow

and I – I am their branch, their tree.
My song is of the generations, it echoes
the old dialogue of the years; it is the tribal
chorus that no one may sing alone.

LAURIS EDMOND

Mini Van

In the back, with no seats or windows,
just more grey metal. In the end I curl up
on my coat and listen to the road smooth
and bumpy, slow till he puts his foot down
on the new bypass by Hucknall. This was where
mum worked before the war, a butcher's sooner
than be in service. Though I don't know it yet.
And we're still alive, both of us.
Unseen dark-eyed trees are a way home

through Sherwood Forest, where one day
I'll run with the Harriers. But I'm not
a teenager yet, and this is Mick's van,
our Mick driving us large as life
from Nottingham to a houseful of the dead
still living none of them more than an hour
from where they were born. It is
one winter Saturday, with the tea just mashed
and a bit of dinner waiting for us.

I'm tired of everyone being dead.
I'm tired of being in this van.

PETER SANSOM

I Cannot Say I Did Not

I cannot say I did not ask
to be born. I asked with my mother's beauty,
and her money. I asked with my father's desire
for his orgasms and for my mother's money.
I asked with the cradle my sister had grown out of.
I asked with my mother's longing for a son,
I asked with patriarchy. I asked

with the milk that would well in her breasts, needing to be
drained by a little, living pump.
I asked with my sister's hand-me-downs, lying
folded. I asked with geometry, with
origami, with swimming, with sewing, with
what my mind would thirst to learn.
Before I existed, I asked, with the love of my
children, to exist, and with the love of their children.
Did I ask with my tiny flat lungs
for a long portion of breaths? Did I ask
with the space in the ground, like a portion of breath,
where my body will rest, when it is motionless,
when its elements move back into the earth?
I asked, with everything I did not
have, to be born. And nowhere in any
of it was there meaning, there was only the asking
for being, and then the being, the turn
taken. I want to say that love
is the meaning, but I think that love may be
the means, what we ask with.

SHARON OLDS

Childhood

These criss-cross lines printed on the snow
are bones of trees laid bare by the moon.
We should not be looking so hard

at what a tree would rather keep to itself.
Would we not fear to be shown
how like replicas we are, and how mechanical?

Let's play that game again, stepping out
along the branches – pretending to tip –
as if we still believed we couldn't fall.

KATHARINE TOWERS

daughters

woman who shines at the head
of my grandmother's bed,
brilliant woman, i like to think
you whispered into her ear
instructions. i like to think
you are the oddness in us,
you are the arrow
that pierced our plain skin
and made us fancy women;
my wild witch gran, my magic mama,
and even these gaudy girls.
i like to think you gave us
extraordinary power and to
protect us, you became the name
we were cautioned to forget.
it is enough,
you must have murmured,
to remember that i was
and that you are. woman, i am
lucille, which stands for light,
daughter of thelma, daughter
of georgia, daughter of
dazzling you.

LUCILLE CLIFTON

The trouble

between mothers and daughters
        is how to forgive

the one to whom
        you owe too much

what you see when you look
in the mirror

how you forget you were in her
and she is in you

or the way
she loves you

and cannot, will not
leave you alone

JANE CLARKE

I Wish I Had More Sisters

I wish I had more sisters,
enough to fight with and still
have plenty more to confess to,
embellishing the fight so that I
look like I'm right and then turn
all my sisters, one by one, against
my sister. One sister will be so bad
the rest of us will have a purpose
in bringing her back to where
it's good (with us) and we'll feel
useful, and she will feel loved.

Then another sister
will have a tragedy, and again
we will unite in our grief, judging
her much less than we did the bad
sister. This time it was not
our sister's fault. This time
it could have happened to any

of us and in a way it did. We'll
know she wasn't the only
sister to suffer. We all suffer
with our choices, and we
all have our choice of sisters.

My sisters will seem like a bunch
of alternate me, all the ways
I could have gone. I could see
how things pan out without
having to do the things myself.
The abortions, the divorces,
the arson, swindles, poison jelly.
But who could say they weren't
myself, we are so close. I mean,
who can tell the difference?

I could choose to be a fisherman's
wife, since I'd be able to visit
my sister in her mansion, sipping
bubbly for once, braying
to the others, who weren't invited.
I could be a traveler, a seer,
a poet, a potter, a flyswatter.
None of those choices would be
as desperate as they seem now.
My life would be like one finger
on a hand, a beautiful, usable, ringed,
wrung, piano-and-dishpan hand.

There would be both more and less
of me to have to bear. None of us
would be forced to be stronger
than we could be. Each of us could
be all of us. The pretty one.
The smart one. The bitter one.
The unaccountably-happy-
for-no-reason one. I could be,
for example, the hopeless

one, and the next day my sister
would take my place, and I would
hold her up until my arms gave way
and another sister would relieve me.

BRENDA SHAUGHNESSY

I wish I had more mothers
(after Brenda Shaughnessy)

I wish I had more mothers
enough to have one who wasn't exhausted,
and another who could have sat typing, night after night,
spell-checked the papers, while another would sit on my bed
when my sisters were fighting, know it was deadly and serious
and they couldn't both be right. One mother could've been
effortlessly elegant, dabbed at cologne with her fingers,
knocked them dead at funerals with her ethereal smile,
the black lace of her hat. We could have been haunted
by the smell of her when we sorted her clothes.
There could have been lipstick, a nonsense of underthings,
frothing in rose. Another mother could have been
the dreamer, she could have gone wherever she thought
might be sweeter; without us. One could have painted,
appeared at lunch with flake white on her cheekbones,
or the bridge of her nose. I could have walked away from
the gloating mother-knows-best and gone to another.
I could have given up on the one who smoothed it over
without wanting to know what it was. I could have turned
to the mother who knew every bit of it, because she'd done it
alone and herself. I could have hugged the mother, cuddly
but absent minded, who let her soft flesh fall from her corset,
but left her shopping where she'd bought it, round the town.
I could have kept the one who'd no idea where we were,
what time we'd promised to come home, lied for us as a reflex,
but not the one who wept when it all got beyond her and said

153

we'd all made her life so difficult and really let her down.
I could have left the one who thought prayer was the answer
to pray on her own, could have had a mother who could cook,
who haggled in the market, who came home flourishing
something exotic that wasn't green. There'd be a mother for
each sister and my brother. I could have had all these mothers
round for coffee, made little cakes, but in the chatter and laughter
and the clatter of their cups, no one would learn anything or
come home different, but I'd have tried. I'd want the one who cried
in the pantry the first Christmas I was nursing, to have told me
and let me feel loved. I'd be able to laugh at the one that rang
to tell me my new boyfriend needs a baby, as if I ought to try
harder – forget about the cancer or the thirty years too late –
because I'd have the one who thought I was a triumph through
every failure, whose mind was still sharp and tender, who could
listen, who still had enough of a whistle to call up a dog.

ANN GRAY

Want

When I was twelve, I wanted a macaw
        but they cost hundreds of dollars.

If we win the lottery? I asked.
        Macaws weren't known to be great talkers,

but they were affectionate.
        Yes, my mother said. *If we win the lottery.*

I was satisfied, so long as it wasn't impossible.

The macaw would be blue.

GRETCHEN MARQUETTE

With Stars

My mother speaks from the dark – why
haven't I closed my eyes? Why don't I
sleep? And when I say I can't, she
wraps the quilt around me and leads me
to the window. I am four years old and
a star has the power of wishes.
We stare out together, but she sees past
their fierce shimmering sameness, each
point of light the emblem
of some lost, remembered face. What
do they want? I ask. 'Not to be
forgotten,' she says, and draws me close.
Then her gaze sifts the scattered brilliance.
Her hand goes out – 'There! that one!' so
her own mother, dead years back, looks down
on us. Sleep then like a hammer
among the orbiting dead.

Tonight it is the stars reminding
keeps me up past midnight.
My mother's voice, as in that childhood room,
is with me so surely I might rush out
and find that window, those stars
no further than the next doorway, and her
there waiting – awake all night
because I was awake. 'Go
to sleep,' I'd say. 'They want me
awake tonight.' And she'd know who I meant –
those others still living and afar
because I think them there. And why not
give the dead this benefit of separations?
There were so many nameless before.
But oh, if one falls, *if* –
how can that child ever fall asleep
until sunrise?

TESS GALLAGHER

155

I Stop Writing the Poem

to fold the clothes. No matter who lives
or who dies, I'm still a woman.
I'll always have plenty to do.
I bring the arms of his shirt
together. Nothing can stop
our tenderness. I'll get back
to the poem. I'll get back to being
a woman. But for now
there's a shirt, a giant shirt
in my hands, and somewhere a small girl
standing next to her mother
watching to see how it's done.

TESS GALLAGHER

Hers

My mother said she knew, just knew I was going to be a girl,
two boys before me and two boys after, fodder for a hungry farm,
but I was hers. She taught me her tricks of the trade: it'll look
like dinner is nearly ready if the table is set when he comes in,

bread and butter will fill them up, add three drops of vinegar
to water so your mirrors and windows will gleam, cool
your fingers before rubbing lard into flour for pastry, a handful
of ground almonds will keep your fruit cake moist,

darn a few socks every night and never leave the ironing
for more than a week, don't cut off rhubarb stalks with a knife,
just twist them clean from the crown, and always hold onto
the children's allowance; a woman must have something of her own.

JANE CLARKE

Shoulders

A man crosses the street in rain,
stepping gently, looking two times north and south:
because his son is asleep on his shoulder.

No car must splash him.
No car drive too near to his shadow.

This man carries the world's most sensitive cargo
but he's not marked.
Nowhere does his jacket say FRAGILE,
HANDLE WITH CARE.

His ear fills up with breathing.
He hears the hum of a boy's dream
deep inside him.

We're not going to be able
to live in this world
if we're not willing to do what he's doing
with one another.

The road will only be wide.
The rain will never stop falling.

NAOMI SHIHAB NYE

New Road

How long have we been standing
in the rain? Small son, novice mum
both air-drying our own tears –

watching a drowned ritual where
each wordless man knows his role
his turn, his tool, his time. There is

the thick hot pouring of tarmac
obliterating smell with its cleanness,
the deft sprinkling from a finger-

blackened watering-can, while the
Wackerplate, too loud for trivialities,
empties mind to make itself space

and the rapt passage of the steam-roller –
so heavy it rumbles in your ankles –
sounds the deep notes of sleep after rage.

How long will we stand here and wait?
Watching, as the Blaw-knox lays
watching, as the old road fades,

its crumbled markings, worn lettering
cross habits, wheel-skid patterns
and weary camber. Attentive men

with rakes and shovels make it go away.
Now the painters, with chalk line, come
to make bold, clear, straight signs.

OLIVIA McCANNON

My Father Asks Why

How could he have known?
The nights I forced myself
to stay awake doing sit-ups,
up and down, up and down...

And when I nearly passed out
the skinny saint chanted
and numbers lay across the plate
of my mind. She never let me
rest, and my parents being
somehow bound to me
never slept. At first light,
when the world hatched,
I unrolled my body from cramps,
and ran in light clothes,
knowing that my body
ate itself in the cold,
pared itself down, like a sculpture,
to something that was always
'nearly perfect'.

My father couldn't have known
that all the while I still
believed I was going to win,
bone, blood, and chill.

Father, I only think to number
another mile, going round and round
the neighbourhood, like a rumour.

The world burns out, and flips over,
turns inside out, the cold side
of a hospital pillow, a dead life.

LEANNE O'SULLIVAN

The Cord

I used to lie on the floor for hours after
school with the phone cradled between
my shoulder and my ear, a plate of cold
rice to my left, my schoolbooks to my right.

Twirling the cord between my fingers
I spoke to friends who recognised
the language of our realm. Throats and lungs
swollen, we talked into the heart of the night,

toying with the idea of hair dye and suicide,
about the boys who didn't love us, who
we loved too much, the pang of the nights.
Each sentence was new territory, a door

someone was rushing into, the glass shattering
with delirium, with knowledge and fear.
My mother never complained about the phone bill,
what it cost for her daughter to disappear

behind a door, watching the cord
stretching its muscle away from her.
Perhaps she thought it was the only way
she could reach me, sending me away

to speak in the underworld. As long as
I was speaking she could put my ear
to the tenuous earth, allow me to listen,
to decipher. And these were the elements

of my mother – the earthed wire,
the burning cable – as if she flowed
into the room with me to somehow say:
Stay where I can reach you, the dim room,

the dark earths. Speak of this
and when you feel removed from it
I will pull the cord and take you
back towards me.

LEANNE O'SULLIVAN

Supple Cord

My brother, in his small white bed,
held one end.
I tugged the other
to signal I was still awake.
We could have spoken,
could have sung
to one another,
we were in the same room
for five years,
but the soft cord
with its little frayed ends
connected us
in the dark,
gave comfort
even if we had been bickering
all day.
When he fell asleep first
and his end of the cord
dropped to the floor,
I missed him terribly,
though I could hear his even breath
and we had such long and separate lives
ahead.

NAOMI SHIHAB NYE

a song in the front yard

I've stayed in the front yard all my life.
I want a peek at the back
Where it's rough and untended and hungry weed grows.
A girl gets sick of a rose.

I want to go in the back yard now
And maybe down the alley,
To where the charity children play.
I want a good time today.

They do some wonderful things.
They have some wonderful fun.
My mother sneers, but I say it's fine
How they don't have to go in at quarter to nine.
My mother, she tells me that Johnnie Mae
Will grow up to be a bad woman.
That George'll be taken to Jail soon or late
(On account of last winter he sold our back gate).

But I say it's fine. Honest, I do.
And I'd like to be a bad woman, too,
And wear the brave stockings of night-black lace
And strut down the streets with paint on my face.

GWENDOLYN BROOKS

The World Is Your Beautiful Younger Sister

Seeing her as seldom as you do, it doesn't change,
The ire, the shame, the fists you must remember

To smooth flat just thinking what they did,
What they promised, then took – those men

Who offered to pay, to keep, the clan of them
Lording it over the others like high school boys

And their kids brothers. Men with interests to protect,
And mute marble wives. Men who let her

Beam into their faces, watching her shoulders rise,
Her astonishing new breasts, making her believe

It was she who gave permission.
They plundered her youth, then moved on.

Those awful, awful men. The ones
Whose wealth is a kind of filth.

TRACY K. SMITH

Outgrown

(for Zoe)

It is both sad and a relief to fold so carefully
her outgrown clothes and line up the little worn shoes
of childhood, so prudent, scuffed and particular.
It is both happy and horrible to send them galloping
back tappity-tap along the misty chill path into the past.

It is both a freedom and a prison, to be outgrown
by her as she towers over me as thin as a sequin
in her doc martens and her pretty skirt,
because just as I work out how to be a mother
she stops being a child.

PENELOPE SHUTTLE

Empty Nest

Dear child, the house pines when you leave.
I research whether there is any bird who grieves
over its empty nest.

                    Your vacant room
is a still-life framed by the unclosed door;
read by sunlight, an open book on the floor.

I fold the laundry; hang your flower dress
in darkness. Forget-me-nots.

*

Beyond the tall fence, I hear horse-chestnuts
counting themselves.
                    Then autumn; Christmas.
You come and go, singing. Then ice; snowdrops.

Our home hides its face in hands of silence.

I knew mothering, but not this other thing
which hefts my heart each day. Heavier.
Now I know.

*

This is the shy sorrow. It will not speak   up.

I play one chord on the piano;
                         it vanishes, tactful,
as dusk muffles the garden; a magpie staring from its branch.
The marble girl standing by the bench.

From the local church, bells like a spelling.
And the evening star like a text.
And then what next...

CAROL ANN DUFFY

All at Once

All at once my ability
to retain warmth was
gone. Now the kids
have moved out, I sniffed,
funny that. I buried myself
under more blankets. The fire
roared. The warmer of us two
could no longer take the chill
off me. I shivered and
shuddered as if facing death.

Which I was. Death and I
were standing on a bank.
Between us, nothing but
a considerable distance.

ANNA ENQUIST
translated from the Dutch by David Colmer

Swallow Twice

Given the smallest prompt, Father will describe
how I skulked just beyond the lamplight's reach

watching the ring of men ripe with beer and laughter
push thick fingers into the mountain of spiced meat

roasted with onions, ginger and chillies like an altar
I fought to worship at, swiping through their arms

at the chunks – a mouse attempting to feast with kings.
Frustrated, Father stopped their speech

so I could reach in, greedily choose the choicest piece,
ignore his warnings and tear at the muscle, strain

against the flesh till its elasticity slipped my fingers
and the chunk, chillies and all slapped into my eyes.

Father thumped my back as I coughed on the pepper
/ swallow twice he urged / dropping the wailing mess

of me on Mother's knees. What Father didn't know
is I imagined the key to their impenetrable talk

lay in the cubed meat and I longed to be like them.

In the circle of friends I have, most of our conversations
revolve around music, the heft and sway of the changing

world, the rapid rate of our redundance, how best
to pretend we know it all and when beer loosens

what inhibitions are left after shredding meat
with bare fingers, laughter cloaks our weaknesses:

our inabilities to provide for those we love, who love us,
we who still know nothing of what our lovers want,

how frightening it is to be have nephews growing up
who want to be like us, like men.

INUA ELLAMS

Never

He never taught me how to hold
a pair of clippers. I never saw him
dab cologne on his cheeks. I don't know

the smell of his sweat, or if our fingers
look alike. I didn't learn to drink
by draining whatever wine he might have left
or sharing an ice cold can. He never
wrestled me down, so I never grew up
to return the favour. I didn't learn to love
music thumbing through his vinyl LPs.
I never woke him. He never once raised
his voice at me. I never heard him laugh
and although I remember him at the end
of a long distance call, once,
I don't remember his voice
or what it might have sounded like
saying my name.

JACOB SAM-LA ROSE

The Other End of the Line

After he passed, my mother spoke about him
as if he were still there. She complained
if he didn't come to her in dreams.
You haven't gone to see him yet, she said,
meaning it had been some time since
I'd stood over his grave. For me, there was more
silence. The telephone receiver off the hook,
no one there at the other end of the line.
*The person you are trying to reach
is currently unavailable*, said the automated
voice. And there was so much left to say.

JACOB SAM-LA ROSE

Prayer of the Backhanded

Not the palm, not the pear tree
Switch, not the broomstick,
Nor the closet extension
Cord, not his braided belt, but God,
Bless the back of my daddy's hand
Which, holding nothing tightly
Against me and not wrapped
In leather, eliminated the air
Between itself and my cheek.
Make full this dimpled cheek
Unworthy of its unfisted print
And forgive my forgetting
The love of a hand
Hungry for reflex, a hand that took
No thought of its target
Like hail from a blind sky,
Involuntary, fast, but brutal
In its bruising. Father, I bear the bridge
Of what might have been
A broken nose. I lift to you
What was a busted lip. Bless
The boy who believes
His best beatings lack
Intention, the mark of the beast.
Bring back to life the son
Who glories in the sin
Of immediacy, calling it love.
God, save the man whose arm
Like an angel's invisible wing
May fly backward in fury
Whether or not his son stands near.
Help me hold in place my blazing jaw
As I think to say, *excuse me*.

JERICHO BROWN

As a Human Being

There is the happiness you have
And the happiness you deserve.
They sit apart from one another
The way you and your mother
Sat on opposite ends of the sofa
After an ambulance came to take
Your father away. Some good
Doctor will stitch him up, and
Soon an aunt will arrive to drive
Your mother to the hospital
Where she will settle next to him
Forever, as promised. She holds
The arm of her seat as if she could
Fall, as if it is the only sturdy thing,
And it is since you've done what
You always wanted. You fought
Your father and won, marred him.
He'll have a scar he can see all
Because of you. And your mother,
The only woman you ever cried for,
Must tend to it as a bride tends
To her vows, forsaking all others
No matter how sore the injury.
No matter how sore the injury
Has left you, you sit understanding
Yourself as a human being finally
Free now that nobody's got to love you.

JERICHO BROWN

Tooth

You know how it happens: the first wince,
the lingering sting. It sharpens, deepens
until the pain won't let you sleep and you find yourself
in a waiting room, fingernails pinched into slick palms.

A chair tilts you back. Mouth ajar, you hear the latex gloves
– snap snap – and see the syringe. You hold your breath
as anaesthetic heats the flesh of your cheek.
A metal clamp is thrust between your teeth
and the tugging begins, until something in you relents.
The bloodied tooth is tugged from bone, torn clear
from the jaw it was born in. Blood spurts into stuffed gauze.
The dentist lifts the tooth, asks if you want to keep it.
You shake your head: *No*. No – you'll keep
                                        the empty socket, the hole.

Later, what seems strangest is how your tongue,
still numb, slips in and out of the gap,
as it did when you lost your first child-tooth.
This time, though, there will be no patted head, no fairy,
no new tooth. Absence festers in you like an abscess –
the un-held hand, the un-patted back. This time, you are left
with a pocketful of feeble painkillers and cold rain that rolls
under your collar as you wait for the bus home.
Is this what it is to be an adult? Yes. You are alone.

DOIREANN NÍ GHRÍOFA

from Correspondences: a poem

The same question endlessly repeated,
fingers grasping the same crumbling edge,
one of the first signs of illness
never allowing a lesion to form.
How to cope financially, how to make
nothing into something. When I was still a child
you asked my brothers and I to sit with you
at the table; *I implore you,*
it is all I ask: do what you love, only
choose work you love, no matter what it is.
Not like me, making nothing
out of nothing. Though at least you came out ahead
on one side of the ledger, the side of love dark
with pencil marks, the black of my mother's hair
as she sat in the row ahead at the concert hall
the night you met. Unlike me, with both
blank pages. *How are you coping*, you asked,
over and over, *financially*.
The dreaded endless question born of worry and
helplessness. At least, I always joked, when
you have nothing, nothing can be taken from you,
but we both knew that was bad math, that there was
always something to be taken from you,
not lost, but taken. And so that was the one question
on which you alighted, in the last months
before that decade of silence,
an endless painful longing to rescue,
the repetition of the plough horse,
majestic head bent to earth,
turning the same direction
at the end of each row.

[...]

the morning light, the same crimson
monks wear in Drepung or
hanging in the windows of Lisbon,
the pressback chair, the rug
sewn from scraps, the face of a child
torn from a magazine and tacked to the wall for her
forsaken expression,
the books on the plank-and-brick shelves,
the hundreds of LPs, every orchestra and
soloist in their cardboard
sleeves with spectacular covers I spent
my childhood living into,
every particular of driftwood and stone,
snowshoes, books on animal tracks, astronomical
maps, the memoirs of political prisoners and
Life with the Painters of La Ruche, edible
plants and woodcraft, pages of tortured
solace, survival in the wilderness;
always, from the moment we arrived
there you were, your spirit saturating
every blessed molecule,
even, exactly where you last left it,
years before,
an unbearable phrase of music
in the air

Not only what a soul remembers
but all it forgets,

as if all you know and all you don't know
have changed places;

cloud shadow on the hills,
the sudden downpour in the vale of Borrowdale,
turning the blue slate black,
bare arms in the rain;
animals turned to stone in the blue lias beds;

the name that can't be understood
without its story;
the narrow-bladed paddle and
all the water it displaces;
the help and helplessness
of love;

the photos and the millions
of indifferent eyes that have looked upon
their shaven nakedness;

the ghost life that lives itself
beside us, the shadow of what happened
and what didn't happen;

If ever I lose
my memory of you, walk beside me
like a stag; like a bird heard, unseen

and then
we came and you were no longer there
everything in its place
your presence gone

we waited, went out, returned
but still nothing held
the light after rain,
for I looked there too
in the rain that fell

[...]

each word embedded,
the mud of another country on its shoes,
an upstairs lamp so we won't bump our heads on
darkness, each word a fall
into inarticulate space, each word
a stub, a placeholder for the

inexpressible solute or solvent,
the fragment that is every object, every
cry, all the invisible freedoms
contained in a pair of socks, in warm clothes,
the infrastructure each object implies, of
industry, experience, chance, corruption,
loneliness, love; impossible to understand an object
without its story,
the brutal, the blessed particularity,
I think of the poet who wrote sixty pages of
rhyming verse fermented in classical philosophy and
Hindu gods, each word a barricade (as I am now)
against it; no matter what questions we build, whether
war, or illness, no matter the syntax or
mysticism, medical terms,
historical analysis, no matter,
because *to touch*
means *always*

the warm skin under the flannel shirt,
the soft hair under the tweed cap,

smell of wet pavement on that cool morning,
the ragged book left open by the bed,
every noun and verb a slow peristalsis
through our understanding,
each word so worn with use,

wanting to keep the surface as simple as possible,
without acrobatics or overstatement,
as invisible as a landmark in the desert,
the place where the bus driver releases the airlock,
an exhalation, and the traveller with his sack
steps down into the wilderness, an expanse
of sand without any singularity to the foreign eye,
though he walks resolutely,

without hesitation, into it,
knowing the way,
based on a single grain, a slant of light,
an angle, an intensity, a calibration of
an ever-changing element, a body
language, like the moment of
looking into that face and finding
yourself suddenly, or was it slowly

or like the moment of
looking into that face and finding
yourself suddenly or was it slowly
alone,
who is that woman with the baby,
pointing to me and to your grandchild

and when your language ceased,
a gap ever widening, swaying and closing, swaying and
opening between us, every word with the
inarticulation of the sea when there is
no shore to break and therefore bring
its rhythm, the swaying deck from which you
reached out to that coffin, to that child,

I began the piling of words,
to dig myself out
to dare myself
that single word

[...]

ANNE MICHAELS

The Quilt

The quilt's a ragtag syzygy
of everything I've been or done,
a knotted spell in every seam,
the stuff that pricks and pulls. The quilt

began in '96. I scrapped
the blotch batiks and brocatelles
each backward-bending paisley hook
that tied me to my town. The quilt

came with me when I packed and left
– a bad patch, that – you'll see I've sewn
a worried blot of grey and black
to mark a bruisy year. The quilt

advances, in a shock campaign
through block-fluorescent souvenirs
of seedy clubs and bad psytrance
and peters out in blue. The quilt

came with me when I ditched the scene
and dressed myself as someone new
– or someone else, at any rate
and someone better, too – I felt

a charlatan in borrowed suits,
and flower prints, and pastel hues,
but things had turned respectable,
and so I stitched that in. The quilt

has tessellated all of it.
Arranged, like faithful paladins,
are half a dozen bits and scraps
from those who took a turn, then split –

the dapper one, the rugby fan,
the one who liked his gabardine,
the one who didn't want to be *another patch in your fucking quilt*
but got there all the same. The quilt

is lined with all the bitter stuff
I couldn't swallow at the time –
the lemon-yellow calico
I never wore again. The guilt

snuck into every thread of it
and chafed all through the honeymoon.
I scissored out the heart of it
and stitched it, fixed it, final, here –

with every other bright mistake
I wear, like anyone.

ABIGAIL PARRY

Family Portrait

At our table we don't say grace.
We sit silent in the face of our questions,
a crown of mosquitos swarming our heads.

In this picture, some hot day in March,
the sun makes a strange halo around my ear,
light exploding in our dining room window.

Outside, the mongrels whine against our door,
two pups forbidden shelter for their impurity,
my weak heart dividing to offer all its scraps.

But what could I offer them, when I knew nothing
of love, and took my corrections with the belt
every evening? There in that city of exile, cobbled

square of salt-rust and rebellion, my father's face looms
its last obstruction, where the dark folds of bougainvillea
remain unclimbing; the one clipped flower

of my objection. That withering bloom still hangs limply
in its tangled brooch; my dress, my hands, bruised and falling
loosely about my thighs, unable to ask for a single thing.

And perhaps it was only the rain howling in my ear,
as I observe my doppelgänger in the shadows of the frame,
setting fire to the curtains while we slept. Poisoning

whatever dark potion fills my father's cup, my mother
at his shoulder with her fixed pitcher, pouring. She was
pregnant then, and still wore the mouth of her youth,

so quiet and unsure of itself, her fingers' twelve points
streaked across the jug's fogged glass. There I am again.
I am not myself – long before I shed my Medusa hair,

before anyone caught my sister eating black bits
of a millipede, shell and yellow fur snagged in her teeth,
I had my crooked guilt. My brother with his dagger

at my throat. This is us. This is all of us.
Before we knew this life would shatter, moving wild
and unwanted through the dark and the light.

SAFIYA SINCLAIR

My Mother's Love

I asked my mother
where she kept her love
and she answered:

My love is a golden bird
in a crystal cage

and that cage is perched
on the head of a fat boa
coiled at the top of a tree

and that tree is surrounded
by scorpions
and tigers and bears.

So I went in search of the tree
and fought the beasts
around its trunk.

I fought the fat snake.
But when I opened the cage

I found a goldcrest
with its wings torn off.

PASCALE PETIT

Her Harpy Eagle Claws

Comfort your mother
Dr Pryce says.

My mama is perched
on top of the wardrobe

growling. She's holding
her spider monkey teddy
in her six-inch talons

the way she used to hold my hand
when we crossed the boulevard

and I let go

because being hit by cars
felt so much safer.

PASCALE PETIT

My Wolverine

When my mother says I was her kit
taken from her too early,
I think not of cats but a wolverine,
my devourer of snowfields, who,
when she can find no more prey,
eats herself, even the frozen bones.
I crawl down the black phone line
as if it's an umbilicus
to the last refuge on our planet,
towards whatever back country
happens to be her territory today.
My nails remember to claw.
I lope up the icefall
she's retreated to, that's melting behind her
as she climbs her precipice, too drunk
on freedom to come down.
She shows me the den where words are born
fighting. I do not blame her.
I hold the receiver against my face
as if it's her muzzle, her reek
of blizzard-breath. I embrace
the backward-barbed teeth that can
fell a moose and gnaw even its hooves.
Kit – she spits the word out

in a half-love half-snarl and I
am her glutton, scavenging on my yelp
when I was torn from her after birth,
and again now – not long before she dies.

PASCALE PETIT

Snakes

All those years when my mother knew exactly
what my grandfather was doing, she knew,
and she let it continue. Her excuse: *It happened to me too.*
After my grandmother had left him, had packed her things
and moved out, he complained of being lonely,
said he wanted a girl to help about the house.
I begged her not to send me, peed on myself, hollered,
rolled in the dirt, told her how he spooned-up
against me at night, his hot breath quickening
around my neck. How frightened
I was of his darkened contorted face. Then the touch
of those rough, callused hands, reaching for
my breasts – the shame of them –
the revulsion of them – I wished they would stay buried
within my body. Then the sudden sharp pain
of those large knobbed fingers between my legs. It was then
that I learnt to hate myself, to feel different,
to know that something was wrong
with me. She taught me to take it, to forgive my grandfather
and take it. She taught me that this was what it meant
to be a woman. I did not know how to name
what my mother and my grandfather had done to me,
until that day at the zoo when I saw them, a family,
curled around each other, the venomous tongues that darted
and flickered, the evil intent in their glowing red eyes.

JACQUELINE BISHOP

181

from **Grunter**

Glass

If anybody touches me I shatter
and bits of glass go everywhere like beeps.
The doctor says *I'm sorry*. I am too.
I'm sorry I can't hear a word he's saying.
I'm sorry I can't stop repeating sorry.
I'm sorry if I'm sorry. I'm a genius.
I'm sorry if I'm sick. *You can go.*

Joy

I'm grunting now but soon I will be screaming:
I scream until the sky itself is screaming.
I scream for how I am.
I scream for joy.
There's only this one mouth in the universe,
only one, it's open, and it's mine.

Fun

I'm screaming at full blast and it's fun –
it's fun to slide head first down the stairs,
it's fun to not get ready for the party,
to watch the Rover pull away without me;
it's fun to only eat defrosting peas,
it's fun to be attacked by wasps and bees,
it's fun to leave the train when no one's looking
and be another person somewhere else;
it's fun to cover walls and floors with loops,
great loops of snot,

or loops of lines of Muscidae;
to have no friends, to read the dictionary,
column after column, all night long;
it's fun to wear my bra inside out,
to chew my arm, to dangle upsidedown,
to bang my great big head until it bleeds;
it's fun to bleed,
it's fun to eat dead flies,
it's fun to lie down naked in the snow
and feel snowflakes brush my lips and nipples,
to run and run round and round the house,
to run across the grounds to the road,
to run across the road to the river,
to nose around underneath the water,
to lie, rolled-up and wet, in someone's boat;
it's fun to rock a wolfhound in my lap
(so bony she digs holes in my belly!),
it's fun to be alone at night with God
who visits me in the form of lint.

Being *them*, however, sounds like hell.
I hear they feel cold when it's cold
and when they feel pain I hear it hurts
and other people – this I can't believe! –
other people are a comfort to them.
Very strange. They never comfort *me*.

Grunter

Don't look at me as if you're always thinking
do I have to grunt – because I do!
Do I have to sit in here and grunt
and flap my hands like budgies?
Yes, I do!
I've got a lot of things I need to grunt about!
Don't tell me I must stop because I won't,
don't ask me what I mean – I mean everything!

And if my grunt offends you, hear my scream:
when I scream it's like I grab your head
and everything goes red and there is nothing,
absolutely nothing you can do
and please don't say there is
because there isn't
and please don't even think about approaching me
and never touch me: I am mine, all mine.

My Condition

Because of 'my condition' we all know
I'm not the same as them but they pretend,
in order to be kind, that I am,
but then we get confused, because I'm not!

Sand

Now my friends have learnt not to touch me,
the next thing I must do is to explain
I do however like to be COMPRESSED!
(But *not by them*! It needs to be a *thing*.
A duvet full of sand for example.)

SELIMA HILL

from Sunday Afternoons at the Gravel-pits

My Father's Chair

I never go towards it. On the contrary
I back away and then a firm hand

guides me from behind until I'm held,
beside myself with rage, between the knees

that grip me like a pair of sliding doors
nobody can open but the opener.

No one Is Allowed

No one is allowed to come near me
and I refuse to love anybody

unless *I really want to* – and I know
I do not *really want to* love him.

The Rock-hard Body of My Father's Daughter

The rock-hard body of my father's daughter
belongs to me, and no one else but me,

and nobody can stop me uprooting it,
walking it alone to the gravel-pits,

squeezing it inside a skintight swimsuit
and shaving off, and plucking off, its hairs.

Rage

I was so enraged by how my father
hadn't got a clue who I was,

it never crossed my mind that I myself
neither knew nor cared who *he* might be.

Hope

I know that if I'm ever to forgive him
I have to give up hope – by which I mean

hope for an entirely different past
to supercede the past I must forgive him for.

The Absence of Love

It's not the *absence* of love; on the contrary,
it is its possibility that maddens us;

that comes so close yet seems so far away;
that flickers with a light we are unworthy of.

Fear

The only thing worth living for is fear,
to fear the thing I fear, which is intimacy,

intimacy fear will defy:
I tell myself the answer is to fear.

My Father's Daughter

Although I didn't choose to be his daughter,
my father, in a way, did choose me –

not me exactly, but the other daughter
I should have been but turned out not to be.

Tongue

First of all I will forget the tongue,
and secondly I will forget the mouth;

and then I will forget the room itself
in which he would secrete me like a cheese.

Although Of Course I Know He Isn't Here

When I flinch like that when someone touches me,
although of course I know he isn't here,

I sometimes think it seems as if he is –
and then I'll quickly think of something else! –

but yesterday, in that split second,
I felt my heart go out to him, I mean

only for a second, which is nothing,
but to me it was like everything:

I saw him, or I thought I saw him, shiver,
as if he were a pool or a whippet.

SELIMA HILL

from **The Red Thread Cycle**

I *On the Third Anniversary of the Rape*

Don't say Tunapuna Police Station.
Say you found yourself in the cave of a minotaur, not
knowing how you got there, with a lap of red thread.
Don't say forced anal entry.
Say you learned that some flowers bloom and die
at night. Say you remember stamen, filament,
cross-pollination, say that hummingbirds are

vital to the process.

Give the minotaur time to write in the police ledger. Lap
the red thread
around the hummingbird vase.

Don't say I took out the garbage alone and he grabbed me by the waist
and he was handsome.
              Say Shakespeare. Recite Macbeth for the tropics.
Lady Macbeth was the Queen of Carnival
and she stabbed Banquo with a vagrant's shiv during J'ouvert.
She danced a blood dingolay and gave her husband a Dimanche Gras
upbraiding.

I am in mud and glitter so far steeped that going back is not an option.
Don't say rapist.

Say engineer of aerosol deodorant because pepper spray is illegal,
anything is illegal
Fight back too hard, and it's illegal,
>your nails are illegal

Don't say you have a vagina, say
he stole your insurance policy/your bank boxes/your first car
downpayment

188

Say
he took something he'll be punished for taking,
not something you're punished for holding
like red thread between your thighs.

II *Nail It to the Barn Door Where It Happened*

This is how you survive it.
When the doctor stitching the torn seam of your sex
pauses to tend a text message,
spit on him.

Learn to drive, just so
you can take yourself to Galera Point.
Stand closer to the edge of the land than you ever have.
Feel the spray lick your one ruined ankle.
You must carry out the unspeakable thing you came here to do.
Do it well.
Leave the tools of your doing to line the brush path back, like a trail
of blackened flambeaux bottles.

When you get back home, take your mother down from the mantelpiece,
and tell her the unspeakable thing.

I have to mention that it will hurt.
I have to mention that it may not cure.

Go to the movies all alone, to the last show that's
showing on its last day, so no one but you will be there.
Even so, the floors will be sticky.
Make love to yourself in the darkness, in any way you can bear it.
You will be sticky, departing.
Grin, even so.

Use your mother's scissors to cut out the words
[father] [minister] [boyfriend] [wife]
Pick the right word, and nail it to the barn door
where it happened.
Take aim. Don't tell me what weapon.

Shatter the wood, saying,
'You did not break me.
You did not break me.
Yesterday, I learned to walk again.'

Your ankle will still be ruined forever.
Blast the bolted doors into hell's abattoir.

SHIVANEE RAMLOCHAN

The Eye in the Wall

> O sweet and lovely wall,
> Show me thy chink, to blink through with mine eyne!

At her house on the hill, he was meant to drop
her off, but followed her to the door, where
she leaned for a minute before fumbling
with the key. That was before the sex began.
He loved her fifteen-year-old pleasure, how easy
it was to make her come, but he couldn't find

his own without hurting her. Like looking
through a hole in the wall, he thinks of her again,
wonders if it was wrong, assures himself it was
right. He still has the photo he took when
he tied her to the legs of a table. Like setting his eye
to a crack, but she cannot see him, doesn't know

he is there. That time in the pine forest, she faced
him under a moonless, cloudy evening, at the edge
of frosted needles, near the brightly lit windows
of a small brick house: he wanted to fuck her where
children might look out at any moment, wanted
to fuck her nastily like his fat father fucked

his thin mother. He could have been a nurse
or a geologist, could have cared for animals
or the elderly. He knows he is kind, compassionate
by nature, so years later, he writes, the words
squirming from the email to tell her: *Sometimes*
I sit quietly and try to remember on long journeys home, or
sometimes at work. On evening drives, I often think of you.

ZOË BRIGLEY

The Ward

The nurse says nothing as
he follows me, keeping the length of two corpses
behind me. I see him only out of the corner
of my eye. He comes in to my room
pushes the door behind him, it shuts
with a papery click

Shhh
he says, putting a finger to his lips. He is not much taller
than me, greasy, with a slipped face and stubble.
He puts a hand on each of my arms
steadies me in case I run
and leans in, smelling of hand sanitiser. Kisses me
long and hard, making sure I kiss back.
He moves his hands to my breasts and feels around slowly.
Then he leaves, closing the thin door.

I peel off my gold top and put it in the bin,
sit in my bra for a minute. Then I put on a sweatshirt
and retch over the sink,
wipe my mouth clean of smeared lipstick
with the blue and white NHS towel, and push open the door.
Walk to the office round the corridor
but he's got there first.

He is talking to a female nurse. She is round
with a silver brooch on her cardigan.
Her hair is peppery grey and wispy

I take her out of the room
and tell her what has happened. He is inside typing
a report about me on the desktop computer.
I can see my name at the top.

She puts on a sympathy face; the corners of her mouth
turn down.
I hear her say
Nicki, dear, you're not well.
Nobody here would harm you.
Why don't you go to your room and have a little lie down.

NICKI HEINEN

Asylum

Even poverty can be glamorous, if you insist.

Piss rusted on elevator floors so gilded I mistake it for a trinket.

Mother burrows her face in my hair. She bites my scalp for a hope.

We try to integrate. It is a dream to have enough for a car. Mother
 says *One day we will drive past palm trees to gas stations and buy
 lemon-salted almonds,* by which she means *One day we'll have a
 house.*

Our failures thread bread crumbs into prayer beads.

We are, by default, religious.

Before I brush her wet face, I am still young. Who wouldn't be humiliated by a cold room the size of a casket? Teeth cracked with ice.

But suddenly, with her in my arms, I am no longer small.

Dirty and hungry like a parasite.

I wish I could carry my mother, my life's true love, toward the mirror.

As if her caravan beauty could console her.

Huddled together like lovers in frost, I watch ants march through her inflamed eye socket, a spectacular procession.

God. Is what we lack a shelter for the fragile to pass through?

Does this refugee camp look like a life to you?

On paper, I have a birthright. To the sadness framing my mother's eyes this is meaningless but it makes me invincible in theory.

In theory, my mother is not a tongue running along the coin lock of a shopping cart, looking for the promise of more.

But when did theory deposit me? When buy me dinner?

Come to me. Let me brush your face.

Poverty contains, by necessity, poetry.

Mother says *Que sera sera, one step after another.*

To return to where we've come from would mean to mourn, to moor, to morning.

Upstairs, the blue uncertainty wafts its clouds like unfurled flags.

The workers hand out flip phones, grape juice, sleeping bags.

Still, we remain silent in the fibrous shatter. Faithful to our gold feet.

At night, I sing a lullaby to Mother, cradle her in my arms.

I feed her a spoonful of glass. By morning, she will be a window.

ARIA ABER

Asylum

You say the old masters never got it wrong,
But when Goya painted the death of the imagination
It was a lost dog against a usurious yellow sky
And the dog, a hapless creature who had drawn itself
Ten miles on two legs, stared in amazement
To see the man who once fed him from his plate
Reduced to this.

So I felt this week, the vile soil and everything upon it –
The beggar guest kicked from the table
Before his own dog, and even the honest unpicking
Of art performed nightly and in seclusion.
Like any Penelope my armour is resignation
Although I thought I would lift the bow myself
And draw.

By the morning he is gone
And what to make of this?
The prostitutes hang from a beam like mice
The suitors are piled unburied in the yard.
And some say that it is now much better
And others, that it is worse.
So order was restored
I stared in amazement

SASHA DUGDALE

'Perhaps Akhmatova was right'

Perhaps Akhmatova was right
When she wrote who knows what shit
What tip, what pile of waste
Brings forth the tender verse
Like hogweed, like the fat hen under the fence
Like the unbearable present tense
Who knows what ill, what strife
What crude shack of a life
And how it twists sweetly about the broken sill:
Pressingness, another word for honeysuckle
But housewives? Has poetry
Ever deepened in the pail
Was it ever found in the sink, under the table
Did it rise in the oven, quietly able
To outhowl the hoover?
Does it press more than the children's supper
The sudden sleepless wail?
Did it ever?
It lives. It takes seed
Like the most unforgiving weed
Grows wilder as the child grows older
And spits on dreams, did I say
How it thrives in the ashen family nest
Or how iambs are measured best
Where it hurts:
With the heel of an iron
On the reluctant breast
Of a shirt?

SASHA DUGDALE

Fictionalising Her

In the third form of primary school,
she pretends her stepfather's hand that stretches over at midnight
   does not exist.

In the third form of junior school,
she pretends her gym instructor's arm around her waist
   does not exist.

In the third form of high school,
she pretends the old guy who clings to her hips on the bus
   does not exist.

In her third year of college,
she pretends the foot of her room-mate's boyfriend under the card table
   does not exist.

On her wedding night,
she pretends the one-month-old foetus in her belly
   does not exist.

Three years into her marriage,
she pretends the flirting texts on her husband's mobile
   do not exist.

Seven years into her marriage,
she pretends the plump wife of her boss
   does not exist.

Eighteen years into her marriage,
she pretends the boy who caresses her son in the room
   does not exist.

After twenty-eight years of marriage,
she pretends the ever-enlarging tumour in her womb
   does not exist.

After thirty years of marriage,
she pretends she is fortunate and all the tormenting loneliness in
   her life
 does not exist.

Three minutes before death,
she pretends death is painful and her aversion to this world
 does not exist at all.

XIDU HESHANG
translated from the Chinese by Liang Yujing

Personal

Don't take it personal, they said;
but I did, I took it all quite personal –

the breeze and the river and the color of the fields;
the price of grapefruit and stamps,

the wet hair of women in the rain –
and I cursed what hurt me

and I praised what gave me joy,
the most simple-minded of possible responses.

The government reminded me of my father,
with its deafness and its laws,

and the weather reminded me of my mom,
with her tropical squalls.

Enjoy it while you can, they said of Happiness
Think first, they said of Talk

Get over it, they said
at the School of Broken Hearts.

But I couldn't and I didn't and I don't
believe in the clean break;

I believe in the compound fracture
served with a sauce of dirty regret;

I believe in saying it all
and taking it all back

and saying it again for good measure,
while the air fills up with *I'm-Sorries*

like wheeling birds
and the trees look seasick in the wind.

Oh life! Can you blame me
for making a scene?

You were that limousine, the moon
climbing an onramp of pearl gray cloud.

I was the dog, chained in some fool's backyard:
barking and barking,

trying to convince everything else to wake up
to take it personal too.

TONY HOAGLAND

4

After Frank O'Hara

He was an essential contact-man between the worlds of painting and poetry. And he suggested a rich and fascinating dialogue between them.

EAVAN BOLAND

A remarkable new poetry – both modest and monumental, with something basically usable about it – not only for poets in search of a voice of their own but for the reader who turns to poetry as a last resort in trying to juggle the contradictory components of modern life into something like a liveable space.

JOHN ASHBERY

Frank O'Hara (1926-66) was – and still is – one of America's most influential poets. Inspired by the work of the Abstract Expressionist painters he knew in New York, his poetry has a similar fluidity, exuberance and immediacy, disorientating, provisional and evocative of hectic city life. His other influences were writers, musicians and visual artists, including Rimbaud and Apollinaire, Paul Klee, Max Ernst, Gertrude Stein, and Picasso who made him 'tough and quick'; and he loved to collaborate with artists, who in turn found in him a catalyst for taking their own work to another level. His poem 'Why I Am Not a Painter' (213) embodies 'a complex meditation on how art forms may mutually influence each other, but also evolve by exploring their mediums in the most radical of ways' (Mark Ford).

O'Hara is the quintessential poet of living life to the full, living for the moment. The inscription on his gravestone reads 'Grace / to be born and live as variously as possible', a line from his poem 'In Memory of My Feelings'. Many of his poems compress passing events and sensations of a single day or a few hours into an apparently casual riff on what he was doing and feeling at that particular time, as in 'The Day Lady Died' (198), one of what he called his 'I do this, I do that' poems, written on hearing news of the death of Billie Holliday in July 1959. Other poets have since adopted this mode for writing their own responses to the deaths of later cultural icons, often with a knowing nod back to O'Hara, as in John Burnside's 'The Day Etta Died' (201) recalling an adolescent slow dance to Etta James's 'I'd Rather Go Blind'. O'Hara must hold the record for the most name checks in other poets' poems.

The Day Lady Died

It is 12:20 in New York a Friday
three days after Bastille day, yes
it is 1959 and I go get a shoeshine
because I will get off the 4:19 in Easthampton
at 7:15 and then go straight to dinner
and I don't know the people who will feed me

I walk up the muggy street beginning to sun
and have a hamburger and a malted and buy
an ugly NEW WORLD WRITING to see what the poets
in Ghana are doing these days
                                        I go on to the bank
and Miss Stillwagon (first name Linda I once heard)
doesn't even look up my balance for once in her life
and in the GOLDEN GRIFFIN I get a little Verlaine
for Patsy with drawings by Bonnard although I do
think of Hesiod, trans. Richmond Lattimore or
Brendan Behan's new play or *Le Balcon* or *Les Nègres*
of Genet, but I don't, I stick with Verlaine
after practically going to sleep with quandariness

and for Mike I just stroll into the PARK LANE
Liquor Store and ask for a bottle of Strega and
then I go back where I came from to 6th Avenue
and the tobacconist in the Ziegfeld Theatre and
casually ask for a carton of Gauloises and a carton
of Picayunes, and a NEW YORK POST with her face on it

and I am sweating a lot by now and thinking of
leaning on the john door in the 5 SPOT
while she whispered a song along the keyboard
to Mal Waldron and everyone and I stopped breathing

FRANK O'HARA

Canary

(for Michael S. Harper)

Billie Holiday's burned voice
had as many shadows as lights,
a mournful candelabra against a sleek piano,
the gardenia her signature under that ruined face.

(Now you're cooking, drummer to bass,
magic spoon, magic needle.
Take all day if you have to
with your mirror and your bracelet of song.)

Fact is, the invention of women under siege
has been to sharpen love in the service of myth.

If you can't be free, be a mystery.

RITA DOVE

The Day Etta Died

I was marking a stack of essays
on Frank O'Hara

and each had a Wiki-
paragraph to say

who Genet was, and who
was Billie Holiday

– just as this poem stumbles to its end, predictably
remembering the cold December night

I slow-danced with Annabelle Gray to 'I'd Rather Go Blind'
at the Catholic Club Xmas Party,

trees lit with frost outside and cherry-coloured
streetlamps round the playground at Our Lady's,

and here and there, on windows dark with soot
our blurred reflections, sightless in the glass

yet guiding each other, soundlessly, into the sway
of the future, almost swooning from the close

proximity of skin
and muddled breathing.

JOHN BURNSIDE

The Day Amy Died

It was a Saturday in July 2011. Coffee and papers,
which is usually a treat but there'd been this shooting
in Norway. Did you hear about that, even?

Then the pub, where I heard about you.
Ash had run the *Race for Life* and I was five ciders down.
A woman came at 16.30 and said:
                                    'Amy Winehouse is dead',
and everyone at every table checked phones or Blackberries,
BBC or Twitter; muttering 'tragic'
and 'her dad doesn't know yet',
and the skin on my face went very chill and tight,

and it was a warm Dalston night –
you could see the Gherkin and hipsters eating
Turkish chopped-salads and a girl in vintage polka-dots,
black kids, Tesco full of lesbians –
and when Rich and I took a back-route, smoking weed,
looking at the pavement and sky, I was feeling my
blood. I was thinking of you and if it's better to live
to 27 than never live,

and then at Luke and Suzi's we said 'tragic' and
they fed me curry and, okay, more wine,

and when I came back, 00.30, I couldn't help logging in
to look and it said *92 feared dead now in Norway* and
all over Facebook there were links to your videos –
your stopped face, but we could press play
and you'd jerk to life: tiny, feral, your arms
vandalised like toilet cubicles. Our cartoon.

Underneath they'd written *OMG* and *tragic* and *like Janis*
or *like Billie* and *stupid selfish overrated bitch*

and it's easy to say that shit is inevitable,
but I won't, Amy.
I won't.

CLARE POLLARD

The Day Lou Reed Died

It's not like his songs are going to simply
evaporate,

but since the news I can't stop
listening to him

on endless shuffle – familiar, yes, inside
me, yes, which means

I'm alive, or was, depending on when
you read this. Now

a song called 'Sad
Song', the last one on *Berlin*,

sung now from the other side, just talk,
really, at the beginning, then

the promise
or threat, *I'm gonna stop wasting*

my time, but what else
are we made of, especially now? A chorus

sings *Sad song sad song sad song sad*

song. I
knew him better than I knew my own

father, which means
through these songs, which means

not at all. They died on the same day, O
what a perfect day, maybe

at the same moment, maybe
both their bodies are laid out now in

the freezer, maybe side by side, maybe
holding hands, waiting

for the fire or the earth or the man
or the salt –

if I could I'd let birds devour whatever's left
& carry them into the sky, but all I can do

it seems
is lie on the couch & shiver, pull a coat

over my body as if it were all I had, as if I
were the one sleeping outside, as if it were my

body something was leaving, rising up
from inside me

& the coat could hold it inside
maybe a little longer.

NICK FLYNN

The Evening of the Day Pavarotti Died

I poured some Carnation Milk into a cup of coffee
And sat outside to watch the light fading
On the tree in the cemetery at the back of our garden.

My wife couldn't get over it. 'You never have milk
In coffee, do you?' she said. She often
Ends her sentences with the rising hint of a question.

We both listened and from Mr Lowe's house next door
And from Steve's house up the street we heard
The last note of Nessun Dorma rising and hanging

There like light on a tree. If you want perfection, come here:
The tree, the note, and yes, even the Carnation Milk
In the coffee in the bright blue cup. Then the squirrel

On the shed was too much, like an orchestra taking
One too many bows when you've already stood up to go.

IAN McMILLAN

The Day No One Died
(after Frank O'Hara)

It's a day to drink a large soda
in Bangalore, gulmohar flowers livid on the left
and there on the right. I take the creaking 278,
a woman with one cataract eye's handing a bag
of bananas to the conductor at Mekhri circle.
She knows it too, today's the day
                              no one dies. The soda bottle's
hissing a bit like laughter in my hand when
I pass through Cantonment railway station

without a platform ticket, the policeman watching but
maybe too hot to move. I'm predicting the overbridge
will collapse soon but I walk on it every time.
My doctor's back from Bombay, yawning, henna
on her hands. Ma planned to boycott the wedding
but didn't, she says as she watches
the inside of me on her screen
and then I'm in a rickshaw to Lavelle Road
to see photographs of empty lots in the gallery,
alone with them, not sure why they're all sunny lots.
Someone in the guestbook has written, 'We were fooled.'
I like it that I can sit in Koshys, eat peach melba,
read till the waiter brings back the afternoon menu.
Then I'm out again, drizzled on by the big wet men
sculpture on Mallya Road, turning
onto Kasturba Road and there in the May dusk and 6 o' clock
traffic, the black leaves of a rain tree are, I'm not exaggerating,
like a thousand small quivering birds about to take off.

ANJUM HASAN

Autobiographia Literaria

When I was a child
I played by myself in a
corner of the schoolyard
all alone.

I hated dolls and I
hated games, animals were
not friendly and birds
flew away.

If anyone was looking
for me I hid behind a
tree and cried out 'I am
an orphan.'

And here I am, the
center of all beauty!
writing these poems!
Imagine!

FRANK O'HARA

Autobiography

When I was a child
I counted the looper moths
caught in the dusty mesh
of our window screens.

Fed them slowly into the hot mouth
of a kerosene lamp, then watched
them pop and blacken soundlessly,
but could not look away.

I had known what it was to be nothing.
Bore the shamed blood-letter of my sex
like a banishment; wore the bruisemark
of my father's hands to school in silence.

And here I am, still at the old window
dying of thirst, watching my girlself asleep
with the candle flame alive in my ear,
little sister yelling fire!

SAFIYA SINCLAIR

Frank O'Hara Five, Geoffrey Chaucer Nil

I think on the whole I would rather read
Frank O'Hara than Geoffrey Chaucer, and
this fine, non-smoking morning could well be
the right time to try out a new (uh hum)

poetic form. It's the funniest thing:
I am *here*, thirty years of age, having
put booze and all sorts of, say, 'dubious
substances' behind me, now sweating it

all out in a small, constipated room
with a plump tomato of a woman,
conjugating Middle English verbs. I have
developed a line, a very brief line,

in gestures of friendliness, and in my
trousers an idea is taking shape.

GEOFF HATTERSLEY

Poem

Frank O'Hara was open on the desk
but I went straight for the directory.
Nick was out, Joey was engaged, Jim was
just making coffee and why didn't I

come over. I had Astrud Gilberto
singing 'Bim Bom' on my Sony Walkman
and the sun was drying the damp slates on
the rooftops. I walked in without ringing

and he still wasn't dressed or shaved when we
topped up the coffee with his old man's scotch
(it was only half ten but what the hell)
and took the newspapers into the porch.

Talking Heads were on the radio. I
was just about to mention the football
when he said 'Look, will you help me clear her
wardrobe out?' I said 'Sure Jim, anything.'

SIMON ARMITAGE

I Want to Be like Frank O'Hara

but I've never leaned unhurriedly
on a club doorway listening
to Billie Holiday. Most of my time
in this city I've been a mother and I know
I've spent too much time in Sainsbury's
Dalston branch even if it does
have its own inimitable vibe
and a huge range of root vegetables.
My own roots sink deep in the garden and
I can't bear to leave
in case I miss a single bloom
or one of those odd powder-blue butterflies
passing through on its way to Hackney Marshes.
I swing in the hammock to the echo of police sirens,
but I've never leaned on a club doorway,
my poems in my pocket like Frank.
My books are stuffed with shopping lists
and I can't believe that's Frank.
Although once at 11 a.m. looking
for the new GP surgery in Green Lanes,
I stuck my head in the doorway
of a Turkish men's club and they scattered

from their chess like leaves.
I felt a bit dangerous then, like Elvis in '56.
I think Frank would have liked it,
the way one brave man approached me slowly,
his hands out in front as if
he was about catch something.

MARTINA EVANS

Kiss me quick

When I think a boy is beautiful
I feel like Frank O'Hara, crooning
over St Sebastian in his orange shirt.

Everyone I want is stuck with arrows.
My first kiss came immediately
after I quit church, I knew

I was going to hell for it and then I did.
I never cried so much in my life.
I don't know how to avoid

gorgeous men. There is always
another one and I always love him.
I can't stop producing bouquets

from my empty sleeves.
I am wearing all these poems
to the wedding disco.

I am meeting someone
in the middle of the dance floor,
oh god, I hope it's not you.

PHOEBE STUCKES

Katy

They say I mope too much
but really I'm loudly dancing.
I eat paper. It's good for my bones.
I play the piano pedal. I dance.
I am never quiet. I mean silent.
Some day I'll love Frank O'Hara.
I think I'll be alone for a little while.

FRANK O'HARA

Someday I'll Love Roger Reeves

Until then, let us have our gods and short prayers. Our obligations.
Our thighbone connected to our knee bone.

Our dissections and our swans. Our legs gashed
upon a barbwire fence and our heels tucked behind a lover's knees.
Let us have a stalk of sugarcane to suck

and another to tear our backs with what it knows of disaster
and a tadpole's folly. Let us have mistakes

and fish willing to come to a bell rung across a body of water.
Let us have our drawbridges and our moats. Our heavens
no higher than a pile of dried leaves. Let us have irrelevance

and a scalpel. A dislocated ankle and three more miles to run.
A plastic bottle to hold nothing but last names and a chill.

If none of this will be remembered, then let us keep speaking
with tongues light as screen doors clapping shut
on a child's finger. For this is love. To press

one frame against another
and when something like a finger is found between this pressing,

to press nevertheless. For this is our obligation.
Let us forget our obligations. For this is love.
Let us forget our love. Our eyelids' need for beginnings

and ends and blood. Our coils of hunger
that turn another into dried honey on our hands.

And what if this goes on forever – our ours?
Our drafts and fragments? Our blizzards and our cancers?
Then let us. Then, let us hold each other toward heaven

and forget that we were once made of flesh,
that this is the fall our gods refuse to clean with fire or water.

ROGER REEVES

Someday I'll Love Ocean Vuong
(after Frank O'Hara / after Roger Reeves)

Ocean, don't be afraid.
The end of the road is so far ahead
it is already behind us.
Don't worry. Your father is only your father
until one of you forgets. Like how the spine
won't remember its wings
no matter how many times our knees
kiss the pavement. Ocean,
are you listening? The most beautiful part
of your body is wherever
your mother's shadow falls.
Here's the house with childhood
whittled down to a single red tripwire.
Don't worry. Just call it *horizon*
& you'll never reach it.
Here's today. Jump. I promise it's not
a lifeboat. Here's the man
whose arms are wide enough to gather
your leaving. & here the moment,

just after the lights go out, when you can still see
the faint torch between his legs.
How you use it again & again
to find your own hands.
You asked for a second chance
& are given a mouth to empty out of.
Don't be afraid, the gunfire
is only the sound of people
trying to live a little longer
& failing. Ocean. Ocean –
get up. The most beautiful part of your body
is where it's headed. & remember,
loneliness is still time spent
with the world. Here's
the room with everyone in it.
Your dead friends passing
through you like wind
through a wind chime. Here's a desk
with the gimp leg & a brick
to make it last. Yes, here's a room
so warm & blood-close,
I swear, you will wake –
& mistake these walls
for skin.

OCEAN VUONG

Why I Am Not a Painter

I am not a painter, I am a poet.
Why? I think I would rather be
a painter, but I am not. Well,

for instance, Mike Goldberg
is starting a painting. I drop in.
'Sit down and have a drink' he
says. I drink; we drink. I look

up. 'You have SARDINES in it.'
'Yes, it needed something there.'
'Oh.' I go and the days go by
and I drop in again. The painting
is going on, and I go, and the days
go by. I drop in. The painting is
finished. 'Where's SARDINES?'
All that's left is just
letters, 'It was too much,' Mike says.

But me? One day I am thinking of
a color: orange. I write a line
about orange. Pretty soon it is a
whole page of words, not lines.
Then another page. There should be
so much more, not of orange, of
words, of how terrible orange is
and life. Days go by. It is even in
prose, I am a real poet. My poem
is finished and I haven't mentioned
orange yet. It's twelve poems, I call
it ORANGES. And one day in a gallery
I see Mike's painting, called SARDINES.

FRANK O'HARA

Why I Am Not a Painter

> I am not a painter, I am a poet.
> Why? I think I would rather be
> a painter, but I am not.
>
> FRANK O'HARA

Through a chink in the door my eyes take in the room
at the level of a receding horizon.

Loops and lines sprout through vanishing points
to trace what escapes.

Make sure that considerations are measurable: weigh them
in a hand that you clench like a fist

and strike a table. Listen to its sound
echoing in the room next door.

Close a door to make something happen –
a form of certainty in the faded

house that has shifted slightly. The floors
are buckling and the windows and doors

show cracks. These are the hinges
of an existence I call my own.

MARIA BARNAS
translated from the Dutch by Donald Gardner

My Life as a Painter

The three small birds my father brought me
on a plate had been shot by him a week before,
then plucked, gutted and pot-roasted (not by him
but by my grandfather), and my father sat down
opposite me, asking me to sample each, then tell
him which I preferred. One was a snipe, one a
crake, one a wood-pigeon. I tasted them all,
picked out the lead shot, and liked the pigeon.
My father laughed and said it was his least favourite.
Or maybe he claimed to enjoy all the birds equally.

I often find a wish going through me to remake myself
as a painter. Those three birds would be perfect
for my first work. I wouldn't depict my father on
the hill with the shotgun or Rossa, the red setter,
running to collect the birds. No, I'd stay faithful
to the old concept of the still life or, in French,

nature morte. Birds on a plate, nothing else.
I might add a few colours that weren't there.
And I'd follow up with a long, flat portrait of three
spectacularly blue-moulded loaves, all of them rye.

MATTHEW SWEENEY

Describing Paintings

(to Daniel Stern)

We usually catch only a few details –
grapes from the seventeenth century,
still fresh and gleaming,
perhaps a fine ivory fork,
or a cross's wood and drops of blood,
and great suffering that has already dried.
The shiny parquet creaks.
We're in a strange town –
almost always in a strange town.
Somewhere a guard stands and yawns.
An ash branch sways outside the window.
It's absorbing,
describing static paintings.
Scholars devote tomes to it.
But we're alive,
full of memory and thought,
love, sometimes regret,
and at moments we take a special pride
because the future cries in us
and its tumult makes us human.

ADAM ZAGAJEWSKI

translated from the Polish by Clare Cavanagh

5

Harmony and discord

Love is the charge behind the lyric, technical mastery is its muscle.

JOHN MONTAGUE

The fifth Sikh guru, Guru Arjan Dev, encapsulates this well with his words:
'Without music, how can one dance? Without a voice, how can one sing?
Without strings, how can the rebab be played? Without the name of the
Almighty, all affairs are in vain.' For me, music is an integral part of
culture and identity.[...] Music doesn't exist in a vacuum, and in the
absence of context, meanings can sadly be misunderstood or even lost.

JASVIR SINGH

LOVE AND MUSIC come together in poetry, as in the first words in Shakespeare's
Twelfth Night, spoken by the lovelorn Duke Orsino: 'If music be the food of
love, play on.' The poems in this section cover both, separately and together,
starting with passion and ending with heartbreak, as in the selections in *Staying
Alive* (7: 'In and out of love', 249-94), but in this book we play on, with poems
showing how music is central to our being, to life itself as well as to love.

This section also complements the selections in *Being Alive,* which cover
the nature of love (4: 'Love Life', 179-210), gender, and the nature of relation-
ships (5: 'Men and Women', 211-56); as well as widening the focus in *Being
Human* (9: 'More to love', 465-95) on how human understanding and intimacy
are created not out of order or perfection but through acceptance of difficulty,
inadequacy, imperfection, making do, shortage of time.

These poems also cover other aspects of love: love between women; love
between men; love embodied in voicing a commitment to one another, as in
the poems by Jane Clarke, Miriam Nash and Seamus Heaney (230-32); and
lasting love, lifelong friendship, love's survival in domesticity.

The actor Mark Rylance has read out poems by American poet Louis
Jenkins when honoured at awards ceremonies. He wrote a play with him,
Nice Fish, telling the story of an ice-fishing expedition, based on Jenkins's
prose poem collection *Nice Fish,* which includes 'Fish Out of Water' (255).

217

A Declaration of Need

I need you like a novel needs a plot.
I need you like the greedy need a lot.
I need you like a hovel needs a certain level of grottiness to qualify.
I need you like acne cream needs spottiness.
Like a calendar needs a week.
Like a colander needs a leek.
Like people need to seek out what life on Mars is.
Like hospitals need vases.
I need you.
I need you like a zoo needs a giraffe.
I need you like a psycho needs a path.
I need you like King Arthur needed a table
that was more than just a table for one.
I need you like a kiwi needs a fruit.
I need you like a wee wee needs a route out of the body.
I need you like Noddy needed little ears,
just for the contrast.
I need you like bone needs marrow.
I need you like straight needs narrow.
I need you like the broadest bean needs something else on the plate
before it can participate
in what you might describe as a decent meal.
I need you like a cappuccino needs froth.
I need you like a candle needs a moth
if it's going to burn its wings off.

JOHN HEGLEY

A Lock of Her Hair

As a hoodoo-voodoo, get-you-back-to-me tool,
this hank's thankless task is vast,
a head down to the ground impossibility, possibly,

218

since what I'm thinking of is your toe pad pinknesses too,
your soup hots and round-and-rounds, the fine
and perfect poundage of you on my paws, the very cause
and problem I moan for and bemoan
the absence of. For Love, above the head
this reddish coil once lavishly wore, there's an air so far away
it's sad for me to even think the same sun's rays play
where it was and do to you what I would do
if I were there or you were here. Still, some thrills
remembered do resemble thrills, one hopes, and the ropes
of it that gently fell around me bound me so well
no hell of miles can defile this dream I dream. I mean
the anyway DNA I can find of you. I mean the home
of bones and blood that holds the whole of you
and which this fizzed-up missive means to conjure, missy,
my world in a curl, girl, this man oh man half man I am
when you're gone.

ROBERT WRIGLEY

High Land

I don't remember who kissed who first,
who touched who first, who anything to whom.
All I remember in the highland night –
the sheep loose outside,
the full moon smoking in the sky –
was that you led me and I led you.
And all of a sudden we were in a small room
in a big house with the light coming in
and your legs open; mine too.
And it was this swirling, twirling thing.
It's hard to fasten it down;
it is hard to remember what was what –
who was who when the wind was coming in.

JACKIE KAY

Low Tide, Late August

That last summer when everything was almost always terrible
we waded into the bay one late afternoon as the tide had almost
            finished
pulling all the way out

and sat down in the waist-deep water,
I floating on his lap facing him, my legs floating around him,
and we quietly coupled,

and stayed, loosely joined like that, not moving,
but being moved by the softly sucking and lapping water,
as the pulling out reached its limit and the tide began to flow slowly
            back again.

Some children ran after each other, squealing in the shallows, near
            but not too near.

I rested my chin on his shoulder looking toward the shore.
As he must have been looking over my shoulder, to where the water
            deepened
and the small boats tugged on their anchors.

MARIE HOWE

You were a bird

You were a bird before we met. I know that
because over your skew front teeth
your mouth makes a pointy beak.

I saw you first in Dickens' London,
an evening of frosted windows
and hot steaming steak.

That night we were drinking,
the chimneys were smoking,
and my lips swelled up

like bread baking in the oven.
I met London in your face,
I smelt wine on your breath

and the shape of your mouth
left me feeling slightly lyrical.
We drank a lot that night

we drank so much
you would have seen it from heaven.
With you there, sitting there in my kitchen,

the cooking pots start to sing.
Now the letterbox is a bird
and the telephone is made of birds when it rings.

KATHARINE KILALEA

The Arms of a Marvelous Squid

'Let not your heart be troubled,' the wise man said,
'for love is stronger than you know.'
I was sixteen, seeking lessons in rainbow posters,
love was stronger than I knew. So was fear.
So was sorrow that hauls a heart's bellrope
again and again. So were the bonds
in a drop of water; so was the force of gravity
leading the drop from eye to mouth
or pulling a car with bad brakes downhill
or abetting a body stood on a chair
with a rope around its neck.
So was the force of life in microscopic creatures

221

deep in solid Antarctic lakes,
or boiled in acid on the Pacific floor,
or duking it out between sickness and health
in a human intestine. And the life
in the devious roots of dandelions,
an elephant's trunk, or a flea's hind legs.
Stronger than I knew was the desire sometimes
to move quietly through harmless days,
eating from a plate, buying stamps or a toothbrush.
Which was more remarkable,
the breadth and depth of my ignorance,
or the strength in the arms of a marvelous squid
that hung in my vision, uncurled as if
about to dissolve, then whipped one length
around my wrist, preventing me
from running away, preventing me
from rising to breathe,
reminding me of love?

SARAH LINDSAY

for women who are difficult to love

you are a horse running alone, feral
and he tries to tame you
compares you to an impossible highway
to a burning house
says you are blinding him
that he could never leave you
forget you
want anything but you
you dizzy him, you are unbearable
every woman before or after you
is doused in your name
you fill his mouth
his teeth ache with memory of taste

his body just a long shadow seeking yours
but you are always too intense
frightening in the way you want him
unashamed and sacrificial
he tells you that no man can live up to the one who
lives in your head
and you tried to change didn't you?
closed your mouth more
tried to be softer
prettier, more quiet
less volatile, less awake
but even when sleeping you could feel
him travelling away from you in his dreams
so what did you want to do love
split his head open?
you can't make homes out of human beings
someone should have already told you that
and if he wants to leave
then let him leave
you are terrifying
strange and beautiful
something not everyone
knows how to love.

WARSAN SHIRE

Colosseum

I don't remember how I hurt myself,
The pain mine
Long enough for me
To lose the wound that invented it
As none of us knows the beauty
Of our own eyes
Until a man tells us they are

Why God made brown. Then
That same man says he lives to touch
The smoothest parts, suggesting our
Surface area can be understood
By degrees of satin. Him I will
Follow until I am as rough outside
As I am within. I cannot locate the origin
Of slaughter, but I know
How my own feels, that I live with it
And sometimes use it
To get the living done,
Because I am what gladiators call
A man in love – love
Being any reminder we survived.

JERICHO BROWN

Of My Fury

I love a man I know could die
And not by way of illness
And not by his own hand
But because of the color of that hand and all
His flawless skin. One joy in it is
Understanding he can hurt me
But won't. I thought by now I'd be unhappy
Unconscious next to the same lover
So many nights in a row. He readies
For bed right on the other side
Of my fury, but first, I make a braid of us.
I don't sleep until I get what I want.

JERICHO BROWN

Marriage of Equals

You hated the theatre and I hated the museums.
I didn't notice the butterflies.
You didn't notice the homeless.
I felt oppressed by Auden's old boy study castles.
You planted sapling projects in grey rockeries.
I got obsessed with poignant lines of graffiti.
You understood Oyster cards and booking in advance.
I had to wrench my head back from cauldrons of wine.
You had one beer in contentment.
My friends were idealists who started off yodelling.
Your friends were realists who started off hissing.

Your world was steadily increasing.
My government didn't exist.
You felt the bank balance of the nation in the tips of your fingers.
I bought rare, coffee-spoilt poetry books with crippled spines
from extortionate magpies in Iowa.
You saw the good in Thatcher.
I watched Ken Loach films in a dark room warmed
by the ghost of my grandfather's Yorkshire coal.

I could take or leave the planetarium.
You collided with Andromeda in your insomnia.
I was fine with pills.
You defied shrinks with your in-house mental janitor.
I sat down on the Tube when travelling just one stop.
You would never buy mystery meat from a backstreet 'all you can eat'
buffet called 'Puff the Chinese Dragon'.
I had never bought a sprig of ginger.
You blamed Gordon Brown for the future death of the sun.
I blamed the Rich in general while snacking
on a bite-size cube of decorated fruit cake.

I thought of Kirsty MacColl at Christmas.
You thought of your father's erratic moods.
I jogged alone on the treadmill in front of a mirror.

You punched the air with your lacrosse stick in school year-group photos.
I let potential serial killers use my bathroom after closing time.
You always packed a toothbrush.
I owned every Mike Leigh, even the early BBC television stuff.
You found *Career Girls* over-acted and plotless.
I wept outwardly for a week, inwardly for a year.
You didn't know who Adrian Mitchell was.
I couldn't assemble a pop-up tent.

You wouldn't let anyone read your self-penned screenplays.
I recited poems I wrote yesterday in busy restaurants
to embarrassed olive-skinned companions.
You read Sherlock Holmes novels in small print with a magnifying glass.

Your mum said, 'Go get your girl.'
My mum said, 'Stop proposing to slender-necked lampposts.'
You plunged the knife deeply and once.
I supported huge government funding for chocolate sculptures.
You audibly scoffed during my one-act *Hoodie Hamlet*.
I had a subtle nervous twitch triggered by memories of candlelight
and Leonard Cohen's 'The Partisan'.
You built Jerusalem on England's green and pleasant land.
I reinvented the fish pun.
You closed up like the magic portal.
I took the long slide down into the pool.

CAROLINE BIRD

Want

She wants a house full of cups and the ghosts
of last century's lesbians; I want a spotless
apartment, a fast computer. She wants a woodstove,
three cords of ash, an axe; I want
a clean gas flame. She wants a row of jars:
oats, coriander, thick green oil;

I want nothing to store. She wants pomanders,
linens, baby quilts, scrapbooks. She wants Wellesley
reunions. I want gleaming floorboards, the river's
reflection. She wants shrimp and sweat and salt;
she wants chocolate. I want a raku bowl,
steam rising from rice. She wants goats,
chickens, children. Feeding and weeping. I want
wind from the river freshening cleared rooms.
She wants birthdays, theaters, flags, peonies.
I want words like lasers. She wants a mother's
tenderness. Touch ancient as the river.
I want a woman's wit swift as a fox.
She's in her city, meeting
her deadline; I'm in my mill village out late
with the dog, listening to the pinging wind bells, thinking
of the twelve years of wanting, apart and together.
We've kissed all weekend; we want
to drive the hundred miles and try it again.

JOAN LARKIN

Poem in Noisy Mouthfuls

Can't stop eating you, movie-style extra butter microwave popcorn.
Can't stop watching you, rented movie about an immigrant family
from Lebanon. Can't help but weep, seeing the family wave

goodbye to relatives in the Beirut airport – tear salt mixing with
popcorn salt. Can't hide my mess, myself from the friend beside me.
Can't answer his question, *Does it remind you of your family, leaving China?*

I want to say, *No, it's completely different*, which in many ways it is, but
    really
I'm remembering what a writer friend once said to me, *All you write about
is being gay or Chinese* – how I can't get over that, & wonder if it's true,

227

if everything I write is in some way an immigrant narrative or another
coming out story. I recall a recent poem, featuring fishmongers in Seattle,
& that makes me happy – clearly that one isn't about being gay or Chinese.

But then I remember a significant number of Chinese immigrants
live in Seattle & how I found several of the Pike Place fishmongers
attractive when I visited, so I guess that poem's about being gay

& Chinese, too. So I say to my friend, *I'm not sure*, & keep eating
the popcorn. Thank god we chose the giant 'family size' bag. Can't stop
the greasy handfuls, noisy mouthfuls. Can't eat popcorn quietly.

Later, during my friend's smoke break, still can't come up with a worthy
response to his radical queer critique of homonormativity, of monogamy,
domesticity, front lawn glory. *These middle-class gays picking out*

garden gnomes, ignoring all the anti-racist work of decolonisation
that still needs to be done – don't you think they're lame? I say, *Yeah, for sure,*
but think, marriage, house, 1 kid, 2 cats – how long have I wanted that?

Could I give that up in the name of being a real queer? Probably can't.
& it's like another bad habit I can't give up. Eating junk, can't. Procrastinating,
can't. Picking scabs, can't. Being friends with people who challenge

my beliefs & life plans, can't. Reading & believing in Ayn Rand, though?
Can. Brief phase as a Christian because I liked the cross as an accessory? Can.
WWJD? Can. White heterosexist patriarchy? Can. America...can't.

Can't help but think, when we get back to the movie, how it was my father's
decision to move here, not my mother's, just like the parents on screen.
Can't stop replaying my mother's walk onto the plane, carrying me,

though I was getting too old for it, holding me, my face pressed into her
hair, her neck, as she cried, quietly – can't stop returning to this scene of
     leaving,
can't stop pausing the scene, thinking I've left something out again,

something else my mother told me. Like my grandmother at the airport,
how she saw my small body so tied to my mother's body, & still she doubted,
she had to say, *You better not lose him.* & my mother kept that promise

till she couldn't, she lost me, in the new country, but doesn't
that happen to all parents & their children, one way or another,
& don't we need to get lost? Lost, dizzy, stubbly, warm, stumbling,

whoa – that's what it felt like, 17, kissing a boy for the first time.
Can't forget it. Can't forget when my mother found out & said,
This would never have happened if we hadn't come to this country.

But it would've happened, every bit as dizzy, lost, back in China.
It didn't happen because of America, dirty Americans. It was me,
my need. My father said, *You have to change*, but I couldn't, can't

give you up, boys & heat, scruff & sweet. Can't get over you. Trying to get
over what my writer friend said, *All you write about is being gay or Chinese.*
Wish I had thought to say to him, *All you write about is being white*

or an asshole. Wish I had said, No, I already write about everything –
& everything is salt, noise, struggle, hair,
carrying, kisses, leaving, myth, popcorn,

mothers, bad habits, questions.

CHEN CHEN

//

My mother lays the table with chopsticks & ceramic
spoons, expects you to fail at dinner. To the Chinese,

you and I are chopsticks: lovers with the same anatomies.
My mother tells you that *chopsticks* in Cantonese sounds

like *the swift arrival of sons.* My mother tongue rejoices
in its dumbness before you as expletives detonate: *[two*

women] [two men] [disgrace]. Tonight, I forget I am
bilingual. I lose my voice in your mouth, kiss till blood

comes so *sorry* does not slip on an avalanche of syllables
into sorrow. I tell you that as long as we hold each other,

no apology will be enough. Tonight, I am dreaming again
of tomorrow: another chance to eat at the feast of the living

with chopsticks balanced across the bridges of our hands
as we imbibe each *yes*, spit out every *no* among scraps of

shell or bone. Father says: *Kids these days are not as tough
as we used to be. So many suicides in one week.* How many

times have you and I wondered about leaving our bodies
behind, the way many of us have already left? My friend's

sister loved a woman for ten years and each word she says
to her mother stings like a papercut. Each word she does

not say burns like the lines she etches carefully into skin.
I have stopped believing that secrets are a beautiful way

to die. You came home with me for three hundred days –
to show my family that dinner together won't kill us all.

MARY JEAN CHAN

Vows

I can't promise it's chiselled from gold
in spirals that speak of forever.

I can't tell you it's wise as a mountain
with pines that reach for heaven.

I can't promise it's flawless as honey
gathered by bees in bell heather.

I can't say it's simple as silk
spun from cocoon into treasure.

But I promise it's rooted as rowan
with berries that sing to September.

I promise its to and its fro
will surprise like Glenmalure weather,

a seasoned row boat,
moored or unmoored at your pleasure.

JANE CLARKE

Love Song for a Keeper

If nothing of us lasts past seven years,
each speck of skin replaced, old cells reborn,
then soon the crisscross lines inside your palm
where I pretended to read kids, careers,
won't recognise my thumbprints anymore.
This fleck of face, that furthest tip of tongue,
whole parts of us will never know they touched,
nights when our tiny room swelled up with breath,
till one window exhaled for us at dawn.
Then will our new skin falter in the sudden
cold unknown? Will bones be what we dig for?
As our chests press again, stranger to stranger,
our particles in motion, trembling, raw,
let my flesh blaze to yours, for seven more.

MIRIAM NASH

Scaffolding

Masons, when they start upon a building,
Are careful to test out the scaffolding;

Make sure that planks won't slip at busy points,
Secure all ladders, tighten bolted joints.

And yet all this comes down when the job's done
Showing off walls of sure and solid stone.

So if, my dear, there sometimes seem to be
Old bridges breaking between you and me

Never fear. We may let the scaffolds fall
Confident that we have built our wall.

SEAMUS HEANEY

The Embrace

As you lie beside me I edge closer
taking sleep from your lips
as one wick draws flame from another.
And two night-lights are lit
as the flame takes and sleep passes
between us. But as it passes
the boiler in the basement shudders:
down there a fossil nature burns,
down in the depths prehistory's
sunken fermented peats blaze up
and slither through my radiator.
Wreathed in a dark halo of oil,
the bedroom is a close nest
heated by organic deposits,

by log pyres, leafmash, seething resins...
And we are the wicks, the two tongues
flickering on that single Palaeozoic torch.

VALERIO MAGRELLI
translated from the Italian by Jamie McKendrick

Aubade

It's Saturday but you haven't slept in.
Your side of the bed's still warm.
My hangover is like a smashed windscreen.
I hear a repeated noise down the corridor.
One surface determinedly rubs another.
While asleep I picked my lip till it bled
– a side effect of the medication,
like the gravid if sledgehammer-obvious nightmare.
Your body walks in completely naked.
This is how you prefer to clean the bathroom
and though my plan was for inertia
I understand today we're to redeem the time.
The sound of the curtains yanked apart
is the morning clearing its throat.

VIDYAN RAVINTHIRAN

Leaving Early

My Love,

            tonight Fionnuala is your nurse.
You'll hear her voice sing-song around the ward
lifting a wing at the shore of your darkness.

233

I heard that, in another life, she too journeyed
through a storm, a kind of curse, with the ocean
rising darkly around her, fierce with cold,
and no resting place, only the frozen
rocks that tore her feet, the light on her shoulders.

And no cure there but to wait it out.
If, while I'm gone, your fever comes down –
if the small, salt-laden shapes of her song
appear to you as a first glimmer of earth-light,
follow the sweet, hopeful voice of that landing.
She will keep you safe beneath her wing.

LEANNE O'SULLIVAN

Note

If we become separated from each other
this evening try to remember the last time
you saw me, and go back and wait for me there.
I promise I won't be very long,
though I am haunted by the feeling
that I might keep missing you,
with the noise of the city growing too
loud and the day burning out so quickly.
But let's just say it's as good a plan as any.
Just once let's imagine a word for the memory
that lives beyond the body, that circles
and sets all things alight. For I have
singled you out from the whole world,
and I would – even as this darkness
is falling, even when the night comes
where there are no more words, and the day
comes when there is no more light.

LEANNE O'SULLIVAN

Some New Thing

The best reason to live is that there is no reason to live.
I walked to your apartment in the late night.
Flowers I didn't plant began to be flowers
and I was a color and then I was none.
Conrad said, let the train take you anywhere,
pass all the old stops. I let the train take me anywhere,
I passed all the old stops. With you I liked being nowhere
and with you I live nowhere now.
The best reason to paint is that there is no reason to paint.
Keith Haring wrote that. It could be about us.
I go into churches and I go into bars:
I feel the time stop.
To feel – you can't stop at some point.
Not a religious thing. Why on earth or why not.
Let's be in a Sunday morning
with no complacencies of the peignoir,
no late coffee or oranges – all he does
is watch the neighborhood dogs getting walked.
No one will let you through if you don't walk your own sadness.
No one will let you touch them if you're a person at all.
One summer we walked the entire island of Manhattan,
we were our own animal.
From Inwood to the water to your small want.
And you. You, you, you
you can read these lines in any order
because I want to leave nothing out
and there's nothing here.
Words are just words. What I feel
I feel twice and risk three of.
Some new thing.
How there's more here without us at all.

ALEX DIMITROV

Lines for a Thirtieth Wedding Anniversary

Somewhere up in the eaves it began.
High in the roof – in a sort of vault
between the slates and gutter – a small leak.
Through it, rain which came from the east,
in from the lights and foghorns of the coast,
water with a ghost of ocean salt in it,
spilled down on the path below.
Over and over and over
years stone began to alter,
its grain searched out, worn in:
granite rounding down, giving way
taking into its own inertia that
information water brought – of ships,
wings, fog and phosphor in the harbour.
It happened under our lives, the rain,
the stone. We hardly noticed. Now
this is the day to think of it, to wonder.
All those years, all those years together –
the stars in a frozen arc overhead,
the quick noise of a thaw in the air,
the blue stare of the hills – through it all
this constancy: what wears, what endures.

EAVAN BOLAND

Yes

Love, yes there is always a body involved
which makes it and makes it, makes it

tricky sometimes. But it doesn't matter, we've been
together for so long that we've stashed ourselves
inside each other, won't get lost can't get away any more.

Of course, omens get under the skin, dance along
when you dance, run when you run, hang out

on the sofa too, just sitting there and later Fail
makes off with your dreams, a winter afflicts
the old river that wants to stream. But it

doesn't matter and the sphinx who poses
the riddle *who of who is most* is nothing

to get worked up about, we'll just take each other
by the hand and where the road ends we will sleep.

HESTER KNIBBE
translated from the Dutch by Jacqueline Pope

Uxor Vivamus...

The first night that I slept with you
And slept, I dreamt (these lines are true):
Now newly married we had moved
Into an unkempt house we loved –
The rooms were large, the floors of stone,
The garden gently overgrown
With sunflowers, phlox, and mignonette –
All as we would have wished and yet
There was a shabby something there
Tainting the mild and windless air.
Where did it lurk? Alarmed we saw
The walls about us held the flaw –
They were of plaster, like grey chalk,
Porous and dead: it seemed our talk,
Our glances, even love, would die
With such indifference standing by.

Then, scarcely thinking what I did,
I chipped the plaster and it slid
In easy pieces to the floor;
It crumbled cleanly, more and more
Fell unresistingly away –
And there, beneath that deadening grey,
A fresco stood revealed: sky-blue
Predominated, for the view
Was an ebullient country scene,
The crowning of some pageant queen
Whose dress shone blue, and over all
The summer sky filled half the wall.

And so it was in every room,
The plaster's undistinguished gloom
Gave way to dances, festivals,
Processions, muted pastorals –
And everywhere that spacious blue:
I woke, and lying next to you
Knew all that I had dreamt was true.

DICK DAVIS

Making a Meal of It

No point in murmuring
Against the life you live,
No point in hungering
For what Fate cannot give;

No point in calling up
Vast, empty words like Fate –
The table's set, sit down
And eat what's on your plate.

DICK DAVIS

To My Husband

If we were never going to die, I might
Not hug you quite as often or as tight,
Or say goodbye to you as carefully
If I were certain you'd come back to me.
Perhaps I wouldn't value every day,
Every act of kindness, every laugh
As much, if I knew you and I could stay
For ever as each other's other half.
We may not have too many years before
One disappears to the eternal yonder
And I can't hug or touch you any more.
Yes, of course that knowledge makes us fonder.
Would I want to change things, if I could,
And make us both immortal? Love, I would.

WENDY COPE

One Day

One day, my love, the good times will be over,
Never to return. And it could come
Quite suddenly – the news that either one
Of us is ill, unlikely to recover.
How will we deal with that – day after day
Of grief and sickness? Will we both be brave
And kind in everything we do and say
And, failing that, be able to forgive?
We'll have to do our best to stay afloat,
Despite our anger, tiredness and fear,
Trusting in our love, a sturdy boat
That's served us pretty well, year after year.
We'll hope it can survive the stormy weather
And bring us safely into port, together.

WENDY COPE

Objecting to Everything Today

Objecting
to everything today.

Crumbs
in the bed,
on the counter-top,
to eating as a necessary occupation.
Hairs in the bath, twined in the brush,
dog-hairs on the couch. And his shoes
where he tossed them,
askew under it.
The importunate dog,
the cold
drear outside
and having to take him out.
And the water too hot! Objecting
to the daily
attritional messiness
of living. And to myself
more than anything.

Yesterday's
newsprints on the chair, books
I'm in the middle of I don't want to finish.
No, don't say it!
Don't say I have a cold coming on!

Objecting to the newsreader
as he briskly reads out a rape, another
murder. To that brash
light in the sky.
And the same light failing.

I am not the raped one.
He is not the murdered.

And still today I'm objecting
to living.

The luxury of us with few troubles.

ANNE HAVERTY

A Visit

I still remember love like another country
with an almost forgotten landscape
of salty skin and a dry mouth. I think
there was always a temptation to escape
from the violence of that sun, the sudden
insignificance of ambition,
the prowl of jealousy like a witch's cat.

Last night I was sailing in my sleep
like an old seafarer, with scurvy
colouring my thoughts, there was moonlight
and ice on green waters.
Hallucinations. Dangerous nostalgia.
And early this morning you whispered
as if you were lying softly at my side:

Are you still angry with me? And spoke my
name with so much tenderness, I cried.
I never reproached you much
that I remember, not even when I should;
to me, you were the boy in Ravel's garden
who always longed to be good,
as the forest creatures knew, and so do I.

ELAINE FEINSTEIN

241

Wedding Cake Decorations

A small white wife
with a small white face;
a thin white groom
on a round, white base.

They have no shoes
because they have no feet:
their maker thought them obsolete.

They cannot run away!

The married man
and his married wife
are stuck this way.

Let's hold each other tight,
they say.

So they hold each other
all through the day,
and all through the
frightening night.

TARA BERGIN

Couple

Sharers of skin,
dreamers of one another's landscapes.

Thieves of one another's thoughts.
rivals for destiny's attention.

Convicts serving time
in the prison of one another's arms.

Savage antagonists marooned
on a planet no wider than a bed.

RANJIT HOSKOTÉ

Windows
(for Alex)

She is opening tab after tab on her laptop screen
so the one with his name in it gets smaller and smaller,
squeezed down by little pieces of the internet
until he is just three letters in the corner,
a peep of light, the last Tetris block before death.

He said that if her arms had grown really long
for whatever reason he'd have carried them down the street
like a train. He said she reminded him
of a statue in Rome that had him in raptures.
He had a photo of it framed.

What's the use of trying to be pretty and dreaming
of ridiculous dresses when love is just an apple
being eaten from the inside?
And now she's tearing up a post-it note and making it rain
bright pink into the bin. Is this what heartbreak feels like –
like rain falling through your head?

All she wants is to see the collection of walking sticks
from Tutankhamun's tomb. To be in Egypt on the deck of a boat
in a cold pool, completely alone, and fine with it.

In the bath, she rolls over and over.
She stands behind the glass balcony door surveying
the windows of the highrise opposite, the lives behind them.
The lights extinguish one by one, to a gallery of frames
with the paintings stolen, and a walled-in quiet.

REBECCA PERRY

Love is a place

From my seat on the train I gaze at the landscape
and suddenly, fleetingly, a vineyard goes by
which is the lightning-flash of some truth.
It would be a mistake to alight from the train
because then the vineyard would vanish.
Love is a place, and there is always something
that reveals it to me: a distant field,
a conductor's empty stand with only a rose on it,
and the musicians playing on their own.
Your room as day was breaking.
And, of course, the singing of those birds
in the cemetery, one morning in June.
Love is a place.
It endures beyond everything: from there we come.
And it's the place where life remains.

JOAN MARGARIT
translated from the Catalan by Anna Crowe

The Love

Where does it go? Depots mainly, on the edge
of Kent and Essex. Try the Dartford Crossing –
sewage plants, substations, heavy traffic –
a perfect place for murder.
They keep it stocked in wooden crates on endless
shelves on floor after floor in subterranean
bunkers: love contained like unsold cargo
or un-pulped books; the self-help kind, flat-packed love
for easy storage, love damp and jaundiced.
Love worn on no one's sleeve, love rattling
like shattered ceramics on the tusks of a forklift.
How does it get here? It just comes for early
career researchers, who mill about the aisles

dressed in protective suits, who unearth
platonic love from cases, like plutonium,
careful not to spill a drop of all this used
and wasted love. They've heard the rumours,
spots, blindness, madness, mania, jealous rages,
fits and giggles, genocide. Winners
of the Turner Prize shipped in to build collages
chronicle its decline, or replicate Rodin's
The Kiss from never-worn engagement rings,
dredged from drains, rivers, pawn shops,
and love-locks clipped from the Pont des Arts
to ease the weight of love. Musicians digitise
the sound, moans like warping steel or wood,
the chorus of an altered mass. Meanwhile,
the poets, wearing rubber gloves, read charred
and tea-stained letters, cached emails
from dumped lovers, to recycle Eros
from the mulch of this organic compost.

JOHN CHALLIS

Happy Ending

After they had not made love
she pulled the sheet up over her eyes
until he was buttoning his shirt:
not shyness for their bodies – those
they had willingly displayed – but a frail
endeavour to apologise.

Later, though, drawn together by
a distaste for such 'untidy ends'
they agreed to meet again; whereupon
they giggled, reminisced, held hands
as though what they had made was love –
and not that happier outcome, friends.

FLEUR ADCOCK

Epilogue

Let us not repeat the easy lies about eternity
and love. We have fallen out of love
before – like children surpassing
the borders of their beds, woken
by gravity, the suddenness of tiles.
So it is we have opened our eyes
in the dark, found ourselves far
from all that was safe and soft.
So it is we have nursed red bruises.
If we are amazed at anything let it be this:
not that we have fallen from love,
but that we were always resurrected
into it, like children who climb sweetly
back into bed.

KEI MILLER

Kingdom Come
(for Vona)

That Arts & Crafts house still for sale,
shutters all always shut,

is the safest place to park.
Blaming the market, they shipped north.

Who'd have thought a year
would find me stalking our old selves

while neighbours wheel their trash
to the sidewalk for the morning?

Mostly I mark papers
by light run off the alternator.

Though lately I've been praying, lady,
that whatever kingdom come there is

is a street we owned a place on
where the life we meant to love

and ran screaming from mid-stream
completes itself without us

and it's evening over and over again.
A piece of Plantation House chandelier

is dismantling the last bar of sun
into bit and bobs of iris.

In the yard each lost wish still chimes
even though there's no wind.

There is a barometer stalled on 'Fair',
a slow air remastered on the squeezebox.

The sea, gone miles out of its way, is there
as a screensaver reflected in the screendoor.

And our heirs are there in the ping-pong
and hip-hop of the garage's murk.

And I, in some shape or form,
am there as well. And you are there.

CONOR O'CALLAGHAN

Ghost Poem

Crowded at my window tonight, your ghosts
will have nothing to speak of but love
though the long grass leading to my door
is parted neither by you leaving

nor by you, coming here. The same ghosts
keep in with my blood, the way
a small name says itself, over
and over, so one minute is cavernous

compared to the next, and I cannot locate
words enough to tell you your wrist
on my breast had the same two sounds to it.
You are a sky over narrow water

and the ghosts at my window
are a full day until I shed their loss.
I want to tell you all their bone-white,
straight-line prophecies

but the thought of you, this and every night,
is your veins in silverpoint mapped
on my skin, your life on mine,
that I made up and lived inside, as real,

and I find I cannot speak of love
or any of its wind-torn ghosts to you
who promised warm sheets and a candle, lit,
but promised me in words.

VONA GROARKE

Gold Hoop Earrings

Someone did this to me, I loved him
but that doesn't matter. Having an affair

is just getting all dressed up to cut yourself.
My brain used to shut itself off and go quiet

and fuzzy, the moment he put his hands
on me or took them off. I've tried to imagine

how he felt but I was too busy falling down
my own set of drains. I'm going to spend my life

correcting his attraction to me. I'm different now.
I'll never wear lingerie again. I'm going to acquire

some gold hoop earrings and find someone
to film me talking and talking. I am going

to leave the country, and become
an impressive nightmare, just watch me.

PHOEBE STUCKES

Attempt

This is what I remember: the paramedic said
we can't help you unless you've already died,
we have to know you are serious. I think his name

was Dennis, I said it feels pretty *fucking* serious Dennis.
I thought death might render me serene but it didn't.
I wasn't going down without a fight. I wanted to steal

the backless cotton nightgown they gave me to wear.
It was soft, and pink, I wanted to shove it in my handbag
and run. As usual, I cried all my makeup off. I flirted

with the junior doctor. He said I had young woman's
syndrome, which means your veins are hard to find.
I said, you have no idea, and puked. My head split

all the way along its seams, it took my mother an age
to arrive. When they sent her out she did not go,
she hung around all night. I did not die.

PHOEBE STUCKES

For Love

I would not go there again for money;
for the way the sky closes over you there,
for months without sun, for the beaten look
of those streets, heaved brick, painted storefronts,
and stark fronts of houses, for streets where the day
goes to die in gutters heaped with old black snow,
and for what people have known about each other forever
and will not amend. I would not go there even
to die, to add one single ounce of sacrifice
to the tombs of Main Street, graveyards of old farmland,
the cursed diesel factory, whose machinery crushed
my grandfather's spine when its cables snapped overhead,
stretched thin, made weak by overuse and uncaring.
I would not give another death, another curse
to that sorry history. Enough that it has eaten,
mangled and eaten, my grandfather, worn out
my grandmother, who was a silvered ghost weaving nests
of her own white hair for the birds, stopped my lucky father
whose luck ran out, and hauled him back, and caught
his quick, nervy brothers, who went to war and came home
and subsided into wisecracks and darkening philosophies.
Enough that my father's sisters have gone mad,
leaning over the oilcloth to read their fortunes in the cards,
their sweet, worried faces grown old. I would not go there,
even to satisfy my wish to join them, my longing to be there
in the long afternoons beside them, when the snow
hangs in the empty air, whirled about, driven sideways,
like the souls of my family given for nothing. Not for my need
to give a name to our lives, to be again, most truly, myself –
even to save myself, I would not give satisfaction to that angry ground.
I would not go there again. For love, I would not go.

CYNTHIA HUNTINGTON

Working Class Voodoo

This is me holding a voodoo doll.
This is me waving the doll over the hob.
This is me being silly, doll down my pants,
shrugging like a nineties sitcom doofus.
This is also me, going a bit mad, in the garden.
Ha-ha... Look at the sky! Weird isn't it?
That's my dear old mum, bless her, screaming.
Without her my daughter wouldn't have nice clothes.
There's dad, half cut, staring at a black cloth.
We never came to blows and I'm proud of that.
They're always asking what happened, oh
what happened, son, what happened?
The voodoo doll is not meant to represent
anyone in particular, although I'm sure
you're sharp enough to notice it bears
a striking resemblance to the snake man
who rattles beside my wife and sells
her telly for dope; who sometimes tells
my daughter to wipe herself on a towel
because they can't afford toilet paper;
who isn't bothered the divorce isn't fixed yet.
We are talking about the biggest creep in town,
living with my daughter, doing heroin
next to the bedroom where she wets herself.
I could kill him I could kill him I could.
Anyway, this is me throwing the doll
as far as I can, then running after it
on all fours with the most beautiful sunset
exploding cake and bottles of pink wine.
I mean clean powder and a holy syringe.
I mean glory, glory, my girlfriend's smile.
Finally, this is me in my doctor's office.
She wants to increase the medication,
thinks it will improve my quality of life.
She says perhaps it's not that I left a home,
or that I left a wife & child, it's because

I walked away from love, and those of us
who walk away from love are haunted
and we must learn to live again, bound
by the rules of the haunted cult of walking away.
You know, I wrote a poem about how much I hate
our abusive neighbours, just before it was published
they mysteriously moved out. Isn't that spooky?
And my wife looks at me like I fucking murdered her.
And her boyfriend smokes it he doesn't inject!
And my daughter kisses the freckles on my arm.
She says, 'Why did you leave us daddy?'
She tells me their budgies die from hunger.
She says daddy is so forgetful, his brain must be
a half-crushed sandcastle, waiting for the sea.
Then there's this doll, posing for a photograph.
This is me holding a match and a can of petrol.
The truth I beg you the truth the truth the truth.
Haunted for the haunted for the haunted forever.
I sometimes wonder if I wrote a broken family
into existence, using poems like this, and that,
someday, maybe, I could write them back.

BOBBY PARKER

Love-Smitten Heart

Coming out of Liverpool as the sun set
I begged my heart to stop but the train galloped on, dragging
all the corpses I keep tethered to my imaginary umbilicus.

I have bought a knife and I keep it with me at all times.
There is no one to call on when the world turns black.
I'm dying cruelly in my love-smitten heart.

I'm dead on the outside and regretfully alive in the middle.
I think of how dearly I would tend to your dead body.
I'm mortally pierced and I will not survive.

I write every poem as though it is my last poem,
expecting it to be my last. I'm often duped into climbing down and
    enduring.
When I am unafraid then you really should worry.

I feel my eyes set deeply and painfully in my head.
Music keeps my empathy raw and lubricated, though I don't care
if I ever again feel anything.

I want my heart cold in a cold cage of a body in a cage.
I don't imagine I will have the opportunity to regret it.
I've reached the very bottom darling and I know that you know it.

So many empty beds.
Beds left alone and
beds climbed out of – your body still fighting the cold there.

I am going to book a hotel room in my own name.
The sun will come through the window when I am no longer there.
The sun will rise until it doesn't.

The sun will set whether I rise or not.
Nothing has ever been simpler and you are blind to the facts.
There is constant pain I cannot manage and it won't die.

I call your number from the bench on the memorial park,
Pendle mounting fiercely in the background, and all the lights blinking.
Once there was a power-cut and I stared into the closed eye of the dark.

The police came this morning and threatened me.
They said nothing is so bad and they know what people like me do.
The policewoman went upstairs and questioned Elizabeth through the
    bathroom door.

The policewoman said, is there not somewhere else I can go, to
    someone else.
She said her mother had bipolar and she put her through hell.
I had to bite my lip and look in the other direction.

The policeman said I need to see a doctor, need to be sensible and
    take the medication
my doctor prescribes me, that Sunday mornings are not the time to
    ring the police.
My husband says bipolar disorder doesn't stop beyond nine to five.

The policeman stands over me aggressively, says it's just a blip,
that if I go walkabout he will issue a high risk missing person's report.
He uses the word 'daft' half a dozen times.

I hate how my husband describes my suicide attempts.
I listen to him on the phone desperate and describing my state of mind
using language, terminologies and a discourse I don't want to belong to.

I'd kiss him every minute of the day but it would make him sore.
I'd make him promises I can actually keep but they will become the
    promises I regret.
I need the freedom to go away and hurt,

just go with the wave until it takes me out. A sense of finality spurs
    me on.
I survive on nostalgia and the promise of pain.
The pain is a plan where there is no real hope or vision of a future
    where I am not alone.

We all die, is what I want to tell them.
We all know this, though grief is irrational and impossible and also
    unavoidable.
I won't be able to hold you through it.

My half of the bed will remain cold and my face indented on the pillow.
Your bare back and its pains will crease and fold.
In the morning I will be a shadow barely touching your body.

MELISSA LEE-HOUGHTON

Fish Out of Water

When he finally landed the fish it seemed so strange, so unlike other fishes he'd caught, so much bigger, more silvery, more important, that he half expected it to talk, to grant his wishes if he returned it to the water. But the fish said nothing, made no pleas, gave no promises. His fishing partner said, 'Nice fish. You ought to have it mounted.' Other people who saw it said the same thing, 'Nice fish...' So he took it to the taxidermy shop but when it came back it didn't look quite the same. Still, it was an impressive trophy. Mounted on a big board the way it was, it was too big to fit in the car. In those days he could fit everything he owned into the back of his Volkswagen but the fish changed all that. After he married, a year or so later, nothing would fit in the car. He got a bigger car. Then a new job, children... The fish moved with them from house to house, state to state. All that moving around took its toll on the fish, it began to look worn, a fin was broken off. It went into the attic of the new house. Just before the divorce became final, when he was moving to an apartment, his wife said 'Take your goddamn fish.' He hung the fish on the wall before he'd unpacked anything else. The fish seemed huge, too big for this little apartment. Boy, it was big. He couldn't imagine he'd ever caught a fish that big.

LOUIS JENKINS

No End to Images

No end to tissues of tears beside the bed
or to avenues of trees and cathedrals,
no end to bee-eaters in the rose apples
or summer on the balcony in Neukölln,
no end to the pharmaceutical clouds over Kraków
No end to the hour I stood and shook
like a leaf in the shower's privacy,

no end to my name, snagged like a burr,
no end to the body which is colossally small
with its pains and plainer longings.
No end to grief, never any end to that.
No end to the silver train stalled in Budapest
where I wept in the empty sleeper,
no end to iron shoes along the Danube,
to history, the convalescent light
that falls on my desk so evenly,
no end to the gardens of Europe
with their murderous symmetry,
no end to picnics on the forest's edge
or piazzas of pure Carrara marble,
to cruelty, madness, oblivion,
massacres and women's scarves,
the hunger of wolves, ripening stonefruit,
no end to fear and secret police,
and no end to Bach fugues on the turntable
whose ideas resolve so cleanly
into a life infinitely more gentle and orderly
than our fraught morning fights
or the cries we send echoing at night
down the hollow halls of love.

SARAH HOLLAND-BATT

'Very simple love that believes in words...'

Very simple love that believes in words,
since I cannot do what I want to do,
can neither hug nor kiss you,
my pleasure lies in my words
and when I can I speak to you of love.
So, sitting with a drink in front of me,
the place filled with people,

if your forehead quickly creases
in the heat of the moment I speak too loudly
and you never say don't be so loud,
let them think whatever they want
I draw closer melting with languor
and your eyes are so sweetly veiled
I don't reach for you, no, not even the softest touch
but in your body I feel I am swimming,
and the couch in the bar's lounge
when we get up looks like an unmade bed.

PATRIZIA CAVALLI
translated from the Italian by J. D. McClatchy

Like when we went to the cinema that time

We go to the park and you don't touch me
In the hard bright fizz of the sun we don't touch

We lie side by side. The grass is so green
we shudder, it's hot, and still we don't touch,

it's burning. We stare at the sky though a tree,
and it's so blue it hurts, just like the gap

between us which crackles and spits, we feel each
spark of grass wake up and prickle

between us, crying out, begging please to be
crushed but we don't touch, oh we don't touch

NATALIE SHAW

from Impossible Loves

2

Impossible love is the happiest of loves.
Or can be.
The only way to find happiness in impossible love
is never to believe impossible love is possible.
You could just be the impossible love of your impossible love.
But that would be a miracle.

4

Music sustains impossible loves,
nurtures them with the ethereal presence of a song,
a song that is ours even though I listen to it only when alone.
Impossible love allows a guitar string
perfect equilibrium,
gets drunk on the sweet nostalgia of a polonaise,
quivers with a voice between a moan and a song.
Then impossible love becomes a guitar, a piano
or is the sound of a voice.
Music is the present tense of impossible loves.

DARIO JARAMILO
translated from the Spanish by Richard Gwyn

Mozart on the Motorway

I close the window,
ward off the din of other cars
and go along in my capsule at eighty kilometres an hour,
with Mozart,
where time and space, hours and kilometres don't count
and a clarinet might be the prime cause,

the explanation of everything,
the heart of the matter.
Mozart on the motorway.
The world is bright and happy.

DARIO JARAMILO
translated from the Spanish by Richard Gwyn

Ceilidh

A ceilidh at Carrigskeewaun would now include
The ghost of Joe O'Toole at ease on his hummock
The far side of Corragaun Lake as he listens to
The O'Tooles from Inishdeigil who settled here
Eighty years ago, thirteen O'Tooles, each of them
A singer or fiddler, thirteen under the one roof,
A happy family but an unlucky one, Joe says,
And the visitors from Connemara who have rowed
Their currachs across the Killary for the music,
And my ghost at the duach's sheepbitten edge
Keeping an eye on the lamps in the windows here
But distracted by the nervy plover that pretends
A broken wing, by the long-lived oystercatcher
That calls out behind me from Thallabaun Strand.
The thirteen O'Tooles are singing about everything.
Their salty eggs are cherished for miles around.
There's a hazel copse near the lake without a name.
Dog violets, sorrel, wood spurge are growing there.
On Inishdeigil there's a well of purest water.
Is that Arcturus or a faraway outhouse light?
The crescent moon's a coracle for Venus. Look.
Through the tide and over Owennadornaun
Are shouldered the coffins of the thirteen O'Tooles.

MICHAEL LONGLEY

Aran

(for Tom and Peggy Mac Intyre)

He is earthed to his girl, one hand fastened
In hers, and with his free hand listens,
An earphone, to his own version
Singing the darkness into the light.
I close the pub door gently and step out
And a gull creaks off from the tin roof
Of an outhouse, planing over the ocean,
Circling now with a hoarse inchoate
Screaming the boned fields of its vision.
God, that was the way to do it,
Hand-clasping, echo-prolonging poet!

Scorched with a fearful admiration,
Walking over the nacreous sand,
I dream myself to that tradition
Generations off the land –
One hand to an ear for the vibration,
The far wires, the reverberation
Down light-years of the imagination
And a loved hand in the other hand.

The long glow springs from the dark soil, however –
No marsh-light holds a candle to this.
Unearthly still in its white weather
A crack-voiced rock-marauder, scavenger, fierce
Friend to no slant fields or the sea either,
Folds back over the forming waters.

DEREK MAHON

The Rolling Wave

(for Caoimhín Ó Raghallaigh)

Only when the others had left for the village
To drink and sing and dance in the New Year,
And the empty house had begun to answer

The wind in the birches that gave the valley
Its name and shaped its oldest stories,
Only then did he take down the fiddle and play.

It was the same tune. Again and again note-
And-pitch perfect, he played *The Rolling Wave*
As he had always done, predictable as the tides.

He tried all the variations he had picked up
Here, there and everywhere, stylish ornaments
That hung like baubles on the tune. Despair

Practised its scales on him. Faintly then,
He heard the sea flexing under the wind.
Swell after swell broke on the shingled coast,

Not the water rolling forward in the wave
But the wave rolling through the unmoving
Water, pitching its perfect notes to the sky.

So he played, not the tune itself but the tune
Being itself. And the house played with him,
Its timbers resonating like tightened strings,

Until he stood, his bow still drawn across
The still quivering air, in the new stillness
Inside his music, unmoving, transformed.

PADDY BUSHE

The Given Note

On the most westerly Blasket
In a dry-stone hut
He got this air out of the night.

Strange noises were heard
By others who followed, bits of a tune
Coming in on loud weather

Though nothing like melody.
He blamed their fingers and ear
As unpractised, their fiddling easy

For he had gone alone into the island
And brought back the whole thing.
The house throbbed like his full violin.

So whether he calls it spirit music
Or not, I don't care. He took it
Out of wind off mid-Atlantic.

Still he maintains, from nowhere.
It comes off the bow gravely,
Rephrases itself into the air.

SEAMUS HEANEY

That Note

Like Miles Davis' dark Arkansas roads
the tone I was after lay listless and dreaming
as we rode the sea lanes deep in Dublin Sound.
On either side of the waters we were crossing
lay cable, freight line, pipes of city joy,

and barely visible, though gleaming and new,
an audible pitch of beads and corded wire –
weird acoustics slumbering in their alloy.

And I knew it was there, like the shudder
in a mass light-years away shows
the hidden path of a polished ball of ice,
come this way with its heart on fire.
And that solder, that rich conspiracy of brass
and copper, a flame in the blood unlike
the one art melancholy of a cedar grove,
or the straight-on certainty of a 30s autobahn,
so it feels like time itself, or a bolt
from its legions, has come to this span we inhabit,
to count on and improvise, that note.

GERARD FANNING

Song

A rowan like a lipsticked girl.
Between the by-road and the main road
Alder trees at a wet and dripping distance
Stand off among the rushes.

There are the mud-flowers of dialect
And the immortelles of perfect pitch
And that moment when the bird sings very close
To the music of what happens.

SEAMUS HEANEY

Music Heard with You

Music I heard with you was more than music…
CONRAD AIKEN

Music heard with you
will stay with us always

Grave Brahms, and elegiac Schubert,
a few songs, Chopin's fourth ballad,

A few quartets with heart-
breaking chords (Beethoven, adagia),

the sadness of Shostakovich, who
didn't want to die.

The great choruses of Bach's Passions,
as if someone had summoned us,

demanding joy,
pure and impartial

joy in which faith
is self-evident.

Some scraps of Lutosławski
as fleeting as our thoughts.

A black woman singing blues
ran through us like shining steel,

though it reached us on the street
of an ugly, dirty town.

Mahler's endless marches
the trumpet's voice that opens that Fifth Symphony

and the first part of the Ninth
(you sometimes call him 'malheur!').

Mozart's despair in the Requiem,
his buoyant piano concertos –

you hummed them better than I did,
but we both know that.

Music heard with you
will grow still with us.

ADAM ZAGAJEWSKI
translated from the Polish by Clare Cavanagh

Listening to Bach's B Minor Mass in the kitchen

Finally, I'm done with the phone calls and everything else
and when I switch on the radio it feels like lying in salt water –
all I need to do is breathe: Bach will keep me afloat.
I'm mixing yeast into flour, making rolls for my daughter's
birthday breakfast in the morning, kneading and kneading
the dough then setting it to rise; arranging in a glass
the last of the tiny pink roses with a sprig of green,
finding the blue candles and ironing the tablecloth,
the one my granny embroidered, sweeping the floor,
thinking about the hot August night of the birth,
and about the people we met on Westray last week,
and the presents I still need to wrap, and Bach himself
who is like a mountain covered in wildflowers,
and the singers in the Albert Hall who, the conductor says,
get close to godliness through this performance;
and I'm wondering, as all those voices fill my kitchen
with the Mass, if this is what he means: the sense
of time and place dissolving, so what divides us
from the past and elsewhere, and from each other,
falls away, and everything's connected and we are all
drops of water in this enormous breaking wave.

ELIZABETH BURNS

The silence of the world before Bach

There must have existed a world before
the Trio Sonata in D, a world before the A minor Partita,
but what was that world like?
A Europe of large unresonating spaces
everywhere unknowing instruments,
where *Musikalisches Opfer* and *Wohltemperiertes Klavier*
had never passed over a keyboard.
Lonely remote churches
where the soprano voice of the Easter Passion
had never in helpless love twined itself round
the gentler movements of the flute,
gentle expanses of landscape
where only old woodcutters are heard with their axes
the healthy sound of strong dogs in winter
and – like a bell – skates biting into glassy ice;
the swallows swirling in the summer air
the shell that the child listens to
and nowhere Bach nowhere Bach
skating silence of the world before Bach

LARS GUSTAFSSON
translated from the Swedish by John Irons

Chaconne

We know, everyone knows, that he spoke with the Lord
in countless cantatas and passions, but there's also
the chaconne from the second partita for solo violin:
here, perhaps only here, Bach talks about his life,
he suddenly, unexpectedly, reveals himself,
swiftly, violently casts out joy and sorrow
(since it's all we've got), the pain of losing his wife and children,
the grief that time must take everything,
but also the ecstasy of hours without end

when, in some dim church's musty air,
lonely, like the pilot of a plane delivering mail
to foreign countries, he played the organ and sensed beneath his fingers
its pneumatic acquiescence, its rapture, its trembling,
or when he heard the choir's single, mighty voice as if
all human strife were gone for good
– after all, we dream about it too,
telling the truth about our life,
and we keep trying awkwardly,
and we'll go on trying, but where are they,
where can our cantatas be, tell me,
where is the other side.

ADAM ZAGAJEWSKI
translated from the Polish by Clare Cavanagh

Even the Vanishing Housed

But what if the world's
strict questions were not this
unanswerable yellow, that rampant red,
or the black-hearted, pried-open blue?
If the disciplined welter
were not heady with white-scented bloom?
Would love bend like the tulips then
from its quick-flying carriage?
Would tenderness wring the heart still
of its burdens, leaving only the dark-salted
circles on stone-colored ground?
It is the way humans know –
through the earth, through the things of the earth,
lips stained by what they have tasted,
the sweet sap-run, the tart-rinded fruit.
Leave to dogs and the angels
the music that lies beyond hearing.
Though the infinite palace is infinite, it is precise.

JANE HIRSHFIELD

Schubertiana

1

In the evening darkness in a place outside New York, an outlook point
    where one single glance will encompass the homes of eight million people.
The giant city over there is a long shimmering drift, a spiral galaxy seen
    from the side.
Within the galaxy coffee-cups are pushed across the counter, the shop-
    windows beg from passers-by, a flurry of shoes that leave no prints.
The climbing fire escapes, the lift doors that glide shut, behind doors
    with police locks a perpetual seethe of voices.
Slouched bodies doze in subway coaches, the hurtling catacombs.
I know too – without statistics – that right now Schubert is being played
    in some room over there and that for someone the notes are more real
    than all the rest.

2

The endless expanses of the human brain are crumpled to the size of a
    fist.
In April the swallow returns to last year's nest under the guttering of this
    very barn in this very parish.
She flies from Transvaal, passes the equator, flies for six weeks over two
    continents, makes for precisely this vanishing dot in the land-mass.
And the man who catches the signals from a whole life in ordinary chords
    for five strings,
who makes a river flow through the eye of a needle,
is a stout young gentleman from Vienna known to his friends as 'The
    Mushroom', who slept with his glasses on
and stood at his writing desk punctually of a morning.
And then the wonderful centipedes of his manuscript were set in motion.

3

The string quintet is playing. I walk home through warm forests with the
    ground springy under me,
curl up like an embryo, fall asleep, roll weightless into the future,
    suddenly feel that the plants have thoughts.

4

So much we have to trust, simply to live through our daily day without
sinking through the earth!
Trust the piled snow clinging to the mountain slope above the village.
Trust the promises of silence and the smile of understanding, trust that
the accident telegram isn't for us and that the sudden axe-blow from
within won't come.
Trust the axles that carry us on the highway in the middle of the three
hundred times life-size bee-swarm of steel.
But none of that is really worth our confidence.
The five strings say we can trust something else.
And they keep us company part of the way there.
As when the time-switch clicks off in the stairwell and the fingers –
trustingly – follow the blind handrail that finds its way in the
darkness.

5

We squeeze together at the piano and play with four hands in F minor,
two coachmen on the same coach, it looks a little ridiculous.
The hands seem to be moving resonant weights to and fro, as if we were
tampering with the counterweights
in an effort to disturb the great scale arm's terrible balance: joy and
suffering weighing exactly the same.
Annie said, 'This music is so heroic,' and she's right.
But those whose eyes enviously follow men of action, who secretly
despise themselves for not being murderers,
don't recognise themselves here,
and the many who buy and sell people and believe that everyone can
be bought, don't recognise themselves here.
Not their music. The long melody that remains itself in all its
transformations, sometimes glittering and pliant, sometimes rugged
and strong, snail-track and steel wire.
The perpetual humming that follows us – now –
up
the depths.

TOMAS TRANSTRÖMER
translated from the Swedish by Robin Fulton

Allegro

I play Haydn after a black day
and feel a simple warmth in my hands.

The keys are willing. Soft hammers strike.
The resonance green, lively and calm.

The music says freedom exists
and someone doesn't pay the emperor tax.

I push down my hands in my Haydnpockets
and imitate a person looking on the world calmly.

I hoist the Haydnflag – it signifies:
'We don't give in. But want peace.'

The music is a glass-house on the slope
where the stones fly, the stones roll.

And the stones roll right through
but each pane stays whole.

TOMAS TRANSTRÖMER
translated from the Swedish by Robin Fulton

To Be Alive

To be alive: not just the carcass
But the spark.
That's crudely put, but...

If we're not supposed to dance,
Why all this music?

GREGORY ORR

6

Mortal hurt

I've been thinking about poetry's ability to help us grieve – for
ourselves, for each other – and always to bear witness. Suffering is very
often a private thing. But to become more than just suffering, something
transformative, it needs to be shared. This is why we have ritual.
And poetry is a kind of ritual, with its own conventions, its own internal
logic of organising and ordering emotion and different registers of
language. Poetry is the closest grief has to expression in language.
Without it, we would be reduced to a single, unending cry of
inexpressible hurt. With it, we exercise our prerogative to be human,
in conversation with a grief that would otherwise destroy us.

ILYSE KUSNETZ

This section begins with poems on mortality, followed by personal testimonies
of poets who have survived serious illness, including Caroline Bird on her
experiences in a drug rehabilitation clinic (276-77), and Lieke Marsman (279-81),
Jo Shapcott (281) and Julie O'Callaghan (283) on their treatment for cancer.
Sadly, others did not survive. The epigraph above and poem (284) by Ilyse
Kusnetz (1966-2016) are from her second, posthumously published collection,
Angel Bones (2019). Max Ritvo (1990-2016) was diagnosed with Ewing's sarco-
ma at 16, and died at 25; his work appeared in three posthumously published
books: *Four Reincarnations* (2016), *The Final Voicemails* (2018), and *Letters from
Max* (2018). Helen Dunmore (1952-2017) had written half of her final collection,
Inside the Wave (2017), when she learned that her cancer was terminal; 'Hold
out your arms' (316) was her last poem. Lucie Brock-Broido (1956-2018) also
died from cancer. Her poem 'Soul Keeping Company' (337) is one of several
on the passage from life to death. Another is 'Street of Sailmakers' (338) by
Dean Young, who received a life-saving heart transplant in 2011 after living
for a decade with a degenerative heart condition.

Julie O'Callaghan survived cancer herself only to lose her husband, poet
Dennis O'Driscoll (340), to the disease in 2012, silencing her for years until
she was finally able to write the poems of *Magnum Mysterium* (2020), two of
which are included here (341). Bernard O'Donoghue's title, 'Ter Conatus' (323),
is Latin for 'having tried three times', from Virgil's *Aeneid*: when Aeneas is
unable to embrace the shades of his late wife Creusa and his father Anchises.
The Morandi Bridge in Genoa recalled in Eiléan Ní Chuilleanáin's poem (324)
collapsed on 14 August 2019 causing the deaths of 43 people.

This section complements selections of poems on sickness, loss, death and
mortality in *Staying Alive* (3: 'Dead or alive', 117-30; 10: 'Disappearing acts',
369-412), *Being Alive* (10: 'Ends and Beginnings', 443-82), and *Being Human*
(5: 'Fight to the death', 245-306).

The Half-Finished Heaven

Despondency breaks off its course.
Anguish breaks off its course.
The vulture breaks off its flight.

The eager light streams out,
even the ghosts take a draught.

And our paintings see daylight,
our red beasts of the ice-age studio;

Everything begins to look around.
We walk in the sun in hundreds.

Each man is a half-open door
leading to a room for everyone.

The endless ground under us.

The water is shining among the trees.

The lake is a window into the earth.

TOMAS TRANSTRÖMER
translated from the Swedish by Robin Fulton

The Fact That No Birds Sing

When sorrow comes, there is no
language

for it. Sorrow
is blackness, is absence, is yearning – many names

can be used, none of which
equals sorrow. To bear sorrow

is not to want to get up
in the morning, not to manage to lift your foot

from the sidewalk, not to be able to escape
the same stab in your heart that you felt

yesterday, the day before yesterday, two days
before yesterday, every time

you pass those spots in town, those landscapes
of mind, those names

for what you lost: a body, a laughter, a lightness – a pair
of eyes to meet your own. Do those eyes

have a name? Are they called Oscar? Are they called
Kathinka? The fact that O or K is gone

is incomprehensible, incomprehensible, incomprehensible
– is there a name for it? The fact

that K or O shall never place a calming hand
on your forehead brings pain

beyond words – is there a name for it? The fact
that no birds

sing. A blackness
called sorrow. Lasts seldom more than seven years.

JAN ERIK VOLD
translated from Norwegian by the author

Wait

Wait, for now.
Distrust everything if you have to.
But trust the hours. Haven't they
carried you everywhere, up to now?
Personal events will become interesting again.
Hair will become interesting.
Pain will become interesting.
Buds that open out of season will become interesting.
Second-hand gloves will become lovely again;
their memories are what give them
the need for other hands. The desolation
of lovers is the same: that enormous emptiness
carved out of such tiny beings as we are
asks to be filled; the need
for the new love is faithfulness to the old.

Wait.
Don't go too early.
You're tired. But everyone's tired.
But no one is tired enough.
Only wait a little and listen:
music of hair,
music of pain,
music of looms weaving our loves again.
Be there to hear it, it will be the only time,
most of all to hear your whole existence,
rehearsed by the sorrows, play itself into total exhaustion.

GALWAY KINNELL

from **Averno**

You die when your spirit dies.
Otherwise, you live.
You may not do a good job of it, but you go on –
something you have no choice about.

When I tell this to my children
they pay no attention.
The old people, they think –
this is what they always do:
talk about things no one can see
to cover up all the brain cells they're losing.
They wink at each other;
listen to the old one, talking about the spirit
because he can't remember any more the word for chair.

It is terrible to be alone.
I don't mean to live alone –
to *be* alone, where no one hears you.

I remember the word for chair.
I want to say – I'm just not interested anymore.

I wake up thinking
you have to prepare.
Soon the spirit will give up –
all the chairs in the world won't help you.

I know what they say when I'm out of the room.
Should I be seeing someone, should I be taking
one of the new drugs for depression.
I can hear them, in whispers, planning how to divide the cost.

And I want to scream out
you're all of you living in a dream.

Bad enough, they think, to watch me falling apart.
Bad enough without this lecturing they get these days
as though I had any right to this new information.

Well, they have the same right.

They're living in a dream, and I'm preparing
to be a ghost. I want to shout out

the mist has cleared –
It's like some new life:
you have no stake in the outcome;
you know the outcome.

Think of it: sixty years sitting in chairs. And now the mortal spirit
seeking so openly, so fearlessly –

To raise the veil.
To see what you're saying goodbye to.

LOUISE GLÜCK

The End of the Bed

I saw hands reaching out of the bookcases.
I saw the bookcases stretching out of themselves.
I saw a man sitting on the end of the bed.
I saw wolves in the wardrobe.
You tried turning on the lights.
You tried splashing me with water.
You sat me on the sofa with a mug of tea.
I said, 'We all need to journey into a pit.'
Children were staging a play at the end
of the bed. You said, 'Baby, are you telling
me a story?' I said, 'This is *my* story.'
You called 999. I dribbled out my tea.

You said, 'My girlfriend's making no sense.'
I told the paramedics I was twenty-five.
I couldn't remember how to walk.
They were in my living room shining
torches, discussing my pupils.
I was lightly inhabited like a vapour.
I told the neon woman I lived on 'Address Road'.
I got my postcode wrong. And my birthday.
I couldn't remember my mum's maiden name.
I said Queen Elizabeth the First was on the throne.
When asked my dad's name, I listed Alan, Tom, Richard,
Mark, Sam, Luke, William, Graham, Martin, Harry...
In the ambulance I turned to you and said,
'Don't worry baby, I've got this.'

CAROLINE BIRD

A Surreal Joke

One year is blank on my curriculum vitae.
I was in the desert, convalescing,
repairing my septum. I'd tried to die
expensively, dragging it out over
six months, locked in my university
bathroom with a rolled-up scrap of canto.
I forgot how to love my family.
At one point, my arms turned completely blue.

My assigned counsellor told me I used
poetry to hide from myself, unhook
the ballast from my life; a floating ruse
of surreal jokes. He stole my notebook.
I said, they're not jokes. He said, maybe try
to write the simple truth? I said, why?

CAROLINE BIRD

As Marginalia in John Clare's *The Rural Muse*

I wasn't finished. From as far back
as I can recall having heard a voice in my skull

I've wanted to die, or change, or die
changing. Hexagonal window, the moon

penned in it, and a segmented swarm sucking
up peonies. Heat off tar shingles

in June as the blood in one arm
blackened, thickened, went blearily toxic,

I exited earth up an IV tube.
The wall-mounted paper dispenser

narrating nightmares of scale, sores fell
from fingers – get well petals – and grew

back puce. Slug of little light, the bedrail
gleamed. Warmed yoghurt, a summons

button and visual aphasia. Now I've no spit,
no hospice and admit nothing, or,

for long stretches, only what happened
was all that ever could have happened.

Reeds curtain where land abuts lake,
if such limit exists, if ducks aren't taken

by pike mid-thought.

KEN BABSTOCK

The Following Scan Will Last Less Than a Minute

afternoons are
Eurosport replays
of alpine skiing
sponsored by Jack Wolfskin and Milka
brands to whom I am grateful
for facilitating this daily moment of calm

evenings are the joy
I take in loving Simone as much as I do
especially in the face of this overwhelming exhaustion

cancer is so quotidian
you hear about it on Wednesday morning
die on a Tuesday afternoon
no strobe lights
no cloakroom check-in
the sun is shining
a completely ordinary insipid sun
above the A10
and the exit for Praxis

The Following Scan Will Last One Minute

with cancer in your back everything
is suddenly afforded an epic quality

two people in a car
magical!

tying your own shoelaces
the stuff of poetry!

Simone feeding me recovery ward noodles
a fairy tale

279

The Following Scan Will Last Five Minutes

The internet has a great deal to offer
Someone who doesn't wish to dwell
For whom every breath is a distraction

Throbbing lung tumours
The man in the street
Is always right

The nation state has been disarticulated
By her opponents
Then glorified

By her supporters
The man in the street
Is always right

The news repeats itself
The rhythm of drones
The oncologist commences sentencing

There is nothing I need to see
Except, again and again,
A new day with you

The MRI tunnel speaks
The following scan will last five minutes
Poetry fills this empty head

Contrast agent
The stench of anaesthetic
A beach ball in your nose

A volleyball in your stomach
Poetry fills this empty head
The rhythm falters

The news repeats itself
Language without sound
Cancer without catharsis

There is nothing I need to see
Except, again and again,
A new day

LIEKE MARSMAN
translated from the Dutch by Sophie Collins

Of Mutability

Too many of the best cells in my body
are itching, feeling jagged, turning raw
in this spring chill. It's two thousand and four
and I don't know a soul who doesn't feel small
among the numbers. Razor small.
Look down these days to see your feet
mistrust the pavement and your blood tests
turn the doctor's expression grave.

Look up to catch eclipses, gold leaf, comets,
angels, chandeliers, out of the corner of your eye,
join them if you like, learn astrophysics, or
learn folksong, human sacrifice, mortality,
flying, fishing, sex without touching much.
Don't trouble, though, to head anywhere but the sky.

JO SHAPCOTT

Harbinger

Just another day   in hyper-capitalist society –
in my Facebook feed,   news of rabbits and

chickens tortured on meat farms,   but I'm still not
vegan and I'm waiting   to die myself

from cancer I may have gotten   from soil or groundwater
contaminated by nuclear weapons,   and no amount

of posting uplifting stories   is going to fix that.
And lord, let them cease   trying to control women's

bodies, people's genders,   people's desires,
let them stop hating people   because of their color

and ethnicities. I want to shake   the bigots and racists
till their teeth rattle loose   and they lose their bite,

till their tongues   swell up in their mouths
and they're stricken mute.   I want to save

all the slaughtered animals,   save the seas and their
inhabitants – whales, birds,   the tiniest bivalves –

from choking on plastic.   I want to purify the air
of sulfur and carbon dioxide,   scrape the lead

from plumbing pipes,   god I need to do something
besides dying, besides   thinking about death

and the neofascist   politicians who lead
a nation of people   unable to think critically

after 40 years' systemic   dismantling
of the education system   by the rich

so their lackeys   can make it
illegal to prosecute   corporations for poisoning

the air, earth, water – and Jesus,   isn't it
a kind of   mental illness

annihilating what you need   to stay alive
for the accumulation of   blind profit –

and in the process killing   and killing and
murdering me,   along with the people and animals

I can't save but want to,   with all my goddamn
fucking heart, but instead   I'm waiting

to die, trying to find some   last meaning in all
of this. A warning, perhaps.   *You're next.*

ILYSE KUSNETZ

No Can Do

I know I'm a total party-pooper.
But there's no way
I can go to Red Lobster.
I have to stay home.
I have to rest.
I can't move.

Chip is like:
'How come you don't want to
to go out anyplace?'

I'm this huge moose
with no hair,
a cheapo wig and cancer.
And I'm supposed to go
and eat a Seafood Platter?
No can do.

JULIE O'CALLAGHAN

'the posh mums are boxing in the square...'

the posh mums are boxing in the square
roughing each other up   in a nice way
this is not the world into which I was born
       so I'm changing it
I'm sinking deep into the past and dressing my own mum
in their blue spandexes
svelte black stripes from hip to hem
and husbands with better dispositions toward kindness
or at least   I'm giving her new lungs
I'm giving her a best friend   with no problems and both of them pads
some gloves to go at each other with   in a nice way
I'm making it a warm day for them but also
I'm making it rain
the two of them dapping it out in long shadows
I'm watching her from the trees grow
strength in her thighs   my mum
grow strength in her glutes my mum
her back taught upright
her knees
and watching her grow no bad thing in her stomach no tumour
her feet do not hurt to touch   my mum she is hopping
sinews are happening
wiry arms developing their full reach
no bad thing explodes

sweat and not gradual death   I'm cheering
no thing in her stomach no alcohol
no cigarettes with their crotonaldehyde let my dad keep those
no removal of her womb
– and I'm cheering her on in better condition
cheering she is learning to fight for her own body
in spandex her new life
and though there is no beef between them
if her friend is gaining the upper hand
I will call out from the trees
       her name
          Christine!

and when she turns   as turn she must
my mum   in the nicest possible way
can slug her right in the gut

WAYNE HOLLOWAY-SMITH

My Body Effervesces

I am born for the second time.
I am light
as the eyelash of the wind.
I froth, I am froth.

I walk dancing,
if I wish, I will soar.
The condensed lightness
of my body
condenses most forcibly
in the lightness of my foot
and its five toes.
The foot skims the earth
which gives way like compressed air.
An elastic duo
of the earth and of the foot. A dance
of liberation.

I am born for the second time,
happiness of the world
came to me again.
My body effervesces,
I think with my body which effervesces.

If I wish
I will soar.

ANNA SWIR
translated from the Polish by Czeslaw Milosz & Leonard Nathan

285

A Story About the Body

The young composer, working that summer at an artist's colony, had watched her for a week. She was Japanese, a painter, almost sixty, and he thought he was in love with her. He loved her work, and her work was like the way she moved her body, used her hands, looked at him directly when she made amused and considered answers to his questions. One night, walking back from a concert, they came to her door and she turned to him and said, 'I think you would like to have me. I would like that too, but I must tell you that I have had a double mastectomy,' and when he didn't understand, 'I've lost both my breasts.' The radiance that he had carried around in his belly and chest cavity – like music – withered very quickly, and he made himself look at her when he said, 'I'm sorry. I don't think I could.' He walked back to his own cabin through the pines, and in the morning he found a small blue bowl on the porch outside his door. It looked to be full of rose petals, but he found when he picked it up that the rose petals were on top; the rest of the bowl – she must have swept them from the corners of her studio – was full of dead bees.

ROBERT HASS

Poem to My Litter

My genes are in mice, and not in the banal way
that Man's old genes are in the Beasts.

My doctors split my tumors up and scattered them
into the bones of twelve mice. We give

the mice poisons I might, in the future, want
for myself. We watch each mouse like a crystal ball.

I wish it was perfect, but sometimes the death we see
doesn't happen when we try it again in my body.

My tumors are old, older than mice can be.
They first grew in my flank a decade ago.

Then they went to my lungs, and down my femurs,
and into the hives in my throat that hatch white cells.

The mice only have a tumor each, in the leg.
Their tumors have never grown up. Uprooted

and moved. Learned to sleep in any bed
the vast body turns down. Before the tumors can spread,

they bust open the legs of the mice. Who bleed to death.
Next time the doctors plan to cut off the legs

in the nick of time so the tumors will spread.
But I still have both my legs. To complicate things further,

mouse bodies fight off my tumors. We have to give
the mice AIDS so they'll harbor my genes peacefully.

I want my mice to be just like me. I don't have any children.
I named them all Max. First they were Max 1, Max 2,

but now they're all just Max. No playing favorites.
They don't know they're named, of course.

They're like children you've traumatised
and tortured so they won't let you visit.

I hope, Maxes, some good in you is of me.
Even my suffering is good, in part. Sure, I swell

with rage, fear – the stuff that makes you see your tail
as a bar on the cage. But then the feelings pass.

And since I do absolutely nothing (my pride, like my fur,
all gone) nothing happens to me. And if a whole lot

of nothing happens to you, Maxes, that's peace.
Which is what we want. Trust me.

MAX RITVO

Heaven Is Us Being a Flower Together

Victoria, I think death comes at blindness.

I think pupils are sails,
and death is when the wind goes slack.

Winter, by being so white,
it is trying to talk to me –

closing communicated to one who sees death
as white worms
riddling the apple of the eye.

You think death comes at the cessation of touch.
You are a flower bulb
that can feel even in the winter earth.

The cold is a line that will not bend,
drawn through you foot to head.

Heat is a planet
fleeing its own cold line.

I have written this poem inside of you.
I am clutched in with your mother blood,
feeling your bends in the dark,
becoming a soft bend in your body.

We are becoming a bulb
in the ground of the living,
in the winter of being alive.

MAX RITVO

Cachexia

Today I woke up in my body
and wasn't that body any more.

It's more like my dog –
for the most part obedient,
warming to me
when I slip it Goldfish or toast,

but it sheds.
Can't get past a simple sit,
stay, turn over. House-trained, but not entirely.

This doesn't mean it's time to say goodbye.

I've realised the estrangement
is temporary, and for my own good:

My body's work to break the world
into bricks and sticks
has turned inward.

As all the doors in the world
grow heavy
a big white bed is being put up in my heart.

MAX RITVO

Michael's Dream

(FROM *Atlantis*)

Michael writes to tell me his dream:
I was helping Randy out of bed,
supporting him on one side
with another friend on the other,

and as we stood him up, he stepped out
of the body I was holding and became
a shining body, brilliant light
held in the form I first knew him in.

This is what I imagine will happen,
the spirit's release. Michael,
when we support our friends,
one of us on either side, our arms

under the man or woman's arms,
what is it we're holding? Vessel,
shadow, hurrying light? All those years
I made love to a man without thinking

how little his body had to do with me;
now, diminished, he's never been so plainly
himself – remote and unguarded,
an otherness I can't know

the first thing about. I said,
You need to drink more water
or you're going to turn into
an old dry leaf. And he said,

Maybe I want to be an old leaf.
In the dream Randy's leaping into
the future, and still here; Michael's holding him
and releasing at once. Just as Steve's

holding Jerry, though he's already gone,
Marie holding John, gone, Maggie holding
her John, gone, Carlos and Darren
holding another Michael, gone,

and I'm holding Wally, who's going.
Where isn't the question,
though we think it is;
we don't even know where the living are,

in this raddled and unraveling 'here'.
What is the body? Rain on a window,
a clear movement over whose gaze?
Husk, leaf, little boat of paper

and wood to mark the speed of the stream?
Randy and Jerry, Michael and Wally
and John: lucky we don't have to know
what something is in order to hold it.

MARK DOTY

The Body

Twenty years ago, I imagined
passersby on the street naked
stripping their clothes like a breeze and chuckled at them
walking unaware of what I saw:
plenty of sparkling bodies in their imperfections and glory.

Today, as I walk the streets, I no longer see naked
bodies, but their internal organs:
the trembling heart, shrunk to a baby's fist,
of the man staring at small ads for an apartment;
bowels, like sailor ropes in a heavy bag,
of the one tired on a bench;

291

a woman's bones shuffling across the street
like fragile musical instruments;
veins of the young saleswoman at the empty store
with overpriced clothes;
lightning in the spring sky;
lungs; kidneys; liver; spleen; blood and lymph;
an inner ear no longer ringing;
the womb's walls shadowed by the slumber
of unborn babies;
sperm in the reactor on the brink of bursting,
retreats to its mute testicular abyss
between two newsstands; and the man
walking to the market to buy some greens
I see: his brain and a head of cabbage ogle each other
today quite coquettishly.

Twenty years ago, the body you see
had only skin
but now, it has only organs;
so, I guess, that's how to reach
inside.

ANA RISTOVIĆ
translated from the Serbian by Steven and Maja Teref

Long Life

Late summer. Sunshine. The eucalyptus tree.
It is a fortune beyond any deserving
to be still *here*, with no more than everyday worries,
placidly arranging lines of poetry,

I consider a stick of cinnamon
bound in raffia, finches
in the grass, and a stubby bush
which this year mothered a lemon.

These days I speak less of death
than this miracle of survival. I am
no longer lonely, not yet frail, and
after surgery, recognise each breath

as a favour. My generation may not be
nimble but, forgive us,
we'd like to hold on, stubbornly
content – even while ageing.

ELAINE FEINSTEIN

The Excuse

Do they write poems when they have something to say,
Something to think about,
Rubbed from the world's hard rubbing in the excess of every day?
The summer I was twenty-four in San Francisco. You and I.
The whole summer seemed like a cable-car ride over the gold bay.
But once in a bistro, angry at one another,
We quarreled about a taxi fare. I doubt
That it was the fare we quarreled about,
But one excuse is as good as another
In the excess of passion, in the need to be worn away.

Do they know it is cleanness of skin, firmness of flesh that matters?
It is so difficult to look at the deprived, or smell their decay.
But now I am among them. I, too, am a leper, a warning.
I hold out my crippled fingers; my voice flatters
Everyone who comes this way. In the weeds of mourning,
Groaning and gnashing, I display
Myself in malodorous comic wrappings and tatters,
In the excess of passion, in the need to be worn away.

RUTH STONE

At eighty-five, my mother's mind

When she wanders from room to room
looking for someone who isn't there,

when she asks where we keep the spoons,
when she can't chew and spits out her food,

when her last dim light flickers with falling ash
and she exclaims: 'What a dismal end to a brilliant day!'

when she calls her regular laxative an astronaut,
when she can't hear words but fears sounds,

when she says: 'Don't go – I can't bear it when you go,'
or: 'Just run me off the cliff,'
or wants to know how many Disprin ends it,

then I think how at eighty-five
my mother's mind is a castle in ruin.

Time has raised her drawbridge, lopped her bastions.
Her balustrade is crumbled, and she leans.

Yet still you may walk these ramparts in awe.
Sometimes when she speaks, the ghostly ensign flies.

Time cannot hide what once stood here,
or its glory.

Do not think that we are good
or merely tourists.

That which detains us
was once our fortress.

FINUALA DOWLING

Widowhood in the dementia ward

'Oh my God, I'm so pleased to see you,'
she says from her nest of blankets.
'I've been meaning to ask –
How is your father?
How is Paddy?'

'He died,' I say, remembering 1974.

'Good heavens, now you tell me!
How lucky he is.'

'You could join him,' I suggest.

'I didn't like him *that* much,' she replies.

FINUALA DOWLING

Birthday in the dementia ward

We are discussing her eighty-sixth birthday.
She pulls herself up from her cushions:
'I wonder – I would really like my mother to come –
could you arrange that?'

(Your mother was born in 1888,
even if she were Japanese
she could not come.)

'I'll see if I can arrange transport.'

FINUALA DOWLING

Old Age

Later, when I am feeble-minded,
with a lapdog and goose skin,
I'll keep a bottle warm
against me and talk
to you in my sleep.
If you can understand now
what I'm going to say then,
crackling withered stem that I'll be,
I will not feel so broken off,
more like a blown-out dandelion.
Can you hear me babble?
There go my little parachutes.

JUDITH HERZBERG
translated from the Dutch by Shirley Kaufman with Judith Herzberg

The Wrong Beds

Life is a hospital ward, and the beds we are put in
are the ones we don't want to be in.
We'd get better sooner if put over by the window.
Or by the radiator, one could suffer easier there.

At night we dream of faraway places:
The Côte d'Azur, all perfume and light. Or nearer home
a cottage in the Cotswolds, a studio overlooking the sea.
The soul could be happier anywhere than where it happens to be.

Anywhere but here. We take our medicine daily,
nod politely, and grumble occasionally.
But it is out of our hands. Always the wrong place.
We didn't make our beds, but we lie in them.

ROGER McGOUGH

Sneak

Age comes, and then
infirmity, not beating
on the door with knotty

stick, announcing its
arrival with due pomp
and medication, but

insinuating noxious
vapours into lung and heart,
round knee and hip, curling

through the brain like smoke,
invisible yet choking with
an acrid autumn smell.

GERALDINE MITCHELL

How the Body Remembers

Last night I was woken by a loose scrap of siren
and found you, face pressed to the night,
watching some drama unfold on our road,
cobalt strobing the silence

the way it lit up the street that September
in Trastevere, washed over you blue after blue
where you lay among fag ends and chair legs
until they lifted you on to a stretcher

and breath guttered back through your lungs
as we lunged over cobbles in a language
unknown to us and you found yourself
back in a nine-year-old body

297

careening through London's cacophony
of sirens, bomb flares through blue glass,
the City in flames, your eyes wide
with terror and me holding your hand.

GERALDINE MITCHELL

from The Book of Steve

Let's age together like old-growth trees,
our knobby elbows sueded with moss,
draped over each other in a tipsy embrace,
staggering after our thousandth waltz.
We'll toast each year with another ring,
welcome hawks like finials to balding heights.

When the end comes, shall we crash to earth
comic and good-natured about it
as the bridal couple in the video
toppling as they tango the town hall floor?
Thudding to the ferns, we'll sleep like spoons again,
looped with huckleberry, frogs booming at our feet,
nurse-logs to saplings bowering a new age.

ELISE PARTRIDGE

Everyone Is Beautiful Today

He'd drunk a good half of his life away,
        the rest had gone on hangovers.
Friday. He hadn't been sitting reading Schopenhauer,
        thinking of death or how he'd make it later,
and still the worse for wear he stumbled down the street,

saw a pretty face, and then another, and thought:
      everyone is beautiful today, my god,
a person is a well-made thing. And everyone,
      including me, deserves another spring.

Drinking is dying and rising up again from death.
      I guess I must have led a thousand lives
and now I'm ready to bury my head in another year.

Strolling serenely onwards, blithely praising faces,
      sitting down outside a bar and drinking to the light.

MENNO WIGMAN
translated from the Dutch by David Colmer

Age

I have been writing about this townland
For fifty years, watching on their hummock
Autumn lady's tresses come and go and,
After a decade underground, return
In hundreds. I have counted the whoopers
And the jackdaws over Morrison's barn.
Too close on the duach to tractor tracks
The ringed plover's nest has kept me awake,
And the otter that drowned in an eel-trap.
Salvaging snail shells and magpie feathers
For fear of leaving particulars out,
I make little space for philosophising.
I walk ever more slowly to gate and stile.
Poetry is shrinking almost to its bones.

MICHAEL LONGLEY

Refusing at Fifty-two to Write Sonnets

It came to him that he could nearly count
How many Octobers he had left to him
In increments of ten or, say, eleven
Thus: sixty-three, seventy-four, eighty-five.
He couldn't see himself at ninety-six –
Humanity's advances notwithstanding
In health-care, self-help, or new-age regimens –
What with his habits and family history,
The end he thought is nearer than you think.

The future, thus confined to its contingencies,
The present moment opens like a gift:
The balding month, the grey week, the blue morning,
The hour's routine, the minute's passing glance –
All seem like godsends now. And what to make of this?
At the end the word that comes to him is Thanks.

THOMAS LYNCH

As You Get Older

As you get older
and the pen begins to run out

you begin – without thinking –
to thank the god

you do not believe in.
It's the man

who does not believe
believes most

by saying, over and over,
in a repetitive prayer,

I do not believe,
I do not believe in anything out there.

So when you
start

cursing the god that does not exist
and the pen fills with anger

that's when
faith

and tyranny
begin.

DERMOT HEALY

A Lift
(i.m. Dermot Healy)

Tell me, is it all atomised energies
Or do the dead, as Baudelaire says, have bad hours?

The world goes on as wicked as before, or worse
Whatever history says. Because of us

We like to think. I'm not so sure. Remember
The time we said a decade of tunes in the car

To pass the time on the way to Derry, you giving
The first one, no stuttering allowed, me answering.

I'd like one more chat as we cross the border
Four packed in the back, faces solemn for the soldier.

Questions about fiddling styles, the long poem –
You were against it – where I stood on the bodhrán

And always the clouds parted and anything, statues
Soho strippers, homeless boys, a sinking cruise ship

Could appear there, out of nothing, like a flock
Of Maybirds because that's also how life is. Pure magic.

MARY O'MALLEY

For Andrew Wood

What would the dead want from us
Watching from their cave?
Would they have us forever howling?
Would they have us rave
Or disfigure ourselves, or be strangled
Like some ancient emperor's slave?

None of my dead friends were emperors
With such exorbitant tastes
And none of them were so vengeful
As to have all their friends waste
Waste quiet away in sorrow
Disfigured and defaced.

I think the dead would want us
To weep for what *they* have lost.
I think that our luck in continuing
Is what would affect them most.
But time would find them generous
And less self-engrossed.

And time would find them generous
As they used to be
And what else would they want from us
But an honoured place in our memory,
A favourite room, a hallowed chair,
Privilege and celebrity?

And so the dead might cease to grieve
And we might make amends
And there might be a pact between
Dead friends and living friends.
What our dead friends would want from us
Would be such living friends.

JAMES FENTON

Bright Copper Kettles

Dead friends coming back to life, dead family,
speaking languages living and dead, their minds retentive,
their five senses intact, their footprints like a butterfly's,
mercy shining from their comprehensive faces –
this is one of my favorite things.
I like it so much I sleep all the time.
Moon by day and sun by night find me dispersed
deep in the dreams where they appear.
In fields of goldenrod, in the city of five pyramids,
before the empress with the melting face, under
the towering plane tree, they just show up.
'It's all right,' they seem to say. 'It always was.'
They are diffident and polite.
(Who knew the dead were so polite?)
They don't want to scare me; their heads don't spin like weathervanes.
They don't want to steal my body
and possess the earth and wreak vengeance.

They're dead, you understand, they don't exist. And, besides,
why would they care? They're subatomic, horizontal. Think about it.
One of them shyly offers me a pencil.
The eyes under the eyelids dart faster and faster.
Through the intercom of the house where for so long there was
        no music,
the right Reverend Al Green is singing,
'I could never see tomorrow.
I was never told about the sorrow.'

VIJAY SESHADRI

Anaesthesia

They slip away who never said goodbye,
My vintage friends so long depended on
To warm deep levels of my memory.
And if I cared for them, care has to learn
How to grieve sparingly and not to cry.
Age is an exercise in unconcern,
An anaesthetic, lest the misery
Of fresh departures make the final one
Unwelcome. There's a white indemnity
That with the first frost tamps the garden down.
There's nothing we can do but let it be.
And now this *you* and now that *she* is gone,
There's less and less of me that needs to die.
Nor do those vacant spaces terrify.

ANNE STEVENSON

Last Days

(in memory of Gabriele Helms, 1966–2004)

My friend, you wouldn't lie down.
Your wandering IV pole
glided with you, loyal, rattling
on frantic circuits;
crisp pillows didn't tempt;
round, around, around, guppies

cruised the lobby tank,
flickering sunrise-slivers
all guts, mouths urging, urging;
tube lights buzzed like bees
over your pale shoulders;
you wadded your pink gown, yanked

on crimson sweats
matching the bulbs you glimpsed
blazing that Christmas week
through nearby squares downtown; on
through the bluish hours
the night janitor's mop

swung drowsily over the lino,
the nurse tucked one leg up,
barely a monitor blinked;
scout in a cornered valley,
you looped your length of ground
as cancer hurtled to break

the bones that kept you pacing,
carrying your handsbreadth girl
(five-month spindle Buddha,
her brain's coral byways
travelled by your voice);
round, around, around, you

duelled to stay alive until
she could be born.
The doctors that last Tuesday
said it had to be now
and wheeled you off, upright.
Her shivering two red pounds –

you never got to cup them.
Did you hear her cry?
Three days later,
your gray eyes glazed,
blank. We stroked your hands.
What could wrench you down?

Your daughter's walking now;
we dash chasing after.
Round, around, around,
tentative, urgent stumbles....
Someday we will tell her
you refused to lie down.

ELISE PARTRIDGE

In This Life
(i.m. Katherine Washburn)

I had forgotten you were dead. You stumbled suddenly
into my mind, the way you stuttered out of your taxi
one Christmas, en route from Rome to New York.
I thought you the last of the old New Yorkers
unashamed of what you knew, always ready to learn.
By eight in the morning in our basement kitchen
the ashtray was already full, and the coffee cold in our cups
as we talked of Bukovina and Paul Celan's last poems,
Scholem and the *Origins of the Kabbalah.*

Outside, it was still Ireland.

All that winter, we were like a spacecraft
stranded on an alien planet. Not a hi-tech
Hollywood silver machine, but an old rust bucket
from a low-budget movie. Our cracked capsule
was called 'Seaspray', perched on the rocks of Sandycove,
its eyes watering in the wind from the Kish.
The 'Little Big House' we called it, on account
of all the tiny rooms behind the imposing façade,
and there we waited for the great wave
to lift us off the rocks.

That winter we nearly froze, as I scuttled upstairs
with buckets of fuel, but
nothing could cut the chill of inheritance
from the freezing air, or halt the slow fall
of the damp wallpaper, collapsing under the weight
of a century of servile respectability.

Shivering in our kitchen, you looked like a medieval nun,
or rather, a Beguine, a handmaid of the lord in her spare time,
with your dusty black dress and your Plymouth Brethren hair
clutching your Mac Powerbook like a latterday missal
crammed with half-done translations from the *Greek Anthology*
and fiery funeral orations by Rabbi Isaac da Fonseca.

Two weeks later you were dead. And we had to leave that house
spinning off into outer space, clinging to debris.
A politician lives in it now, and fills the rooms
with her own air, ignorant of what was buried there.

Katherine: we sat in the Clarence Hotel, drinking vodka
martinis, laughing at how well we knew each other
though in this life we had hardly met.

MICHAEL O'LOUGHLIN

Prayer

First heard words, delivered to this right ear
Allah hu Akbar – God is great – by my father
in the Queen Elizabeth maternity ward.
God's breath in man returning to his birth,
says Herbert, is prayer. If I continued

his lines from there, from *birth* – a break Herbert
chimes with *heav'n and earth* – I'd keep in thought
my mum on a Hereford hospital bed
and say what prayer couldn't end. I'd say
I made an animal noise, hurled language's hurt

at midday, when word had come. Cancer. Now so spread
by midnight her rings were off.
                                        I stayed on. At her bed.
Earlier, time and rhythm flatlining, I whispered
Thank you   I love you   thank you
                                        mouth at her ear.
She stared on, ahead. I won't know if she heard.

ZAFFAR KUNIAL

Mother's Ninety-fourth Birthday

You keep to your bed.
The doctors say you won't walk again.
We come in pairs mostly –
phantom wings
trying to make you fly.

ADIL JUSSAWALLA

Body, my body

Body, my body, how many hands
of how many strangers have had hold of you?

Death was once a barber's clammy hand.
Then came the arctic chill of a stethoscope.

Still later you broke in a dentist's chair
or a nasty teacher smacked your head.

And then the metros with their teeming flesh,
and surplus crowds who glided past like fish

in alleys and compartments, shops and lifts.
Body, my body, please think of the smell

of rooms the first time, and of amorous sheets,
the spring that became in us. For we're

afraid. And fear lives while the body lasts.
And soon, when I'm laid out, they'll comb my hair.

MENNO WIGMAN
translated from the Dutch by Sean O'Brien
Karlien van den Beukel & Menno Wigman

Spooning Stars

You kept talking about the flame of life
on those visitation days you spent
spooning your father his last meals
of cremated hope and constellations
as his cheeks sunk inwards

and lips curled at the rim
of his teeth where his gums
caught on to the spreading cancer
like catching a secret from an open window.

The crumbs brushed in the silence
when he slept, waking after to ask you
for sangria. You thought he was losing
his mind, his memory, more weight
but he kept a bottle hidden
and you slept beside him
every pitch black night on the ward
where trolley wheels veered under the dead
rubbing your hands for heat
from the last burning embers of his bones
squinting to watch the shiver
                    of his dim pulse
as if it pressed upwards against thin skin
like a trapped star searching its exit
                    through the needle.

JANETTE AYACHI

The Tube

Golly, a nice man wants to put a tube
into my stomach, and his colleagues
are pleading with me to simply let him.

One woman sat by my bed holding
the harmless little tube, as if the sight
of it would make me say *Yes, stick it in.*

Instead, I continued to be noncompliant.
You might as well be holding a noose,
is what I said. The woman smiled and left.

I lay there and closed my eyes, imagining
all the nourishment that would go through
the tube, reversing my super weight loss.

I would now grow fat as a sumo wrestler,
or as the beer drinker I once was, back when
my illnesses lived in hypochondria county.

I could whizz up *boeuf bourguignon* to
baby food, or even thinner, and pump it in.
I could learn to forget what food tastes like.

They claim I could even still eat, with the tube
sticking out of me, but how could I revel in
a Wiener Schnitzel with that encumbrance?

No, that would be like eating on the train
to the black camp, this one with no skeletal
survivors liberated by a victorious militia.

I want to stay off that train as long as I can,
despite all the exhortations to board now.
I want to be myself till the last minute.

MATTHEW SWEENEY

Ship of Death

Watching you, for the first time,
turn to prepare your boat, my mother;
making it clear you have other business now –
the business of your future –
I was washed through with anger.

It was a first survey,
an eye thrown
over sails, oars, timbers,
as many a time I'd seen that practised eye
scan a laden table.

How can you plan going off like this
when we stand at last, close enough, if the wind is right,
to hear what the other is saying?
I never thought you'd do this, turning away,
mid-sentence, your hand testing a rope,

your ear tuned
to the small thunder of the curling wave
on the edge of the great-night sea,
neither regretful nor afraid –
anxious only for the tide.

KERRY HARDIE

Burrow Beach

She really doesn't talk much any more.
Not, I think, because she has nothing to say.
The thoughts are there, but words get in the way.

She has a bed now that makes noise.
The air goes in and out with a quiet thrum,
not like a lullaby that you might hum

to a sleepy child with eyelids growing heavier
but a hospital sound that has invaded her home
like all the other paraphernalia they have on loan

from the health clinic up the hill –
the hoist, commode, chairs with buckles and wheels,
ramps to the front door. All this equipment feels

to me like a crash course in growing old.
I'm now the same age – forty-five –
that she was when her mother died.

So one day all this will be mine:
the blister packs, the overbed table, the pale blue
light of her life washing through

this house like the sea down on the Burrow Beach
that she conjured with her artist's eye from a blank page.
As Thomas exhorted, Rage, rage

against the dying of the light,
and that is what I am doing each day,
raging in my own distilled and private way,

nothing showy – it's not what she would want –
but that doesn't make less bitter or less deep
the sorrow that breaks over me before I sleep.

SARA BERKELEY TOLCHIN

My life's stem was cut

My life's stem was cut,
But quickly, lovingly
I was lifted up,
I heard the rush of the tap
And I was set in water
In the blue vase, beautiful

In lip and curve,
And here I am
Opening one petal
As the tea cools.
I wait while the sun moves
And the bees finish their dancing,
I know I am dying
But why not keep flowering
As long as I can
From my cut stem?

HELEN DUNMORE

Hold out your arms

Death, hold out your arms for me
Embrace me
Give me your motherly caress,
Through all this suffering
You have not forgotten me.

You are the bearded iris that bakes its rhizomes
Beside the wall,
Your scent flushes with loveliness,
Sherbet, pure iris
Lovely and intricate.

I am the child who stands by the wall
Not much taller than the iris.
The sun covers me
The day waits for me
In my funny dress.

Death, you heap into my arms
A basket of unripe damsons
Red crisscross straps that button behind me.

I don't know about school,
My knowledge is for papery bud covers
Tall stems and brown
Bees touching here and there, delicately
Before a swerve to the sun.

Death stoops over me
Her long skirts slide,
She knows I am shy.
Even the puffed sleeves on my white blouse
Embarrass me,
She will pick me up and hold me
So no one can see me,
I will scrub my hair into hers.

There, the iris increases
Note by note
As the wall gives back heat.
Death, there's no need to ask:
A mother will always lift a child
As a rhizome
Must lift up a flower
So you settle me
My arms twining,
Thighs gripping your hips
Where the swell of you is.

As you push back my hair
– Which could do with a comb
But never mind –
You murmur
'We're nearly there.'

(25 May 2017)

HELEN DUNMORE

315

My Mother's Sea Chanty

I dream that I am washing
my mother's body in the night sea
and that she sings slow
and that she still breathes.

I see my sweet mother
a plump mermaid in my dreams
and I wash her white hair
with ambergris and foaming seaweed.

I watch my mother under water
gather the loose pearls she finds,
scrub them free from nacre
and string them on a lost fishing line.

I hear my dark mother
speaking sea-speak with pilot fish,
showing them how to direct barks
that bear away our grief.

I pray my mother breaks free
from the fish pots and marine chores
of her residence beneath the sea,
and that she rides a wild white horse.

LORNA GOODISON

You Are Not
(for my mother)

You are not in these tulips,
not in their flailing stems
or shrivelled yellow petals

that alive you'd have painted;
not in the pearly wintry sky
or the scarred slopes of the hill
that before your legs failed
you'd have climbed;
not in the spiky firs
or eddies and swirls of the river,
or in its still sandy pools
where in your youth
you'd have swum;
not in the first drizzle of snow,
or in the deer that hangs
in the larder with black hooves
and long delicate legs,
not in its heart or liver
that we ate last night for supper
and you would have relished.

You are not anywhere
who loved all the things I love
but I couldn't talk to;
who still loom in my head
like a giantess.
                    Yet I remember
hauling you out of the bath,
tugging on arms I was afraid
of pulling from their sockets;
then drying you and helping you
to dress, before guiding you
down slippery stone steps
to watch flycatcher chicks
leaving the nest, hearing
the *peep peep peep*
of their mother's warning call.

VICKI FEAVER

In the Temple Basement

Standing in the ladies' room line,
in the temple basement, the woman in front of me
said, 'I've been sitting behind you, admiring
your hair.' 'Thank you! White for Rosh
Hashanah!' I say, and then, 'It was
a gift from my mother.' I love to say
my mother to someone I imagine as a normal
person – though who knows. And I love
to see cut flowers age – we are cut
flowers, when they sever the cord, we begin
our dying. She lived to be eighty-five,
I needed every hour of it.
Each time I made her laugh on the phone,
that warm gurgle – and she couldn't reach out with her
long curved polished nails, to stroke me –
we were making something together, like a
girl-made mountain stream among
Sierra onion, and lupine, stonecrop
and leopard lily. And especially
I needed every minute that last evening,
watching her, watching over
her – and beyond her harm! – and wishing her
any good thing, including more life, though she
began to look serene, her lungs
filling, rattling, ceasing, starting, but her
spirit was on its way, and since she had
always believed it, and I think could not have
borne to live without it, it was as
if she was nearing the blue home
of her heavenly father, and then finally opening into
permanent blossom.

SHARON OLDS

The photo that is most troubling is the one I don't want to show you

Breathing, distraction, whatever
I lay down in this field
I stopped agonising because it started to seem as if agonising was
    hurting me
'The dead don't die. They look on and help.'
Excuse these intense but beautiful bouts of emotion
I seem to be gradually coming to some realisations
And I didn't know what to make of it at the time
My mouth opened and I breathed flame
Mother, can you hear me?
He said, *The dead don't die!*
It was dark and something was kind of starry
Ardent...
Something as auspicious as a child born on my birthday
It wasn't in the normal run of things
But I hold her
I hold her the way I reach inside myself and hold all the trouble
Skies suddenly so dark
And the way home on fire
Through the forest, loud and forgetful as a burst of rain
In case you could hear me
On the backs of horses

EMILY BERRY

from Debatable Land

(for my father, wherever)

from Country

Daddy, this is really about you
as everything is these days
beyond the hospital, where you wander
away down the corridors, and sometimes
get outside.
            Then police telephone
to check your address – even before the nurses
appear to have missed you.

ANNEMARIE AUSTIN

What My Double Will

My double will do it: go inside,
seek out the ward, not mind
when he lifts to her the blank eyes
of a bored stranger on the bus
who only notices you enough to
edge an inch nearer the window
when you must sit next to him.

My double will be jaunty, carry
fruitcake and daffodils maybe –
the brandy he used to like become
'impossible with the medication'.
She'll have expected that and
the way a tranquilliser's hammer
has rendered the fog she brings
even more a pea-souper for him.

My double won't care if he asks
about a job she never had in a town
she's never been to. She'll collaborate
when he tells how he piloted a plane
to Africa and back the night before,
killing the enemy all along the way –
so they lie in a swathe from Timbuktu
to Sidi Barani and beyond, let's say.

But I'll stand outside the hospital's
front glass wall like a cigar-store
Indian – wooden, transfixed. I'll carry
air and hold emptiness in my mouth.
And the horror I'm ashamed of will
wash over me like cold rain and wash
over me again, only my double gone in.

ANNEMARIE AUSTIN

Last Christmas Cracker

From the last Christmas cracker I pulled ever
with Dad, it seemed there flew not just the golf-tees
I will never use, but my yellow kite
the line broke from, and the wind wafted
into the tall oak where he climbed to get it;
my blue wooden yacht which grounded itself
in the middle of the council boating lake,
where he waded barefoot through the sludge
to restore it sodden to the concrete shore;
the garage window I broke one Sunday
learning to curve a shot round the linen post;
then, in a terrible rush, all the things
in the future he will not ever set
to rights, now that he has gone away.

STEVEN MATTHEWS

After My Father Died

The sky didn't fall.

It stayed up there,
luminous, tattered with crows,
all through
January's short days,
February's short days.

Now the year
creeps towards March.
Damp days, grass springing.
The poplars' bare branches
are fruited with starlings and thrushes.
The world is the body of God.
And we –
you, me, him, the starlings and thrushes –
we are all buried here,
mouths made of clay,
mouths filled with clay,
we are all buried here, singing.

KERRY HARDIE

from Vrouz

When my father shuffled off this mortal coil
Time would not be stomached like that casserole
And dad a feather then my father was so light
Oh how he could have lasted daddy in that state
Of airiness a man becoming angel and so small
My father shrinking with the hope I'd feel
And even though he was as yellow as a clown-fish
In the month of February ninety-seven at the heart
Of just-before-the-spring when he stopped breathing

Ants still ran about and worked without him
Geese would fly without him just the same the moon
The moon would make its circles and its crescents
The big world without a feather daddy would go on.

VALÉRIE ROUZEAU
translated from the French by Susan Wicks

Ter Conatus

Sister and brother, nearly sixty years
They'd farmed together, never touching once.
Of late she had been coping with a pain
In her back, realisation dawning slowly
That it grew differently from the warm ache
That resulted periodically
From heaving churns on to the milking-stand.

She wondered about the doctor. When,
Finally, she went, it was too late,
Even for chemotherapy. All the same,
She wouldn't have got round to telling him,
Except that one night, watching television,
It got so bad she gasped, and struggled up,
Holding her waist. 'D'you want a hand?' he asked,

Taking a step towards her. 'I can manage,'
She answered, feeling for the stairs.
Three times, like that, he tried to reach her.
But, being so little practised in such gestures,
Three times the hand fell back, and took its place,
Unmoving at his side. After the burial,
He let things take their course. The neighbours watched

In pity the rolled-up bales, standing
Silent in the fields, with the aftergrass
Growing into them, and wondered what he could

323

Be thinking of: which was that evening when,
Almost breaking with a lifetime of
Taking real things for shadows,
He might have embraced her with a brother's arms.

BERNARD O'DONOGHUE

The Morandi Bridge

Let me lean my cheek against this limestone pillar –
I want to press until I feel the buzzing,
the sound the world makes when it isn't going
anywhere, a purr of grey transparent wings

hovering in one place. A humming to itself
because it needs to lie still, stay quiet and
recover, and who will bring help?
                                              The noise
when the bridge fell down in Genova – the road

you and I drove along slowly, heading east
behind a small Fiat, packed and weighed down
with people, cake and flowers for a mother-in-law
that made a Sunday lunch; they were taking their time –

it was lunchtime again each year when we reached the bridge,
and the families were always on the move,
so we'd drive along slowly, those fifteen minutes
high up over the factories and streets –

I would tell you this news if the stones of the world
could carry language, but after eight months, the shock
and the noise inside them still, they cannot move
or even allow a message to pass through.

April 2019

EILÉAN NÍ CHUILLEANÁIN

The call

A moment to rest, at last
the day's visiting done.

Flick through a mag
with unseeing eyes.

There's calm in exhaustion, a break
between work and visiting hours,

glimmer of how life will be
when she recovers: oxygen tank

behind her chair, bed downstairs.
The phone rings. Two lives end.

JAY WHITTAKER

Bed fellow

With the whole bed to choose from
the dog clambers in, so close
I almost fall off the edge.

I move to what used to be my side,
that familiar view across pillows
from which I turned away,

just as I had to sit in her armchair,
occupy her space,
to not see the gap she left.

JAY WHITTAKER

Oxygen Mask

What happened that afternoon? I cannot
remember: no clear sound of your voice,
not one single word or gesture
remain as evidence to ponder
from what I did not know
was the last time I would see you alive.

Ordinary desultory talk;
your room was warm, though only April.
There was another visitor, so
nothing personal was said, nothing
to prick the memory like a burr
you cannot tear from inside your shirt.
Better such pain than a vacant mind
with no power of recall.

I could scream: which might stop me reliving,
over and over, what happened next:
how the shrill phone dragged me from sleep
in the small hours; how I did not arrive
in time; how your hand stiffened and chilled
in mine and your face paled; how I pushed
aside the oxygen mask though the nurse
who brought me a drink had said to leave it
so your jaw would not drop – I remember that.
And then the final kiss.

RUTH FAINLIGHT

Somewhere Else Entirely

Where did you sleep last night,
where did you sleep? I feel
we spent the night together,
but when I wake, always
earlier than the alarm
is set, you're never here.
Strange, the empty bed.

I scan the other rooms
and though I seem to remember
an evening like one of hundreds
of evenings spent together –
so many years together –
peaceful evenings, each
of us at our desk, the sense
of someone else in the flat,
you in your room; then
going to bed: affection,
embraces, intimacy....

Now everything is different.
I walk along the hall,
enter each room, uneasy,
seeking, but find no sign....
Although every room
retains so many memories,
sounds and images, is
saturated with your essence,
I know I'll never meet you here....

Where you sleep, day and night,
is dark and cold and silent:
somewhere else entirely.

RUTH FAINLIGHT

327

Beds

Last night I wondered where you had found to sleep.
You weren't in bed. There was no one in your chair.

Through every window the white, full moon glared.
I walked into the garden, shivering:

'Where are you, my darling? You will catch cold.'
Waking, I let the daytime facts unfold.

ELAINE FEINSTEIN

Screen-saver

I carry your face in a mobile shrine
and take it out on the Underground.

Your digital eyes look into mine.
I change at Farringdon and I have changed.

Touched by you, my skin is kozo tissue,
my hair rose-perfumed ink,

my eyelids are gold leaf.
The woman on my right,

reflected in the window opposite,
takes on the stillness of an icon,

the boy across the way
lifts his cheek to be pure marble

sculpted in living light. Together,
we travel on into the night,

all of us grown precious,
each one of us alive and rare.

IMTIAZ DHARKER

Passport photo

You come in to the photo booth, take off your smile,
untilt your head. As specified, the face

is straight, here is the signature and the date
that says you are forty, thirty, twenty-one.

A flare, a flash. With each one, the destination
changes. I watch you grow young.

The plastic walls remould themselves and melt
to snow, sunlight on a blinding shield of sea,

a sky burnt white beyond white
where anything is possible,

and you are standing on the edge
of the person you are about to be.

Out of this cramped space, this six-foot box,
when you are freed, where will you go,

over what seas, to what far islands?
After the siren songs and the lotus flesh,

the only kiss, the kiss of salt on your lips,
and the grain of your face thrown wide open,

how far will you go to look for home?

IMTIAZ DHARKER

Say his name

Not standing by graves.

Say his name in conversation,
at tables where glasses are raised.

Say his name where you live,
in the company of friends.

IMTIAZ DHARKER

Honesty
(for Imtiaz Dharker)

A flourish of flowers self-seeded
in the shade of an old wall,
nourished on nothing but stone,
dirt, detritus, winter's tears.

From a mulch of dead things
comes a rush of stems,
heart-shaped leaves, Earth's love-gift,
the opulent purples of April,

to keep in the dark when it's over
a purse of seed translucent as bees' wings,
as pages of old books,
as the silver eyes of your lover.

You show me the way it is, to lose, to keep
the light of your life in the lens of a line,
syllables of grief, the world
more luminous seen through tears.

GILLIAN CLARKE

Off Duty

Is my face just right,
am I looking as a widow should?
I pass the funeral parlour
where four weeks ago
the ceremony unfurled.
Now I'm laughing with the children.
The director of the solemn place
is lolling out front, sucking on a cigarette.
We exchange hellos,
and I blush, remembering
how I still haven't paid the bill,
how I nearly left that day
with someone else's flowers.

KATIE DONOVAN

Advice to Women

Keep cats
if you want to learn to cope with
the otherness of lovers.
Otherness is not always neglect –
Cats return to their litter trays
when they need to.
Don't cuss out of the window
at their enemies.
That stare of perpetual surprise
in those great green eyes
will teach you
to die alone.

EUNICE DE SOUZA

Lily

No one would take her when Ruth passed.
As the survivors assessed some antiques,
I kept hearing, 'She's old. Somebody
should put her down.'

I picked her up instead. Every night I tell her
about the fish who died for her, the ones
in the cheerful aluminum cans.

She lies on my chest to sleep, rising
and falling, rising and falling like a rowboat
fastened to a battered dock by a string.

RON KOERTGE

Cat in an Empty Apartment

Die – you can't do that to a cat.
Since what can a cat do
in an empty apartment?
Climb the walls?
Rub up against the furniture?
Nothing seems different here,
but nothing is the same.
Nothing has been moved,
but there's more space.
And at nighttime no lamps are lit.

Footsteps on the staircase,
but they're new ones.
The hand that puts fish on the saucer
has changed, too.

Something doesn't start
at its usual time.
Something doesn't happen
as it should.
Someone was always, always here,
then suddenly disappeared
and stubbornly stays disappeared.

Every closet has been examined.
Every shelf has been explored.
Excavations under the carpet turned up nothing.
A commandment was even broken,
papers scattered everywhere.
What remains to be done.
Just sleep and wait.

Just wait till he turns up,
just let him show his face.
Will he ever get a lesson
on what not to do to a cat.
Sidle toward him
as if unwilling
and ever so slow
on visibly offended paws,
and no leaps or squeals at least to start.

WISŁAWA SZYMBORSKA
translated from the Polish by Stanislaw Barańczak & Clare Cavanagh

Tailoring Grief

The tailor says you have to get measured
to make sure grief fits right on your body.
If grief fits too tight it will suck movement out of you,
make you as still as the dead you are mourning.
I once wore grief so tight on my body my ribs tangled into a bow.

333

The tailor also says wearing an oversized grief will turn you
into a tripping hazard. There is only so much a body can take,
even a plane has weight limits.
We lined up at the tailors to get measured
for my grandfather's funeral. The women for their Aso-oke,
the men for their Agbada. The orange material draped on the table.
It is our culture to celebrate in colour coordination.
I handed the tailor a torn page from *Genevieve* magazine
and pointed out the style I wanted.
Imagine if Mary wore a Gele for the funeral of Jesus,
tied it so tight she was dizzy
enough to feel absent from her body.
I picked up my cloth from the tailor on the seventh day.
The off-shoulder dress exposed my neck
so my dented collarbones could collect my tears.
At the funeral my grandmother wore a dress
with sleeves puffed like swollen lungs.
I held her, the tassels at the end of my dress dangled
like a rain of breathing tubes.
From afar our orange dresses looked like saliva dripping
from the gaping mouth of the sun.
The whole village watched in holy envy:
envy is only effective from afar, does not see the layers
of blood-stained threads that sew this body together.
Give me a culture that requires grief to be sewn
delicately on the body, I'll take it any day.

THERESA LOLA

The Day After – Without Us

The morning is expected to be cool and foggy.
Rainclouds
will move in from the west.
Poor visibility.
Slick highways.

Gradually as the day progresses
high pressure fronts from the north
make local sunshine likely.
Due to winds, though, sometimes strong and gusty,
sun may give way to storms.

At night
clearing across the country,
with a slight chance of precipitation
only in the southeast.
Temperatures will drop sharply,
while barometric readings rise.

The next day
promises to be sunny,
although those still living
should bring umbrellas.

WISŁAWA SZYMBORSKA
translated from the Polish by Stanisław Barańczak & Clare Cavanagh

Helium

> The morning is expected to be cool and foggy.
> WISŁAWA SZYMBORSKA,
> 'The Day After – Without Us'

Imagining what the weather will be like
on the day following your death
has a place on that list of things

that distinguish us from animals
as if walking around on two legs
laughing to ourselves were not enough to close the case.

In these forecasts, it's usually raining,
the way it would be in the movies.

but it could be sparkling clear
or grey and still with snow expected in the afternoon.

Much will continue to occur after I die
seems to be the message here.
The rose will nod its red or yellow head.
Sunbeams will break into the gloomy woods.

And that's what was on my mind
as I drove through a gauntlet of signs
on a road that passed through a small town in Ohio:
Bob's Transmissions,
The Hairport, The Bountiful Buffet,
Reggie's Bike Shop, Balloon Designs by Pauline,
and Majestic China Garden to name a few.

When I realised that all these places
could still be in business on the day after I die,
I vowed to drink more water,
to eat more fresh fruits and vegetables,
and to start going to the gym I never go to

if only to outlive
Balloon Designs by Pauline
and maybe even Pauline herself
though it would be enough if she simply
lost the business and left town for good .

BILLY COLLINS

Trust Me

What can be discussed in words
I beg to state in brief.
A man has only one death:
it may be as light as goose down

or as heavy as a fatted hog.
Gingerly the flowers open
and are crushed in the vat.
What's in your new perfume?
The hills of Africa are in it,
and the cormorants with their mouths full of fish,
a bed of carnations, a swannery in Switzerland,
the citrine sun baking Napa
and a rhino whining at the moon.
An after-dinner argument is in it
and the ever-stronger doses of claptrap
we are forced to take while still alive.
A whole aeroplane, wings and all,
and the lush spaghetti siphoned into lips
poised for a kiss.
Finish it, finish it.

MARY RUEFLE

Soul Keeping Company

The hours between washing and the well
Of burial are the soul's most troubled time.

I sat with her in keeping company
All through the affliction of the night, keeping

Soul constant, a second self. Earth is heavy
And I made no wish, save being

Merely magical. I am magical
No more. This, I well remember well.

In the sweet thereafter the impress
Of the senses will be tattooed to

The whole world ravelling in the clemency
Of an autumn of Octobers, all that bounty

Bountiful and the oaks specifically
Afire as everything dies off, inclining

To the merciful. I would have made of my body
A body to protect her, anything to keep

Her well & here – in the soul's suite
Before five tons of earth will bear

On her, stay here
Soul, in the good night of my company.

LUCIE BROCK-BOIDO

Street of Sailmakers

It's not easy turning into smoke,
not easy blowing away because
even if the mind is an amaryllis
it still struggles like a moth
in a spiderweb. Because
the futility of cathedrals
is more beautiful than heaven?
When he wasn't hearing what
he wanted, Monk, midsong,
would kick his sidemen offstage
until it was just him and the damn
audience wondering who was next.
When my mother died,
I was far away and got farther,
a rectangular shadow on stilts.
Hello, commodious sky, you look high

on fumes. How many times must I
drop bulbs into a hole and still
not know how to be joyous? Years
of washing dishes, watching sunsets
and insects and still no easier
to see what's written in the dark.
Little shiver, I want to preserve you.
Rosebud, I'll try to hold you
forever in my mouth.

DEAN YOUNG

Listening for Lost People

Still looking for lost people – look unrelentingly.
'They died' is not an utterance in the syntax of life
where they belonged, no *belong* – reanimate them
not minding if the still living turn away, casually.
Winds ruck up its skin so the sea tilts from red-blue
to blue-red: into the puckering water go his ashes
who was steadier than these elements. Thickness
of some surviving thing that sits there, bland. Its
owner's gone nor does the idiot howl – while I'm
unquiet as a talkative ear. Spring heat, a cherry
tree's fresh bronze leaves fan out and gleam – to
converse with shades, yourself become a shadow.
The souls of the dead are the spirit of language:
you hear them alight inside that spoken thought.

DENISE RILEY

Then

Hard though I know
you find this to believe,
I was actually alive once.
Alive. And well enough,
at least, to play my part.

I too faced heartaches, disappointments,
embarrassments and vanities
not all that unlike yours, kept up
with the pressing issues of the day,
registered weather's moodiness

on my skin, brooded on the big
life-and-death questions when
I indulged my more reflective traits.
And if it's any consolation,
it feels no less strange to me now

to conceive that I was truly
such a creature once,
and had some small say in how
the world – as it stood at that
time – conducted its affairs.

That my birth would not make
a blind bit of difference,
in the final analysis, does not
negate my life, and counts
for precious little against

the surge of unbounded joy
I felt, on better days, imagining
my highest hopes were still fulfillable.
There was everything to live for then.
It was all before me.

DENNIS O'DRISCOLL

Beyond

Oh Dennis, I dream of you
in the northwest provinces
beyond communication
with the known world.
Who do you speak with?
In what language?
I'm sure you forget all about us
here in the ocean
surrounded by sea monsters.
I eat bowls of food
alone at the table
wondering where you are
my husband.

JULIE O'CALLAGHAN

Cyber You

I need to see you
living and breathing
– I go to You Tube
and there you are being you
(the tiny you)
with the tie I bought you
for Christmas.
Sitting on a chair
on a stage in Santa Fe
asking Seamus questions.
Eternally.

JULIE O'CALLAGHAN

All

And all who died, from winter's sleet,
From flu, from guns, from cells grown wrong,
Still stand, one breath from fingers' reach,
Just out of touch, all colour gone.

The dead grow smaller. From a train
Mist takes the fields, drinks green to grey,
The fog has swept across their face.
In yard or park, they walk away,

Then wait in rooms, without a fire,
With tea uncleared, without a fuss;
In cushioned chairs, now closer drawn,
Nod to each other, not to us.

But in mid age it is not strange
To glimpse them, in the windy street,
Quiet at the kerb, who are all dead,
From guns, cruel cells, or winter's heat.

ALISON BRACKENBURY

7

Interesting times

If poetry can't come to terms with the vocabulary of science and technology,
it is leaving out a large part of human life and is so much the poorer.

R.S. THOMAS

POETS HAVE LONG BEEN KNOWN for celebrating or lamenting technological
progress in the modern world, most memorably, Stephen Spender (1909-95),
glorifying the new electricity pylons in 'The Pylons', how 'far above and far
as sight endures / Like whips of anger / With lightning's danger / There
runs the quick perspective of the future', giving rise to the dismissive term
Pylon Poets for the new generation of younger left-wing poets of the 1930s.
But technological change over the past three decades has been so fast that
few poets have made it central to their work, apart from those addressing
ecological issues for whom industrialisation is seen as the agent of environmental
catastrophe (see section 10, 479-499). Poets such as Edwin Morgan responded
to the novelty of computers and science fiction scenarios in the early years,
while others like Miroslav Holub (an immunologist), Peter Redgrove (who
trained as a scientist), Lavinia Greenlaw, Jo Shapcott, Pauline Stainer, R.S.
Thomas, J.H. Prynne and Katrina Porteous (in *Edge*) have all engaged with
scientific concepts in their poetry, but for most poets, technology has
provided the means of writing and promoting their work at the same time as
it has led to the fragmentation of their traditional readership.

A good source for earlier poems on science is the anthology *A Quark for
Mister Mark: 101 Poems about Science*, edited by Maurice Riordan and Jon
Tulley (Faber, 2000). This section mostly covers more recent responses to
the technological marvels of a later modern age, with poems about drones and
mobile phones, call centres and cashpoints, TV and CCTV, social media and
social degradation, helicopters policing the sky, and factory workers exploited
by corporations.

We have everything we need

We have each become a small world,
spinning from one collision to another.
We scrub cities off our skins and watch
its roads leave tracks in the bath.

Damp rises, rent rises, high-rises.
Look how the cities' silhouettes grow
new forests for us. What new constellation
of stars guides us home?

We are tower-block light flickers
come evening, crammed into shoe boxes,
basements, living room-come-bedrooms.
Stretch out our feet to turn the TV on.

We reach for our phones, our faces made radiant
by its birdsong. Someone somewhere is mining
for the next iPhone but we can't be sure,
we are compassion in 280 characters.

We are lying lonely next to each other
between paper thin walls. We know
our neighbours' shouts and moans,
an echo chamber of coughs and scrapes.

Rent rises, heat rises, sea rises.
Put the kettle on, scald dinner in microwaves.
Droughts happening somewhere, but we can't be sure.
Tesco Metro fluorescence – open 24 hours.

I wonder what will this all look like in 50 years' time.
How will our cities will exhale then?
How will we wear our loss?
How will we sleep when we cannot turn off the alarm?

SELINA NWULU

Insomnia

Scratch of a match
fierce in the dark. The alarm clock,
night-vigilant, reads twenty minutes to four;
wide awake, as so often at this dead hour,
I gaze down at the lighted dock,
trawler and crated catch,
as if on watch.

The bright insects
of helicopters drop to the decks
of gas rigs ten miles out in the heavy waves,
their roaring rotors far from our quiet leaves,
before midnight, and the ship that shone
at dusk on the horizon
has long since gone.

Nothing stirs
in garden or silent house,
no night owl flies or none that we can hear;
not evening the mild, traditional field-mouse
runs nibbling, as you'd expect, under the stairs.
Boats knock and click at the pier,
shrimps worship the stars.

The whole coast
is soporific as if lost
to echoes of a distant past –
the empty beach house with no obvious owner,
the old hotel like a wrecked ocean liner
washed up one stormy night
and left to rot.

That woman from
the Seaview, a 'blow-in'
of some kind from a foreign shore,
seems out of her element and far from home,

the once perhaps humorous eyes grown vague out here.
What is she? A Lithuanian, or a Finn?
We've met before

beside some flat
road bridge and bleak strand road,
two men in black at the corner staring hard,
far off in the stricken distance perhaps a shipyard,
chimneys, power plants, gasometers,
oil refineries, Gothic spires
and things like that –

where a cloud climbs
and swirls, yellow and red
streaking the estuary, and a soul screams
for sunken origins, for the obscure sea bed
and glowing depths, the alternative mud haven
we left behind. Once more we live in
interesting times.

DEREK MAHON

Helicopters

Over time, you picture them
after dark, in searches

focusing on streets and houses
close above the churches

or balancing
on narrow wands of light.

And find so much depends upon
the way you choose

to look at them:
high in the night

their minor flares confused
among the stars, there

almost beautiful.
Or from way back

over the map
from where they might resemble

a business of flies
around the head wound of an animal.

COLETTE BRYCE

Drones

Friends, we're living in a golden, fleeting moment
wherein rich people are buying very expensive toys
that fly higher than airplanes. The toys can land anywhere –
on your fire escape, in your yard – and photograph you
through your curtains with a surveillance camera, record
things you're saying with a high-powered microphone.
Scientists originally built the toy to murder people
in other countries, and now rich people in this country
want to buy them. Why? I have absolutely no idea, but
I can't wait to kill one: shoot it with a shotgun, shoot it
with the hose, wing it with rocks, pick the wings off,
light it on fire, and stomp on it wearing steel-toed boots.
Rich people will be outraged that their toys are being
destroyed, then lobbyists will make destroying the toy
illegal, so we must move fast. The cleverest of us
already are: down in our basements, under the gun.

JENNIFER L. KNOX

Belfast Waking, 6 a.m.

A maintenance man
in a small white van attends
to the city's empty confessionals,
wipes glass walls and pincers litter
(the crisp polystyrene casing
of a burger) like evidence
of the utmost significance,

wrinkles his nose at the tang of urine,
furrows his brow at a broken syringe
then finally turns to the stoical machine,

the dangling receiver's plaintive refrain
please replace the handset
and try again,

unclogs the coin-choked gullet with a tool
and a little force
like a shoulder to a wheel
or an act of necessary violence.

Sites of anonymous threat
or sanctuary, they are out of place
in the cool new century,
but he likes the way

they continue to protect
their odd rectangular blocks of light
whether the people visit them or not.

Above his head, everything is changing;
black diluting
into the blue of a morning's
infinitely slow expression.

The gradual realisation of a steeple, a ripple
of birdsong on the surface of the dawn,
a dawn that is breaking its heart over Belfast.

Béal Feirste. Redbrick terraces. Tightrope wires
and telegraph poles. The liquid slink
of a feline or a fox, one gutter
to the other, then under a fence.

A refuse vehicle's cavernous jaw
reverses massively out of an avenue,
its amber, interrupted beam
glancing hatchbacks stationed in a line.

Footsteps nearing, footsteps fading.
An upturned collar, the clearing of a throat.
A muffled *whump* as a car door shuts.
Its smooth ignition.

The moment, precise,
when the streetlamps of Belfast
quietly go out, a unanimous decision,
and the windowpanes start filling up with sky
at the advent of the ordinary
business of the day.

COLETTE BRYCE

On Patrick Street

This part of the path was once a place apart, a tall glass box
with a door that creaked in like pleats of an accordion.

Not long ago, we stood here, where a cord looped long
and pressed a heavy black handset between shoulder and neck.

Here, we fumbled through coins, shoved them
clunk by clunk into a slot, pressed digits

until we heard our need chime in some distant room.
Then, the lift, the click, the answer of the voice we waited for.

There were times, walking past, you might see someone
through glass, rubbing their brow, or laughing, head thrown back,

until knuckles rasped on the door. At dusk it glowed,
lit from within. We don't speak about how it left or where it went.

We hurry past that place on the footpath now, small square
of empty cement, with plastic pressed to our ears, repeating:

Where are you?
I'm here.

DOIREANN NÍ GHRÍOFA

Flight radar

From the top of the Shard the view unfolds
down the Thames to the sea, the city laid
by a trick of sight vertically in front of me.
At London Bridge Station, trains slide in

and out in a long slow dance. It is not
by chance that I am here, not looking down
but up to where you are on Flight 199,
coming in to land. I have learned to track you

on my mobile phone. However far you go,
I have the app that uses the radar to trace
your path. There you are now, circling down
around this spire where I stand, my face reflected

over your pulse in the glass. You cannot see.
You have no radar for me, no app to make you
look back or down to where I am lifting my hand.
Darling, I will track your flight till it is a dot

that turns and banks and falls out of sight, looking
into the space where you were. Fingers frozen
on the tiny keys, I will stay where I am
in the dying light, the screen still live in my palm.

IMTIAZ DHARKER

CCTV

Exalted on towers and posts and fitted with articulated necks
that tilt, cock and swivel like the necks of owls, silent and absolute.

Like owls, they have a zealous gaze that does not falter, through no matter
how long a night. Unlike owls they sometimes hunt in pairs or threes,

perched at the corner of a flat roof, protected in cages or bulletproof housing,
some with a mohican of spikes. Not gregarious – no, not that at all –

and for all their cutting-edge robotics, they are nothing without the database.
They are not gods but Recording Angels. They come not flaming, sheathed
    in light,

but just as dread: all actions witnessed at thirty frames per second,
compressed by algorithm, returned by co-ax cable.

Theirs is the platform and the underpass, the building site and the park gates,
the bridge, the bus stop, the school playground and the cash machine.

Theirs is the shop doorway where you hope for darkness to cover you;
theirs is the scar on your hand and the make of your watch and your eyes.

JEAN SPRACKLAND

Call Centre Blues

The only thing lonelier than silence is talking
to someone who hates you. The tables are a skyline
of energy drinks, wet wipes for the headset mic, though
we fall ill anyway. Cackling microbes leap into our mouths
from the plastic like gap year teens into a lagoon.
Mr Poole in Swindon doesn't have any money
for Syria and *anyway what about the problems here?*
Nobody wants to hand over cash to a voice
pumped with an anus-rocket of commission
and aspartame. You speed through the script
until Captain Dave up front pulls you up to listen
to your call, pausing to pull apart each cheery phrase
as if parting a scalp for lice. You can hear crumpling
in your insides, the strained pep, the pistol
of an overdraft at your temple. *Listen to Tabitha,*
says Dave. While Panto season sleeps, Tabitha's here,
permanently rouged, her faux-cockney gabble
like a trampoline you want to cut a hole in, though
this you don't say, because Tabitha is queen here,
high fiving newbies, lapping the room at each sell.
You get back on your calls, hunger for natural light.
You want, so desperately, to take no for an answer.

JASMINE ANN COORAY

Bed Blocker Blues

What me worry I should care
Shit for brains – wire for hair
I seen the future and I ain't there
Things are gonna get worse

Velcro slippers and a spandex waistband
Washed up on planet wasteland
Zipped up like a nylon spaceman
Things are gonna get worse

Things are gonna get worse nurse
Things are gonna get rotten
Make that hearse reverse nurse
I am trying to remember everything that I've forgotten

A menace in the box I was good in the air
Now I can't get up from an easy chair
The doctor told me oh yeah
Things are gonna get worse

Things are gonna get worse nurse
Things are gonna get crappy
Colour me perverse nurse
Bad news always makes me happy

The money's gone there's only muck
Social services pass the buck
How bad does it have to suck
Things are gonna get worse

Things are gonna get worse nurse
Things are gonna get dismal
Smite me with a curse nurse
Make it something real abysmal

All that's left is the taste of soup
Afternoon re-runs of *F-Troop*
And a painful frame with a built-in stoop
Things are gonna get worse

Things are gonna get worse nurse
I ain't optimistic
Struck down by inertia nurse
In a bungalow smelling of piss and biscuits

Life's a bitch it's a bit rich
Doubled up with a permanent stitch
Any kind of effort would be so last ditch
Things are gonna get worse

Young people make me swear
You can't take me anywhere
I'm like a breath of stale air
A walking one-man medical scare
Things are gonna get worse

Hail seizure, hello stroke
So many pills a bloke could choke
I can't decide from what to croak
Things are gonna get worse

Things are gonna get worse nurse
Murder by logistics
Take me back to the first verse
The last one's just too pessimistic

Euthanasia – that sounds good
A neutral Alpine neighbourhood
Then back to Britain all dressed in wood
Things were gonna get worse – apparently

JOHN COOPER CLARKE

Pity

Pity we killed all the monsters. It might have been
A help to ask a sphinx or a centaur,
A siren, a deep-sea triton or some such cross between
Our miserable species and another
What it feels like. Too late now. Goodbye
Creation, we are all going to die.

Our tinnitus is in the five oceans, the air
Spasms with our constant jabber, our shit trails
Eternally in icy space but here we are
Still ignorant beyond our broken fingernails.
All's in the sights of the camera and the gun
But we've no neighbourhood, no conversation.

Dying from the centre, if we still had a rind
Of greenmen, ariels, mermaids, beings that passed
Through into knowledge of some other kind
We might not be killing and dying quite so fast.
We seed our hard selves over the countryside.
Don't play with us. All who did have died.

DAVID CONSTANTINE

Sweeping the States

they move in swift on the Swift
Plants in six states & sift
through the faces to separate
the dark from the light

like meat & seat them in
the back of vans packed tight
like the product they pack
& who's to pick up the slack

the black & white can't cut it
so the beef stacks sell single
to feed the pack   the flock
who block passages & clog

the cogs of the machine   the process
not so swift to give & grant a wish
of a place   a stake in the land
handling the steaks for the rest

to take in   to sate the mouths
of the stock who have stock
in the business of beef & beef
with the brown who ground them

JACOB SAENZ

Midlands kids,

we were raised in cars, grew up on the back seats
of the long-gone marques of British manufacturing,
Morris, Austins and Talbots, slightly crap even new,
third- or fourth-hand, pockmarked, and in summer
distinguished by the waft of hot leatherette, the oil-black
tang of four-star fumes and the rust-red frothing of a had-it
head-gasket that had sent the radiator broiling over.

Those people we once thought to be, then – misplaced
down the gap in the back seat that so ingeniously folded forward,
or left tucked like secrets in the chrome pop-out passengers' ashtrays;
just as each promised holiday and magical mystery tour silvered
in the wing-mirrors momentarily before vanishing far out
on the hot horizon, like the car plants, company overalls, jobs for life,
the legendary square steering wheel of a paintshop-fresh Allegro.

JANE COMMANE

NOTE: Sarah Howe's poem opposite is a response to the death of Xu Lizhi (1990-2014), a Chinese poet and Foxconn factory worker from Shenzhen who committed suicide, aged 24. Published by friends after this death, his poem 'I Swallowed a Moon Made of Iron' reads (in rough translation): 'I swallowed a moon made of iron / They call it Screw / I swallowed the industrial effluent, orders of unemployment / The youths lower than machines have untimely died young / I swallowed the toil, swallowed the displacement, / Swallowed the overpasses, swallowed the life full of limescale / I can't swallow any more / All I've swallowed down are surging out of my throat, / Spreading out across the territory of my country and becoming / A poem of shame.' (19 December 2013) [Ed.]

On a line by Xu Lizhi

I swallowed a moon made of iron
you sang
the one who would stare from a fourth-storey sill
waiting for the brunt lick of dormitory fan

to come round again
pitched in the grimy glass
your still-young face electroplates with lunar currents
it clogs the sky

overtime dense as a dentist's drill
you are shower-capped again in the assembly line
your eyes acid-etched circuitries
where fatigue's fluorescent scrim settles like dawn

you float between
the rows ministering to never-ending components
their hands a flight of chrome
tongue soldered by thirst

you sway
could almost reach
the cartoon bulb twitching hot above your head
later in your bunk

among strangers hauled from sundry provinces
who fart like dogs in their sleep
you write down a line about the screw that fell
with an unheard plink

to the factory floor
words I read on a screen that reels at my touch
and choke
then tap the next link

SARAH HOWE

Death of a Cellphone

I'd witnessed before the death of a cellphone.
It was while I was waiting for a train at Yeongdeungpo-gu Office
    Station.
Just as the train was entering the station
a cellphone suddenly threw itself down onto the tracks.
It was the cellphone that had been talking to a young woman,
right in front of me as I waited for the train.
The other passengers screamed.
The train came to a sudden stop, but ran on over the cellphone.
For some time the doors did not open.
Station attendants came running hastily
and the corpse of the cellphone was carried away on a stretcher.
Whose face do we see when we become infinitely abject?
Is it the face of those we could not forgive, could not love?
Bloodstains remained on the tracks
but the train took on the passengers and went staggering off.
Waiting for the red light of the 'Power On' to turn on once again,
the cellphone lies on heaven's supper table
together with those who have killed themselves.

JEONG HO-SEUNG
translated from the Korean by Brother Anthony of Taizé with Susan Hwang

Politics

The greatest events
take place with the utmost simplicity.
It was simple, wasn't it,
to transform manual workers
into political activists:
change cranes into gallows.

SABEER HAKA
translated from the Farsi by Nasrin Parvaz & Hubert Moore

Mulberries

Have you ever seen
mulberries,
how their red juice
stains the earth where they fell?
Nothing is as painful as falling.
I've seen so many workers
fall from buildings
and become mulberries.

SABEER HAKA
translated from the Farsi by Nasrin Parvaz & Hubert Moore

Hole in the Wall

I lean in close and smell its faint bilge note.
I screen my digits but the hole in the wall
knows who I am. One time, it ate my card.

If the high street were a reef, it'd be its shark
and we'd be like those smaller fish that swim
right in to clean its teeth. And if some Hole

in the Wall Gang come and try to tear it out,
when fear moves on the waters of the reef,
it squirts a special dye and clamps up tight.

I used to go deeper into the hole
by coming here to keep an evening fed,
to stay tanked up for longer. *Would you like*

a receipt? Proof that I passed this way one night
and dived for pearls wearing a suit with lead
in my boots. *Would you like to check your balance?*

PAUL FARLEY

Song of Myself

(Apocryphal)

I am my own listserve,
advertising job and fellowship opportunities
for myself by myself to myself.

I sing of unpaid internships to my soul, O soul,
and of passing controversies on which to take sides
is to take the side of the self.

I re-post myself and forward myself
and respond to myself with emojis
for I am the screen and its anticipation,

the pleasure of being liked
and of commanding myself to like others.
For all pages are contained in my potential

for sharing, scrolling, even viewing
incognito. I sign in on myself
and log out of myself and yet remain

more than my usernames
and forgotten passwords.
For I am the great web itself

and every parody known to it
is known to me, and every troll
who devastates its comments section

is of myself. I am celebrity culture
and conspiracy theory culture –
the metastasis of meaning

that nurtures both political
gossip and culture wars,
food blogs, parenting blogs,

and cat videos. What you
shall click, I shall click,
and where you shall cut and paste

I shall be cut and paste.
Do I make myself redundant?
Very well then, I make myself

redundant. I am a paywall
(disambiguation)
I contain metadata.

ZOHAR ATKINS

Ode on a Grayson Perry Urn

Hello! What's all this here? A kitschy vase
   some Shirley Temple manqué has knocked out
delineating tales of kids in cars
   on crap estates, the Burberry clad louts
who flail their motors through the smoky night
   from Manchester to Motherwell or Slough,
     creating bedlam on the Queen's highway.
Your gaudy evocation can, somehow,
   conjure the scene without inducing fright,
     as would a *Daily Express* exposé,

can bring to mind the throaty turbo roar
   of hatchbacks tuned almost to breaking point,
the joyful throb of UK garage or
   of house imported from the continent
and yet educe a sense of peace, of calm –
   the screech of tyres and the nervous squeals
     of girls, too young to quite appreciate
the peril they are in, are heard, but these wheels
   will not lose traction, skid and flip, no harm
     befall these children. They will stay out late

forever, pumped on youth and ecstasy,
    on alloy, bass and arrogance and speed
the back lanes, the urban gyratory,
    the wide motorways, never having need
to race back home, for work next day, to bed.
    Each girl is buff, each geezer toned and strong,
        charged with pulsing juice which, even yet,
fills every pair of Calvins and each thong,
    never to be deflated, given head
        in crude games of chlamydia roulette.

Now see who comes to line the sparse grass verge,
    to toast them in Buckfast and Diamond White,
rat-boys and corn-rowed cheerleaders who urge
    them on to pull more burn-outs or to write
their donut Os, as signature, upon
    the bleached tarmac of dead suburban streets.
        There dogs set up a row and curtains twitch
as pensioners and parents telephone
    the cops to plead for quiet, sue for peace –
        tranquillity, though, is for the rich.

And so, millennia hence, you garish crock,
    when all context is lost, galleries razed
to level dust and we're long in the box,
    will future poets look on you amazed,
speculate how children might have lived when
    you were fired, lives so free and bountiful
        and there, beneath a sun a little colder,
declare *How happy were those creatures then,*
    who knew that truth was all negotiable
        and beauty in the gift of the beholder.

TIM TURNBULL

Praise the Young

They are green, too green, so very green,
the girls in their short frocks,
and the boys with their rollies and 2-pack *Karpackie*,
an optimistic condom in the back pocket.

Look at that redhead, proud in her bloom,
strutting her stuff down the arts block catwalk,
and the shrinking, studious primrose over there,
hiding the buds of her shy sensuality
from the grungy lad with his too-frank stare.

I walk amongst them, laden with envy,
alert to them endlessly, breathing their air,
their odours and perfumes, the sweat of their lies,
and under my breath I pour out to them
my unwanted affection and past-it advice –

love will distort you into someone else,
a hive of disappointments, hopes, desire,
just one beat beating, one struck note,
one pulse, one flesh, claustrofuckinphobic.

CAITLÍN NIC ÍOMHAIR
translated from the Irish by Colette Bryce

Ursa Minor

Four thousand and seventy-four friends
on Facebook, pout-perfect teenager,

stares at me through a silicone laptop.
Just before her bud-burst, she sent me

a friend request; status update,
she dreamt a bear ate her last night.

Poor Callisto, running to forest-mother,
don't talk to strangers until you get there.

In her dream, she lived in a house of glass,
in the woods, seen by bears, seen by wolves.

My urge to reply, fleshed with memories
of the shock of being so new, so ripe.

I typed: *love sometimes eats us up.*
We are all animals in moonlight.

Callisto, LOL, smiley face, heart,
don't go into the woods to be torn apart.

Outside he watches her, clicks on her posts,
likes her pictures of new hairstyles, picnics

and drinks with friends. A gust of hot breath
on glass, broken screen. Bite marks.

JESSICA MOOKHERJEE

Be the first to like this

kicking pine cones down the street
climbing the backyard cherry tree
lying in new sheets
waking in darkness   waking to snow
how your chest thickens when you're scared
how your voice bubbles when you're pleased
be the first to like

view of wind turbines from the train
golden tint on a glass of wine
gliding on rollerblades by the sea
waking so warm   waking on the beach
how your eyes flood when you're tired
how you laugh when you're relieved
like bridges creeks Frisbees
silly cat videos and Instagram photos
like strolling with a friend
between folds of trees
and your heart rolls out a big pink wave
and your lips recall something sweet
like skiing and ice-skating
zip-lining above trees at seventy clicks
blood thudding in your ears
like every new experience because it was new
to you   pocketed in your memory
like the first time you fed the ducks
at Stanley Park
and they stormed like villagers
to your feet

THERESA MUÑOZ

Like, the Sestina
With a nod to Jonah Winter

Now we're all 'friends', there is no love but Like,
A semi-demi goddess, something like
A reality-TV-star look-alike,
Named Simile or Me Two. So we like
In order to be liked. It isn't like
There's Love or Hate now. Even plain 'dislike'

Is frowned on: there's no button for it. Like
Is something you can quantify: each 'like'
You gather's almost something money-like,
Token of virtual support. 'Please like
This page to stamp out hunger.' And you'd like
To end hunger and climate change alike,

But it's unlikely Like does diddly. Like
Just twiddles its unopposing thumbs-ups, like-
Wise props up scarecrow silences. 'I'm like,
So OVER him,' I overhear. 'But, like,
He doesn't get it. Like, you know? He's like
It's all OK. Like I don't even LIKE

Him anymore. Whatever. I'm all like...'
Take 'like' out of our chat, we'd all alike
Flounder, agape, gesticulating like
A foreign film sans subtitles, fall like
Dumb phones to mooted desuetude. Unlike
With other crutches, um, when we use 'like',

We're not just buying time on credit: Like
Displaces other words; crowds, cuckoo-like,
Endangered hatchlings from the nest. (Click 'like'
If you're against extinction!) Like is like
Invasive zebra mussels, or it's like
Those nutria-things, or kudzu, or belike

Redundant fast-food franchises, each like
(More like) the next. Those poets who dislike
Inversions, archaisms, who just like
Plain English as she's spoke – why isn't 'like'
Their (literally) every other word? I'd like
Us just to admit that's what real speech is like.

But as you like, my friend. Yes, we're alike,
How we pronounce, say, 'lichen', and dislike
Cancer and war. So like this page. Click *Like*.

A.E. STALLINGS

366

8

Roots and routes

I think all art offers entry points into stories of migration and identity
because art often seeks to humanise people, or to take a zoomed-in view
of something. For example, the conversation changes when you are
talking about abstract numbers or something as big as war, to when you
zoom in on a particular family, living in a particular neighborhood
during a particular day during a particular war. We see the story, the
nuance, the people as people. That's empathy. Or even a range of
emotions – I can't tell you how many times I've read something or seen a
work of art and felt like an artist put voice to something that I had felt
many times but wasn't sure how to articulate.

FATIMAH ASGHAR

ACCORDING TO THE UNITED NATIONS, the number of international migrants
globally reached an estimated 272 million in 2019, an increase of 51 million
since 2010. They now comprise 3.5 per cent of the world's population, com-
pared with 2.8 per cent in 2000. Those are Fatimah Asghar's 'abstract statistics'
in this case. The poems in the second part of this section tell the individual
stories of people displaced from their homes, trying to adapt themselves to
life in unfamiliar countries and cultures.

But first, there are poems about the meaning of home itself; about finding
or leaving home, the feel of home, and growing up as a family in a home
which continues to hold our stories. Also our sense of belonging: the disparity
between who owns our home or land, and who we feel it actually *belongs* to,
the people who may have lived there for generations and worked the land, or
the landlord or landowner whose ownership often derives from historical dis-
possession, as in Jane Clarke's poem 'Who owns the field?' (374).

There are poems here relating to many migrations by people fleeing war,
oppression, political turmoil and hunger, both very recently from conflicts in
the Middle East and Africa, as well as from the Caribbean, Europe and post-
Partition India and Pakistan in earlier decades. Beata Duncan's poem 'The
Notebook' (399) recalls her journey as a child refugee escaping with her brother
from Nazi Germany in 1934. One of the most shocking news images of recent
times was that of a drowned boy washed up on a Mediterranean beach, recalled
in Linda Gregerson's 'Sleeping Bear' (410), one of a number of poems (408-
19) on the plight of migrants which some readers may find disturbing, parti-
cularly those including descriptions of ill treatment or deaths of children.

'Conversations About Home (at the Deportation Centre)' (418) by Kenyan-
born Somali-British poet Warsan Shire is the original prose poem version
from 2011 of her poem 'Home' which went viral in 2015 and 2017.

367

Home

As if we would never arrive,
we check our watches and connections.
So many elsewheres as we
walk into abandoned rooms
that somehow have forgotten us.

A window propped, half-open
on a garden, stares. A bird
as if to say, you're here,
glances its wings against the blue
so far away, then becomes invisible.

How they call to us, the lost places.
Now I carry my life, as a snail might,
slipping across grass and stone:
the shrugged contours of her shell's light spiral,
the glistening of her bridal train.

Like a half-remembered song,
marking us, making us,
words call us back, they call us on.
To know the world in another language
is to never know the world the same.

DERYN REES-JONES

Initiation, II

At the crossroads, hens scratched circles
into the white dust. There was a shop
where I bought coffee and eggs, coarse-grained
chocolate almost too sweet to eat.
When I walked up the road, the string sack

heavy on my arm, I thought
that my legs could take me anywhere,
into any country, any life.
The air, dazzling as sand, grew dense
with light: bougainvillea spilled
over the salmon walls, the road
veered into the ravine. The world
could be those colors, the mangoes,
the melons, the avocado evenings
releasing their circles of moon.
I climbed the pink stairs, entered
the house as calm and ephemeral
as my own certainty:
this is my house, my key,
my hand with its new lines.
I am as old as I will ever be.

NINA BOGIN

Dancing at Oakmead Road

Sometimes I think of its bright cramped spaces,
the child who grew there and the one we lost,
how when we swept up for its newest lover
the empty rooms were still so full of us.

The honeyed boards I knew would yet hold close
our dusts, some silver from my father's head,
the resin of the wood would somehow catch
in patina the pattern of his tread.

That time in the back room, laughing and drunk,
Geraldo and his orchestra, a tune
that had you up and waltzing and me quiet,
my throat so achey at the sight of you,

glimpsing for a second how it might have been
before his mouth went down on yours, before
the War, before the children broke into
the dance, before the yoke of work. Before.

MAURA DOOLEY

Nocturne

After a friend has gone I like the feel of it:
the house at night. Everyone asleep.
The way it draws in like atmosphere or evening.

One o'clock. A floral teapot and a raisin scone.
A tray waits to be taken down.
The landing light is off. The clock strikes. The cat

comes into his own, mysterious on the stairs,
a black ambivalence around the legs of button-back
chairs, an insinuation to be set beside

the red spoon and the salt-glazed cup,
the saucer with the thick spill of tea
which scalds off easily under the tap. Time

is a tick, a purr, a drop. The spider
on the dining-room window has fallen asleep
among complexities as I will once

the doors are bolted and the keys tested
and the switch turned up of the kitchen light
which made outside in the back garden

an electric room – a domestication
of closed daisies, an architecture
instant and improbable.

EAVAN BOLAND

The Last Light

Everything that can be is disconnected.
      Our fire dies. The starlings, nested
in the eaves, have settled. We have cut
      the house adrift to sleep. Now, before

I turn the key, I listen again to my life –
      wind in the roof space, a maternity case
settling on the rafters, waves breaking
      three fields away, a freight train slipping

southwards towards the port; at the stairs,
      our stray stretched out in her shadow;
upstairs, my wife, all my care, asleep.
      Above us, a flight banks in the dark,

beginning its descent. The road, this night,
      goes quiet. I extinguish the last light.

TOM FRENCH

from The Rooms

Somehow a wilderness grows. The grasses
are full of small animals, the nights so absolute
you could haul yourself through blackness to the stars
and stream down like a stray god on the meadow.

The lake shifts and startles, a vixen cries from her lair.
The cottage veers and shakes and makes
like a mad thing for the trees. If there is a dog
he is barking now, shocked head pummelling air.

371

If there are foxes they are running, if the dead
have spilled from their fields they are here now
running headlong into the night. They are lost
and their gods with them, running down the narrow
lanes, leaping into hedgerows and ditches, mingling
with ash branches, rushes, the sleeping machines in their sheds.

*

To be loosed like that, streaming through the black countryside
or stopped somewhere, holed up in a ditch, stretched
on a bale under the whistling galvanise
as you forget the thin strands you died with

and darkness floats your whole life down, the whole span
settles on skin and hair, everything you were
like branches come together, a forest
of small touches. Here you are

yourself completely, so completely
your fingertips reach the lake
your body drifts and falls like mist on the fields
and all your hours rain down...

There's not a blade of grass here that doesn't have your breath on it
before the sun burns you back to darkness again.

*

Who owns this land, these trees, these birds
pouring through the morning? I've come here
emptyhanded to harvest the wind on my face
the secrecies of place. Star-gathering, lake-stalking

pilgrim head plugged in to draw the powers
out of what my leisure falls on

as tractors roar, lights come on in the yards
and machinery shreds the dark. Cattle
thunder past, a sheepdog barks
from the back of a jeep and a two-stroke engine
puts manners on the hedgerows. The whole
powered world is roaring its purpose

where silently I stand and focus my lens
on the bookish meadow with its subplot of swans.

*

The little jetty sinking in the rushes, hard to find.
Who has no house now will hang his hat
on the ramshackle, the provisional, a summer's

quick labour; will sit for hours inheriting a silence
stitched with warblers and lake tunes. Hermit
of the wetlands, sleep on reeds, sleep on water:

everything else can wait. The streets have flown,
the traffic vanished, and only the dark
comes on in the dark. Cock your ear and a tradition

opens: you can still get in, you can sing
until the edicts are unfrozen
the palaces forgotten, until the dogs start barking

and the neighbour's Toyota comes creeping down the lane
to sniff you out and pin you down.

PETER SIRR

Who owns the field?

Is it the one who is named in the deeds
whose hands never touched the clay
or is it the one who gathers the sheaves

takes a scythe to the thistles, plants the beech,
digs out the dockweed, lays the live hazel?
Is it the one who is named in the deeds

or the one who pulls ragwort on his knees,
lifts rocks into a cart, splits larch for stakes,
the one who gathers the sheaves,

slashhooks the briars, scatters the seed,
cuts his hand on barbed wire, hangs the gate?
Is it the one who is named in the deeds

or the one who could surely lead
to where children made a hiding place
in an old lime tree. He gathers the sheaves.

Is it the one who tends cattle and sheep,
and can tell you how the field got its name?
Is it the one who is named in the deeds
or the one who gathers the sheaves?

JANE CLARKE

Anthem

Love begins in a country
Where oranges weep sweetness
And men piss in the street.

374

Your hands are forever binding
Black strands in a plait. Your mother's
Childhood friend has steeped

Your skin in coconut oil, tucked
Her daughter beside you – the night
Is a womb, live with twins.

Heat's body presses every body.
Sharp chop of your uncle's cough
Clocks the hours; your sister's washing,

The rush of your thoughts. Morning
Is nine glass bangles hoisting sacks
Of sugar from the floor. I'm not talking

About a place, but a country:
Its laws are your mother, its walls
Are your dreams. The flag it flies

Is your father, waving.

KIRUN KAPUR

Catching Crabs

Ruby and me stalking savannah
Crab season with cutlass and sack like big folk.
Hiding behind stones or clumps of bush
Crabs locked knee-deep in mud mating
And Ruby seven years old feeling strange at the sex
And me horrified to pick them up
Plunge them into the darkness of bag.
So all day we scout to catch the lonesome ones
Who don't mind cooking because they got no prospect
Of family, and squelching through the mud,

Cutlass clearing bush at our feet,
We come home tired slow, weighed down with plenty
Which Ma throw live into boiling pot piece-piece.
Tonight we'll have one big happy curry feed,
We'll test out who teeth and jaw strongest
Who will grow up to be the biggest
Or who will make most terrible cannibal.

We leave behind a mess of bones and shell
And come to England and America
Where Ruby hustles in a New York tenement
And me writing poetry at Cambridge,
Death long catch Ma, the house boarded up
Breeding wasps, woodlice in its dark-sack belly:
I am afraid to walk through weed yard,
Reach the door, prise open, look,
In case the pot still bubbles magical
On the fireside, and I see Ma
Working a ladle, slow –
Limbed, crustacean-old, alone,
In case the woodsmoke and curry steam
Burn my child-eye and make it cry.

DAVID DABYDEEN

A Letter Home

I long for a comfort that cannot be measured,
forgotten caves where Bach can't reach,
the bell that sounds for a monarchy
not found on any globe, for the feverish
gathering of hunters who oil
and polish their guns. I long for the salt
that tears contain, the marrow that boils
in my bones, long for the miracle opening up
like a mouth when nothing comes out.

If I am the only one listening, the percussion
of grace in my loins is what I become,
pulling the trigger like no one has taught me
and no one would know how to prevent.
Alone on a trail that no map contains
I follow the line of your neck. Your head
is tilted back, I give myself to whatever it is
that strains my muscles and forces me
to bloom like a rifle going off,
scattered and joined in a single place
my Rome, Medina, Jerusalem.

ALEŠ DEBELJAK
translated from the Slovenian by Andrew Zawacki and the author

If China

If china, then only the kind
you wouldn't miss under the movers' shoes or the treads of a tank;
if a chair, then one that's not too comfortable, or
you'll regret getting up and leaving;
if clothes, then only what will fit in one suitcase;
if books, then those you know by heart;
if plans, then the ones you can give up
when it comes time for the next move,
to another street, another continent or epoch
or world:

who told you you could settle in?
who told you this or that would last forever?
didn't anyone tell you you'll never
in the world
feel at home here?

STANISŁAW BARAŃCZAK
translated from the Polish by Magnus J. Krynski

Home

Give me a home
that isn't mine,
where I can slip in and out of rooms
without a trace,
never worrying
about the plumbing,
the colour of the curtains,
the cacophony of books by the bedside.

A home that I can wear lightly,
where the rooms aren't clogged
with yesterday's conversations,
where the self doesn't bloat
to fill in the crevices.

A home, like this body,
so alien when I try to belong,
so hospitable
when I decide I'm just visiting.

ARUNDHATHI SUBRAMANIAM

And if

If you could choose a country
to belong to –
perhaps you had one
snatched away,
once offered to you
like a legend
in a basket covered with a cloth –

and if the sun were a simple flare,
the streets beating out

the streets, and your breath
lost on the road
with the Yadavs, herding cattle,
then you could rest, absorb
it all in the cool of the hills,

but still you might peel back one face
to retrieve another
and another, down to the face that is
unbearable, so clear
so complex, hinting at nations,
castes and sub-castes
and you would touch it once –

and if this Eastern track were
a gusty English lane
where rain makes mirrors
in the holes,
a rat lies lifeless, sodden
as an old floorcloth,
you'd be untouchable – as one

defined by someone else –
one who cleans the toilets,
burns the dead.

MONIZA ALVI

Ceylon

– the word's on the tip of your tongue
(or, as you say it, *tong*), as we take tea.
Waiting for you to speak, I sip mine:
Tetley's tastes of nothing, but I suppose
it's good to know true flavourlessness,
the prose of life we sugar over with verse.
*Cey*lon you say – a trochee not an iamb –

referring to the drink I drink
with two spoonfuls at home and, here, none.
Though by 'home', I mean the house
my parents live in and where I grew up;
like, and unlike, them saying 'back at home'
when they intend Sri Lanka, and not Leeds
where they live and I haven't, not for years.

VIDYAN RAVINTHIRAN

My Sri Lankan family

extends its electronic tentacles across the ocean.
From the outskirts of Sydney, my cousin
Skypes my uncle in Colombo every day.
My parents live in Leeds, just two hours away,
but here they are, trying to fix the mic.
She tells you at length about her divorced friend
who's lonely and whose dog began to bite:
'Its name was Willow, it was a long WILLOW-type dog.'
Crisply, he explains: 'It's a greyhound.'
They're keen to know our plans. Someone has wed
'another Tamil, and of the same caste. Just like back
at home – it's so primitive – on our small island:
is the girl even happy?' And my mother: 'you do not know that,
they are VERY VERY ASIANS. She is on my Facebook.'

VIDYAN RAVINTHIRAN

Our Town with the Whole of India

Our town in England with the whole of India sundering
out of its temples, mandirs and mosques for the customised
streets. Our parade, clad in cloak-orange with banners

and tridents, chanting from station to station for Vasaikhi
over Easter. Our full moon madness for Eidh with free
pavement tandooris and legless dancing to boostered
cars. Our Guy Fawkes' Diwali – a kingdom of rockets
for the Odysseus-trials of Rama who arrowed the jungle
foe to re-palace the Penelope-faith of his Sita.

Our Sunrise Radio with its lip sync of Bollywood lovers
pumping through the rows of emporium cubby holes
whilst bhangra beats slam where the hagglers roar
at the pulled-up back-of-the-lorry cut-price stalls.
Sitar shimmerings drip down the furbishly columned
gold store. Askance is the peaceful Pizza Hut...
A Somali cab joint, been there forever, with smiley
guitar licks where reggae played before Caribbeans
disappeared, where years before Teddy Boys jived.

Our cafés with the brickwork trays of saffron sweets,
brass woks frying flamingo-pink syrup-tunnelled
jalebis networking crustily into their familied-webs.
Reveries of incense scent the beefless counter where
bloodied men sling out skinned legs and breasts
into thin bags topped with the proof of giblets.
Stepped road displays – chock-full of ripe karela,
okra, aubergine – sunshined with mango, pineapple,
lychee. Factory walkers prayer-toss the river of

sponging swans with chapattis. A posse brightens
on park-shots of Bacardi – waxing for the bronze
eyeful of girls. The girls slim their skirts after college
blowing dreams into pink bubble gums at neck-
descending and tight-neck sari-mannequins. Their grannies
point for poled yards of silk for own-made styles.
The mother of the runaway daughter, in the marriage
bureau, weeps over the plush-back catalogues glossed
with tuxedo-boys from the whole of our India!

DALJIT NAGRA

To His Homeland

You put the swagger in my walk
and volume in my speech,
the tidal feeling that tethers me
and floods my thoughts with memories
of ripe mango, my roast breadfruit, my pomerac.
Through the plane windows I watch the clouds
and feel my stress lift as you come in view,
my guava, my coconut water, my red sno-cone.
My passport holds a younger, slimmer me,
creased and cracked, till I renew it
with my red snapper, my stewed chicken, my pelau.
A month in the crumbling house I grew up in
that leaving didn't feel right, though I had to do it,
my tamarind stew, my pepper sauce, my pumpkin.
And when it snows I think of you,
my pommecythere, my sapodilla, my sugar cake.

ROGER ROBINSON

Potato Season

Gjergj didn't say *child*
or *children*, he said *family* – and it was soft
the way he said it, as if he were kissing
each syllable, making the word bigger
somehow, full of aunts and uncles
and cousins and nieces and nephews.
And when he said *six weeks without pay*,
he drew out the word *pay* so that it sounded like *pain*
and I knew we were on the wrong side of Christmas
and Mum was on the wrong side of the desk.
He held a pistol to her head, but all I saw
was sunlight slatting through Portakabin blinds,

making the black in his hand gleam.
The sun made mosaics of my mother's eyes,
her whites snow, edged
with red runnels, as she told him,
go on then, son. But he didn't look at her
riddling her fingers on the desk
as if she were a girl playing the piano,
he tucked the pistol back into his grey coat,
along with the weight of her final syllable,
and stepped out into the fen.

ELISABETH SENNITT CLOUGH

My Son Waits by the Door

We live on a council estate, my son and I.
Nine years old, but he looks much younger.
He has not yet learnt to read the minds

and motives of our neighbours. It's a month
now since they stopped playing with him:
Heather, Helen, Edmond and Simon.

When I bring him home from school he
doesn't take off his jacket, but waits.
When a breeze whistles past the house

he opens the blue door with a smile
to see whether anybody stands outside
asking him to play on the reckless street

with its smut; but no one is there.
A long emptiness howls like a hyena –
his path is now slippery with its saliva.

Weathered by what happened
he stares past the neighbourhood
and makes his way back into the house.

MIR MAHFUZ ALI

We Are of a Tribe

We plant seeds in the ground
and dreams in the sky,

Hoping that, someday, the roots of one
Will meet the upstretched limbs of the other.

It has not happened yet. Still,
Together, we nod unafraid of strangers.

Inside us, we know something about each other:
We are all members of the secret tribe of eyes

Looking upward,
Even as we stand on uncertain ground.

Up there, the dream is indifferent to time,
Impervious to borders, to fences, to reservations.

This sky is our greater home.
It is the place and the feeling we have in common.

This place requires no passport.
The sky will not be fenced.

Traveler, look up. Stay awhile.
Know that you always have a home here.

ALBERTO RÍOS

Going Nowhere, Getting Somewhere

(from 'Five Measures of Expatriation', III*)*

How was it that till questioned, till displaced in the attempt to answer, I had scarcely thought of myself as having a country, or indeed as having left a country? The answer lies peripherally in looming, in hinterland; primarily in the tongueless, palpitating interiority. Trinidad was. Trinidad is. In the same way, some confident speakers do not think of themselves as having an accent. They will say so: 'I don't have an accent! You have an accent!' In those accentless voices compass points spin, ochre and ultramarine flagella fling themselves identifiably towards this that or the other region. It is a motile version of that luxury, solidity, non-reflectivity that is the assumption of *patria*. So different is the expat from the refugee, who has her country on her back, or the migrant, who has countries at his back.

What would I have called home, before I began creating home? Before I had to learn to ravel up longitude, latitude, population, oil rigs, mobile phone masts, prayer flags, legality of fireworks, likely use of firearms, density and disappearance of forests, scarlet ibis, other stripes of scarlet, into a by-listeners-unvisited, communicable, substantial image of 'Trinidad'?

Language is my home. It is alive other than in speech. It is beyond a thing to be carried with me. It is ineluctable, variegated and muscular. A flicker and drag emanates from the idea of it. Language seems capable of girding the oceanic earth, like the world-serpent of Norse legend. It is as if language places a shaping pressure upon our territories of habitation and voyage; thrashing, independent, threatening to rive our known world apart.

Yet thought is not bounded by language. At least, my experience of thinking does not appear so bound.

One day I lost the words *wall* and *floor*. There seemed no reason to conceive of a division. The skirting-board suddenly reduced itself to a nervous gentrification, a cover-up of some kind; nothing especially marked. The room was an inward-focused container. 'Wall', 'floor', even 'ceiling', 'doorway', 'shutters' started to flow smoothly, like a red ribbed tank top over a heaving ribcage. Room grew into quarter. Room became segment. Line yearned till it popped into curve. The imperfections of what had been built or installed: the ragged windowframe or peeling tile: had no power to reclaim human attention to 'floor' or 'wall' as such. Objects were tethered like astronauts and a timid fringe of disarrayed atmosphere was the immediate past that human activity kept restyling into present. The interiority of the room was in continuous flow. Wall, floor became usable words again in a sort of silence.

I had the sense to shut up about the languageless perception. Procedure for living.

Language is my home, I say; not one particular language.

VAHNI CAPILDEO

Chaudhri Sher Mobarik looks at the loch

Light shakes out the dishrag sky
and scatters the water with sequins. *Look, hen!*
says my father, *Loch Lomond!* as if
it were all his doing, as if he owned it,
laird of Lomond, laird of the language.
He is proud to say *hen* and even more *loch*
with an *och* not an *ock*, to speak
proper Glaswegian like a true-born Scot,
and he makes the right sound at the back
of the throat because he can say *khush*
and *khwab* and *khamosh*, because the sounds
for happy and dream are the words that swim
in the water for him, so he says it again,
Hen! Look! The loch!

IMTIAZ DHARKER

Vanishing Act

Only two out of ten people die in Abu Dhabi; the rest simply fail
to have their visas renewed. They are bagged, tagged and placed
on the next available flight to wherever they first came from – the
one-way ticket experience par excellence. Every edifice on this
island is crafted by these almost-nothings. In death, at least, there
is solace: never again to queue for days on end, never again to have
their fingertips inked and pressed by intolerant hands, their blood
screened for undesirable illnesses, their flesh seared by a sun that
wonders what the hell they are doing here.

ANDRÉ NAFFIS-SAHELY

An Island of Strangers

The rooftop was the place to be. I was fifteen
and in love with ash-cans, pigeon coops,
women hanging their laundry. There was a fifty-
foot portrait of the King by the sea,

overlooking a busy junction – always smiling,
like an ad for toothpaste, or mouthwash.
At night, the shore on the west side of town
was the quietest, where hotels, Natashas and *haram*

coalesced into parties. Every half-lit room
was a sure sign of orgasms and the passing
of money from stranger to stranger. Anything
interesting and pleasurable was *haram*. I envied

the King, and his sons, all eighteen of them.
The King was virile, a patriarch, Abraham on Viagra;
his people, on the other hand, were on Prozac.
Everywhere the eye looked was money. The nose

hit only sweat: acrid, pugnacious, pervasive.
Most of the boys I knew sucked Butane, smoked,
saved up for whores, waited for their parole in the summer.
Each back to his own country. Come September

the dissatisfied returned: misfit mutts, at home everywhere
and nowhere. A friend compared cosmopolitanism
to being stuck at summer camp, waiting for parents
who never showed up. In the thirty-third year of his smile,

the King finally died. His mausoleum is a meringue: wavy,
white, and empty. His sons have gone on squabbling, playing
whose is biggest with bricks. One by one, they die in car crashes.
Days of heatstrokes, kif and bloodthirsty Ferraris.

ANDRÉ NAFFIS-SAHELY

The Three Kings

> We'll arrive too late...
>
>> ANDRÉ FRÉNAUD,
>> 'The Three Kings'

If it hadn't been for the desert and laughter and music –
we'd have made it, if our yearning
hadn't mingled with the highways' dust.
We saw poor countries, made still poorer
by their ancient hatred;
a train full of soldiers and refugees
stood waiting at a burning station.
We were heaped with great honors
so we thought – perhaps one of us
really is a king?
Spring meadows detained us, cowslips,
the glances of country maidens
hungry for a stranger's love.

We made offerings to the gods, but we don't know
if they recognised our faces
through the flame's honey-gold veil.
Once we fell asleep and slept for many months,
but dreams raged in us, heavy, treacherous,
like surf beneath a full moon.
Fear awakened us and again we moved on,
cursing fate and filthy inns.
For four years a cold wind blew,
but the star was yellow, sewn carelessly
to a coat like a school insignia.
The taxi smelled of anise and the twentieth century,
the driver had a Russian accent.
Our ship sank, the plane shook suddenly.
We quarreled violently and each of us
set out in search of a different hope.
I barely remember what we were looking for
and I'm not sure if a December night
will open up some day like
a camera's eye.
Perhaps I'd be happy, live content
if it weren't for the light that explodes
above the city walls each day
at dawn, blinding my desire.

ADAM ZAGAJEWSKI
translated from the Polish by Clare Cavanagh

Checking Out Me History

Dem tell me
Dem tell me
Wha dem want to tell me

Bandage up me eye with me own history
Blind me to me own identity

Dem tell me bout 1066 and all dat
dem tell me bout Dick Whittington and he cat
But Toussaint L'Ouverture
no dem never tell me bout dat

> *Toussaint*
> *a slave*
> *with vision*
> *lick back*
> *Napoleon*
> *battalion*
> *and first Black*
> *Republic born*
> *Toussaint de thorn*
> *to de French*
> *Toussaint de beacon*
> *of de Haitian Revolution*

Dem tell me bout de man who discover de balloon
and de cow who jump over de moon
Dem tell me bout de dish ran away with de spoon
but dem never tell me bout Nanny de Maroon

> *Nanny*
> *See-far woman*
> *of mountain dream*
> *fire-woman struggle*
> *hopeful stream*
> *to freedom river*

Dem tell me bout Lord Nelson and Waterloo
but dem never tell me bout Shaka de great Zulu
Dem tell me bout Columbus and 1492
but what happen to de Caribs and de Arawaks too

Dem tell me bout Florence Nightingale and she lamp
and how Robin Hood used to camp
Dem tell me bout ole King Cole was a merry ole soul
but dem never tell me bout Mary Seacole

From Jamaica
she travel far
to the Crimean War
she volunteer to go
and even when de British said no
she still brave the Russian snow
a healing star
among the wounded
a yellow sunrise
to the dying

Dem tell me
Dem tell me wha dem want to tell me
But now I checking out me own history
I carving out me identity

JOHN AGARD

A Different History

Great Pan is not dead;
he simply emigrated
            to India.
Here, the gods roam freely,
disguised as snakes or monkeys;
every tree is sacred
and it is a sin
to be rude to a book.
It is a sin to shove a book aside
            with your foot,
a sin to slam books down
        hard on a table,
a sin to toss one carelessly
        across a room.
You must learn how to turn the pages gently
without disturbing Sarasvati,

without offending the tree
from whose wood the paper was made.

Which language
has not been the oppressor's tongue?
Which language
truly meant to murder someone?
And how does it happen
that after the torture,
after the soul has been cropped
with the long scythe swooping out
of the conqueror's face –
the unborn grandchildren
grow to love that strange language.

SUJATA BHATT

History-Geography

No one is the first to set foot on any soil
You're always borne by souls who passed before
Time was, gods and goddesses
were alive just like you
Their strengths and weaknesses flow through you
into the earth
trodden underfoot by the procession
of the mortal dead

Granted some of you are my history
yet not my geography
Geography is the name of those who occupy the land
and it takes heart to stay

I stayed in my geography with my dead
Yet you denied your very self
Turned official, emptied of truth

I stayed in my geography with my life
to write my own history

KARIN KARAKAŞLI
translated from the Turkish by Sarah Howe & Canan Marasligil

Where I come from

From the earth I come
From the heart of Africa
From the kidneys of Asia
From India with spices I come
From a deep Amazonian forest
From a Tibetan meadow I come
From an ivory land
From far away
From everywhere around me
From where there are trees, mountains, rivers and seas
From here, there, from everywhere
From the womb of the Mediterranean I come
From a mental scar
From closed borders
From a camp with a thousand tents
From a bullet wound
From the face of a lone child
From a single mother's sigh
From a hole in an inflatable boat about to sink
From a bottle of water for fifty to share
From frozen snot in a toddler's nose
From the tear on a father's cheek
From a hungry stomach
From a graffiti that reads, 'I was here once'
From a missing limb
Like a human I come to share the space.

AMIR DARWISH

Minority

I was born a foreigner.
I carried on from there
to become a foreigner everywhere
I went, even in the place
planted with my relatives,
six-foot tubers sprouting roots,
their fingers and faces pushing up
new shoots of maize and sugar cane.

All kinds of places and groups
of people who have an admirable
history would, almost certainly,
distance themselves from me.

I don't fit,
like a clumsily-translated poem;

like food cooked in milk of coconut
where you expected ghee or cream,
the unexpected aftertaste
of cardamom or neem.

There's always that point where
the language flips
into an unfamiliar taste;
where words tumble over
a cunning tripwire on the tongue;
where the frame slips,
the reception of an image
not quite tuned, ghost-outlined,
that signals, in their midst,
an alien.

And so I scratch, scratch
through the night, at this
growing scab of black on white.

Everyone has the right
to infiltrate a piece of paper.
A page doesn't fight back.
And, who knows, these lines
may scratch their way
into your head –
through all the chatter of community,
family, clattering spoons,
children being fed –
immigrate into your bed,
squat in your home,
and in a corner, eat your bread,

until, one day, you meet
the stranger sidling down your street,
realise you know the face
simplified to bone,
look into its outcast eyes
and recognise it as your own.

IMTIAZ DHARKER

The Foreigner

Solitude chooses a car
that dissolves the night's slight provinces,
an elusive, deserted highway
and the wound struck by a song
that comes too close.

Only those nights of burning profile
traverse the world's well-aimed fervor.
The eye's industries suffer the memory
of a time that bends under its portion,
bridges fallen at the passing lights
and the coded vision of days.

Only his name, alert and disloyal,
refuses to yield to the landscape's shadows.
It's he who seeks,
inside his movement, his resistance.

LUIS MUÑOZ
translated from the Spanish by Curtis Bauer

Just a Nobody

The dead man was no one,
just a man in tattered clothes,
no shoes,
just a coin in his pocket,
no id cards, no bus ticket.
He was a nobody,
dirty and skinny,
a no one, a nobody
who clenched his hand before he died.
When they pried open his fingers,
this nobody,
they found a whole country.

HAMA TUMA
translated from the Amharic by the author

In This Country

In this country the foreigner starts losing his memory
    the day he arrives.

He remains speechless in his own language.

The air around translates his silence into English –
It is snowing.

396

Dry leaves are falling.
The sea waves recede.
The river ebbs away.
The tea is getting cold.
Photographs are fading.

He wonders – one shouldn't be in this country.
He keeps on being a stranger here, and
He starts believing in other strangers.

A cog is broken from the wheel of time.
The gramophone record moves on with the needle stuck
    in one track.

In this country the foreigner does not know what he does
    all the time.
He remains unaware   lost in his thoughts.
He wears *maojay* Punjabi shoes with his 3-piece suit.

In this country the foreigner keeps on looking a the photo
    in his old passport
        and gets scared of his own image.

In this country the foreigner is surprised to realise that
    the way back home is rather long
When lost in his hometown the moon shows him the way
It keeps on walking with him till the dawn breaks and he knocks
    on his own door.

AMARJIT CHANDAN

translated from the Punjabi by the author and Julia Casterton

Migrations

Migrations are always difficult:
ask any drought,
any plague;
ask the year 1947.

Ask the chronicles themselves:
if there had been no migrations
would there have been enough
history to munch on?

Going back in time is also tough.
Ask anyone back-trekking to Sargodha
or Jhelum or Mianwali and they'll tell you.
New faces among old brick;
politeness, sentiment,
dripping from the lips of strangers.
This is still your house, Sir.

And if you meditate on time
that is no longer time –
(the past is frozen, it is stone,
that which doesn't move
and pulsate is not time) –
if you meditate on that scrap of time,
the mood turns pensive
like the monsoons
gathering in the skies
but not breaking.

Mother used to ask, don't you remember my mother?
You'd be in the kitchen all the time
and run with the fries she ladled out,
still sizzling on the plate.
Don't you remember her at all?
Mother's fallen face
would fall further
at my impassivity.
Now my dreams ask me
If I remember my mother
And I am not sure how I'll handle that.
Migrating across years is also difficult.

KEKI DARUWALLA

The Notebook

Tom and I sit in our own compartment
as the fields and villages and lakes go by.
I have a little bag with all that is important:
the necklace Granny gave me, three days
of Mamma's sandwiches, my new notebook
with a green silk cover. Shh!

A policeman paces the train's corridor,
a grey uniform and long polished boots.
He demands our papers and examines the photos,
looking carefully at each of us, passing them on.
He writes quickly in his notebook and I
his description in mine. Another policeman

arrives in a black uniform, silver buttons flashing
as we whisk through a tunnel. He is very erect,
wears a gun, a peaked cap like a large beak.
His face is red and he's been shouting.
He checks his notebook as I look into my own.
Tom is very pale and tells me to sit still.

Another frontier, we must climb down
and board another train. It stops and starts
and there are a crowd of strangers with us.
Opening our bags, they flick through my album.
Tom hides all our papers in his new wallet
and I'm too tired to write in my notebook.

There is the sea and safety, wide and empty.
This time Tom helps me to climb the gangway
and I'm seasick, eating Toblerone on the ferry.
But I'm pleased with myself, washing my hands
under the shiny brass taps in the tiny loo.

Curled on the padded seat of the next train,
I wake up and there is a new policeman,
wearing a beehive helmet and shoes.
He smiles at us, his voice buzzing and gentle.
Tom grips our papers and is very quiet.

BEATA DUNCAN

Exit

Airport security was tight
the day we left
my sister in a pram and I
holding my mother's hand.
She was heavy
with gold coins and cash,
rings, necklaces,
anything of worth
that could be snuck, hid,
stuffed in a sock or slipped
into the secret of a heel.
The bigger things
we left behind.
Pinched hard,
my sister screamed
so loud
the chadored guards
just scowled,
and waved us through,
unfrisked.

MINA GORJI

Refugees

Bent under burdens which sometimes
can be seen and sometimes can't,
they trudge through mud or desert sands,
hunched, hungry,

silent men in heavy jackets,
dressed for all four seasons,
old women with crumpled faces,
clutching something – a child, the family
lamp, the last loaf of bread?

It could be Bosnia today,
Poland in September '39, France
eight months later, Germany in '45,
Somalia, Afghanistan, Egypt.

There's always a wagon or at least a wheelbarrow
full of treasures (a quilt, a silver cup,
the fading scent of home),
a car out of gas marooned in a ditch,
a horse (soon left behind), snow, a lot of snow,
too much snow, too much sun, too much rain,

and always that special slouch
as if leaning toward another, better planet,
with less ambitious generals,
less snow, less wind, fewer cannon,
less History (alas, there's no
such planet, just that slouch).

Shuffling their feet,
they move slowly, very slowly
toward the country of nowhere,
and the city of no one
on the river of never.

ADAM ZAGAJEWSKI
translated from the Polish by Clare Cavanagh

Some People

Some people flee some other people.
In some country under a sun
and some clouds.

They abandon something close to all they've got,
sown fields, some chickens, dogs,
mirrors in which fire now preens.

Their shoulders bear pitchers and bundles.
The emptier they get, the heavier they grow.

What happens quietly: someone's dropping from exhaustion.
What happens loudly: someone's bread is ripped away,
someone tries to shake a limp child back to life.

Always another wrong road ahead of them,
always another wrong bridge
across an oddly reddish river.
Around them, some gunshots, now nearer, now farther away,
above them a plane seems to circle.

Some invisibility would come in handy,
some grayish stoniness,
or, better yet, some nonexistence
for a shorter or a longer while.

Something else will happen, only where and what.
Someone will come at them, only when and who,
in how many shapes, with what intentions.
If he has a choice,
maybe he won't be the enemy
and will let them live some sort of life.

WISŁAWA SZYMBORSKA
translated from the Polish by Stanisław Barańczak & Clare Cavanagh

Night Spent in the Temple of a Patient God

I

You chose your exile among rainswept mountains.

Where you lingered last night
was the home of the patient god
The home where a human is equipped with compassion.
No need for temples, I said.
This is simply a place.
The human soul must surely be a temple.
And rain the river of homelessness
reminds us of god and childhood.

II

You chose your exile among rainswept mountains.

The beauty of making mistakes
and the peace of pain.
Everything led you to emptiness.
And you, you looked at the pale flowers of patience and wept
You slept in his arms as though nothing existed.
There shall be a journey made to the mountain and exile chosen
And a human required of god.

We must listen again to that music.
That place was not meant for loving.

BEJAN MATUR
translated from the Turkish by Ruth Christie

The Moon Sucks up Our Grief

(for Hüseyin Kendal)

I

We gathered sounds from everywhere
the sound of mandolins from balconies
the sound of laughter from rooms
our lips mossy with damp
we stayed endlessly silent.

We were water hiding under steep cliffs
shy and touchy

We had no questions to ask of life
no answers but the glances we exchanged.

Some nights as the moon grew big
the path we took
drew our bodies to the mountains
to the mountains to be dispersed

II

The valleys that longed for the shining eyes
of our childhood
asked for our eyes
asked us to leave our eyes behind
without tears.
We never cried.
We left our eyes behind
and our songs.

III

This land was strange to us now.
Laden with turbid clouds of grief
but no rain-soaked earth.
We were tired
waiting for a breath of air on our wounds.

The olive trees were waiting
and the white earth with its nameless insects
were waiting for us.

    IV

Now we had no god.
We were forgotten.
We had left behind our gaze
in the depths
we could not see.
No memories waited for us
nor did we leave any trace as we passed
as though we had been created then and there
the world of vapour and we of grief.

    V

As it sucked up our grief the waxing moon
was waiting somewhere far off.
We walked with touches of the moon
veiling our pain
but we were still tired
we could not emerge from the whispering leaves of the maquis.
We had to lie down and rest
we had to forget our mandolin-dreams
we had to lay our hands to rest on the vapour
and impress our grief on the opening void of our hearts.
The wind at our fingers
deepened by the mandolin strings,
the familiar wind that lingered,
we had to give our selves
to the wind that knew all
the wind that carried all away

One touch of that wind would gather up our remains.

BEJAN MATUR
translated from the Turkish by Ruth Christie

In Lampedusa

On 3rd October
a barge carrying 518 people
arrived in Lampedusa
Having survived a brutal dictatorship
and a journey full of pitfalls
they stood atop their raft in the dead of night
and saw the lights of the promised land
Believing their suffering had reached an end,
they raised a chorus and praised the Virgin Mary.
While waiting for those ships to rescue them,
men and women, children and grownups,
the sick and the healthy began to sing hymns!
ስምኪ ጸዊ0 መባስ ሓፊሪ፣
I wasn't ashamed when I called out Your name,
ማሪያም ኢስ ኣበይ ወዲቄ:
I called out to Mary and didn't fall
ስምኪ እዩኣ'ሞ ስንቂ ኮይኑ:
Your name sustained me throughout my journey
እንሆ ምስጋናይ ተቐበልኒ!
and here is the grateful echo of the song I raise to thank you!
Suddenly the raft
started filling with water;
they began flashing
red lights to sound the alarm;
switched their lanterns on and off!
Alas, all was quiet on the island.
Meanwhile the water rose, stoking fears the ship would sink.
To send a distress call,
they set a sail on fire, and as the
flames began to spread, some frightened people
jumped overboard and tipped the boat.
They were all adrift in the freezing sea!
Amidst that storm, some died right away,
some beat the odds and cheated death,
some who could swim tried to help
some drowned using their last breath

406

to send messages back to their native land,
some called out their names and countries of origin
before succumbing to their fate!
Among the floating corpses
Mebrahtom raised a desperate cry
Yohanna! Yohanna! Yohanna!
But Yohanna didn't answer;
all alone, and in
an extreme act of love,
she brought her son into the world,
birthing him into the fish-filled sea:
yet nobody in Lampedusa
heard the seven ululations welcoming his birth!
ሕሀሀሀሀሀሀሀሀሀሀሀሀሀ
Because after a superhuman struggle
Yohanna died alongside her son,
who never saw the light of day
and perished without even... drawing his first breath!
A baby died
drowned in the salty sea!
The baby was born and died
with its umbilical cord still unsevered!
A woman died while giving birth!
368 people died! 357 Eritreans died!
On 3rd October
3000 feet from Rabbit Island,
in the heart of the Mediterranean,
a tragedy struck the Eritrean people,
one of many they have endured.

RIBKA SIBHATU

translated from the Italian by André Naffis-Sahely

Hundreds of cockroaches drowned today

Hundreds of cockroaches drowned today.
It was just as well they died at sea – no one holds funerals for beetles,
this way there'll be less of a mess.
In the old days, we used to buy the cockroaches,
bring them over the oceans in slightly safer ships,
and we'd have them work in our fields,
snipping cotton for us as the sun seared their shells.
Here's a secret; the cockroaches have never swum too well.
Back then, we'd throw the sick ones over the side
but now money drowns them,
and we smirk as their brown lungs fill with salt and silt,
we sing as they sink.

MUSA OKWONGA

The Boat that Brought Me

Behind these eyes that look like mine
old names are fading away,
the past lies crumpled in my clenched fist –
a coppery bird in coppery wind,
this vast place has covered me from head to toe.

I am not stripped of word and thought
but sometimes what I want to say gets lost
like a moon smudged with cloud, or when I splutter on a drink.
My tongue trips up when I speak of that journey
though the blood in my veins felt the truth of death.
As I traced my footsteps through the tracery of my old language
Summer whispered to me
and my frozen fingers began to put out shoots
even as I began to love the cold ebb and flow of tides.

Sometimes I miss
the boat that brought me here,
now that I am witness to the icy eyes of a Swedish winter
under these tired old clouds,
while that suitcase still holds a patch of the sky-blue me.

AZITA GHAHREMAN
translated from the Farsi by Maura Dooley & Elhum Shakerifar

The Boatman

We were thirty-one souls, he said, in the gray-sick of sea
in a cold rubber boat, rising and falling in our filth.
By morning this didn't matter, no land was in sight,
all were soaked to the bone, living and dead.
We could still float, we said, from war to war.
What lay behind us but ruins of stone piled on ruins of stone?
City called 'mother of the poor' surrounded by fields
of cotton and millet, city of jewelers and cloak-makers,
with the oldest church in Christendom and the Sword of Allah.
If anyone remains there now, he assures, they would be utterly alone.
There is a hotel named for it in Rome two hundred meters
from the Piazza di Spagna, where you can have breakfast under
the portraits of film stars. There the staff cannot do enough for you.
But I am talking nonsense again, as I have since that night
we fetched a child, not ours, from the sea, drifting face-
down in a life vest, its eyes taken by fish or the birds above us.
After that, Aleppo went up in smoke, and Raqqa came under a rain
of leaflets warning everyone to go. Leave, yes, but go where?
We lived through the Americans and Russians, through Americans
again, many nights of death from the clouds, mornings surprised
to be waking from the sleep of death, still unburied and alive
with no safe place. Leave, yes, we'll obey the leaflets, but go where?
To the sea to be eaten, to the shores of Europe to be caged?
To *camp misery* and *camp remain here*. I ask you then, where?

You tell me you are a poet. If so, our destination is the same.
I find myself now the boatman, driving a taxi at the end of the world.
I will see that you arrive safely, my friend, I will get you there.

CAROLYN FORCHÉ

from Sleeping Bear

What is it about the likes of us? Who cannot take it in
            until the body of a single Syrian three-
        year-old is face down on the water's edge? Or this

week's child who, pulled from the rubble, wipes
            with the back and then the heel of his small
        left hand (this time we have a video too) the blood

congealing near his eye then wipes (this is a problem,
            you can see him thinking Where?) the hand
        on the chair where the medic has put him.

So many children, so little space in our rubble-strewn
            hearts. In alternative newsfeeds I am
        cautioned (there is history, there is such a thing

as bias) that to see is not to understand. Which (yes, I know,
            the poster child, the ad space, my consent-
        to-be-governed by traffic in arms) is true and quite

beside the point. The boy on the beach, foreshortened
            in the photograph, looks smaller than
        his nearly three years would make him, which

contributes to the poignancy. The waves have combed his
            dark hair smooth. The water on the shingle, in-
        different to aftermath, shines.

LINDA GREGERSON

Mediterranean Blue

If you are a child of a refugee, you do not
sleep easily when they are crossing the sea
on small rafts and you know they can't swim.
My father couldn't swim either. He swam through
sorrow, though, and made it to the other side
on a ship, pitching his old clothes overboard
at landing, then tried to be happy, make a new life.
But something inside him was always paddling home,
clinging to anything that floated – a story, a food, or face.
They are the bravest people on earth right now,
don't dare look down on them. Each mind a universe
swirling as many details as yours, as much love
for a humble place. Now the shirt is torn,
the sea too wide for comfort, and nowhere
to receive a letter for a very long time.

And if we can reach out a hand, we better.

NAOMI SHIHAB NYE

After being asked if I write the 'occasional poem'

After leaving Raxruhá, after
crossing Mexico with a coyote,
after reaching at midnight
that barren New Mexico border,
a man and his daughter
looked to Antelope Wells
for asylum and were arrested. After
forms read in Spanish
to the Mayan-speaking father,
after a cookie but no water, after
the wait for the lone bus

to return for their turn, after boarding,
after the little girl's temperature spiked,
she suffered two heart attacks,
vomited, and stopped breathing. After
medics revived the seven-year-old
at Lordsburg station, after she was flown
to El Paso, where she died,
the coroner examined
the failed liver and swollen brain. Then
Jakelin's chest and head were stitched up
and she returned to Guatemala
in a short white coffin
to her mother, grandparents,
and dozens of women preparing
tamales and beans to feed the grieving.
In Q'eqchi', *w-e* means *mouth*.

KIMIKO HAHN

Illegal Immigrant

it is possible
the sun has risen
and over the mountains
the clouds are there still,
that winds are driving
and families arriving
and there is the sound of a party
sound of dancing, chanting,
and glasses smashing,
the laughter exploding
in every minute and people
and happiness and also
me, with my big heart,
in a ship or strapped under
the truck, I am crossing

the border and moment
by moment am entering
with glory England

REZA MOHAMMADI
translated from the Dari by Nick Laird & Hamid Kabir

Flight

What is it about Mohammed Ayaz
that sticks in the mind?

Is it how he squeezed himself
into the wheel bay
    of a Boeing 777,
found somewhere to crouch and cling?

Is it how, at 30,000 ft in the freezing
dark, he turned into a block of ice?

Is it where his twisted body was found,
in a DIY store car park,
    in London,
by a worker – on her way
to load paint tins
    into strong paper bags?

What is it about Mohammed Ayaz
that sticks in the mind?

Is it his foolishness?
Is it his courage?

Is it that his family's debts,
were as high as Mount Mankial?

Harvesting the onion crop,
they had so little time to grieve.

Is it that 3,000 people share
only one telephone
in the broad green valley of Swat?

Is it that routinely the captain
opened the undercarriage
and tipped him out?

And others will fall in this way,
on almost exactly the same spot.

Allah gives and Allah takes away
said his father.
He was meant to die
at this time.

But the son who had fallen
to earth groaned
It was the wrong time.
The wrong way.

MONIZA ALVI

For Lana Sadiq

On her face, all exiles,
all the roads opened to refugees.
Her face is an olive grove in Haifa and an orange orchard in Jaffa
and West Bank fig trees, and prickly pears from Galilee.
The dove lives in her eyes with the flash of stones thrown by children.
On her lips, the smile of the first daisy opening on the foothills,
and the first tent pitched for refugees, and the first orange dried out
    by bullets

and the first anemones budding
on bodies of the first butterflies fallen to earth here, south of us.
In exile, she searches for her children, to bring them back to her.
I didn't say to her: I am like you, a mother too, at the impossible
    road's beginning
Like you, I'll pace those paths, back and forth, to find my children.
Perhaps one day we'll return together.
And what have I gained, and what have I lost?
And what have I done, Father? My brothers don't love me
And don't want me among them.
What victory there for us, what victory for them?

FADWA SOULIEMAN
translated from the Arabic by Marilyn Hacker

Diaspora

Afraid is a country with no exit visas
a wire of ants walking the horizon
embroiders our passports at birth
Johannesburg Alabama
a dark girl flees the cattle prods
skin hanging from her shredded nails
escapes into my nightmare
half an hour before the Shatila dawn
wakes in the well of a borrowed Volkswagen
or a rickety midnight sleeper out of White River Junction
Washington bound   again
gulps carbon monoxide in a false-bottomed truck
fording the Braceras Grande
or an up-country river
grenades held dry in a calabash
leaving

AUDRE LORDE

The Displaced Persons Camp

Lean vigilant faces, sleepless eyes
look up. They sit like children grown
unnaturally, cramped into desks in rows,
and submit to the language of strangers, a stern
new ordering of tenses: is, was,

will be. 'Repeat now, after me.' Each voice
lifts towards clarity, and breaks: waves
on a north shore, a dull bafflement of loss.
'The subtler points – *should, might have been* –
will come in time.' The class dismissed,

they are free to sit, or pace the bare
perimeter. Willowherb flares from the dust.
It is neither peace nor war. Beyond the wire
in wide fields, two boys and a dog
race after their own cries. And stop. And stare.

PHILIP GROSS

Longing

Displaced Persons' Camp, Northern Sudan 1998

I long for the weather.
Here we live in the desert.
At home we have rain and green forests
And I feel very comfortable there.
Always I am thinking about my home.
Here we sleep on sand.
The sand is full of snakes and scorpions.
The children shout in the night.
They think the soldiers are coming at any moment.
My longing is to be back in my own home

Where I don't beg
And because the weather there is fine.
I am used to it from childhood.
And the water at home is not salty.

TERESA SAMUEL IBRAHIM
As told to Patricia Schonstein

The Last Train Across Ariat Bridge
Displaced Persons' Camp, Northern Sudan 1998

Because there was an ambush in my village
and my husband was detained
I decided to flee with the children to the north.
We waited for the train, we slept on the ground.
We had no good bedding or coverings.
Rain started. I started crying
because of the small children crying of rain and hunger.
I took the last train across Ariat with my children and some belongings.
The whistle of the train blew and we had some difficulties.
Everyone was pushing especially the soldiers.
The children were crying from being crushed.
I was crying and arguing with those who were overcrowding.
But they were also helpless.
I remained with my children: Dirty. Weak. Hungry.
We had only groundnuts to eat
and as we passed over Ariat Bridge
it was broken behind us by the rebels.
That was the last train to leave southern Sudan.
It took four days on the way between Ariat and Kosti.
Two nights later we arrived in Khartoum.
There was no place for us. No one was willing to take us
because they also have their problems.
We settled with others in the desert outside Khartoum.
There was no shelter there, only some thorn trees.
The ones who could not take the train
arrived after walking two months.

Some died walking. Some drowned in the flood.
Some reached Khartoum thin with swollen legs
with rashes and cracks.
We ourselves had some blankets and very little money.
Wood was difficult to get.
The only food was okra, some salt, water
and wheat flour given to us by the Catholic Church.
We started cutting dry thorn trees to make rakuba.
This is the quickest way to make a shelter
because if you are moving
you can take it and erect it in the next place.
You cannot say if you will be forced to move again.

TERESA SAMUEL IBRAHIM
As told to Patricia Schonstein

Conversations About Home
(at the Deportation Centre)

Well, I think home spat me out, the blackouts and curfews like
tongue against loose tooth. God, do you know how difficult it is,
to talk about the day your own city dragged you by the hair, past
the old prison, past the school gates, past the burning torsos erected
on poles like flags? When I meet others like me I recognise the
longing, the missing, the memory of ash on their faces. No one
leaves home unless home is the mouth of a shark. I've been carrying
the old anthem in my mouth for so long that there's no space for
another song, another tongue or another language. I know a shame
that shrouds, totally engulfs. I tore up and ate my own passport in
an airport hotel. I'm bloated with language I can't afford to forget.

*

They ask me *how did you get here?* Can't you see it on my body?
The Libyan desert red with immigrant bodies, the Gulf of Aden
bloated, the city of Rome with no jacket I hope the journey meant

more than miles because all of my children are in the water. I thought the sea was safer than the land. I want to make love, but my hair smells of war and running and running. I want to lay down, but these countries are like uncles who touch you when you're young and asleep. Look at all these borders, foaming at the mouth with bodies broken and desperate. I'm the colour of hot sun on the face, my mother's remains were never buried. I spent days and nights in the stomach of the truck; I did not come out the same. Sometimes it feels like someone else is wearing my body.

*

I know a few things to be true. I do not know where I am going, where I have come from is disappearing, I am unwelcome and my beauty is not beauty here. My body is burning with the shame of not belonging, my body is longing. I am the sin of memory and the absence of memory. I watch the news and my mouth becomes a sink full of blood. The lines, the forms, the people at the desks, the calling cards, the immigration officers, the looks on the street, the cold settling deep into my bones, the English classes at night, the distance I am from home. But Alhamdulilah all of this is better than the scent of a woman completely on fire, or a truckload of men who look like my father, pulling out my teeth and nails, or fourteen men between my legs, or a gun, or a promise, or a lie, or his name, or his manhood in my mouth.

*

I hear them say, go home, I hear them say, *fucking immigrants, fucking refugees.* Are they really this arrogant? Do they not know that stability is like a lover with a sweet mouth upon your body one second and the next you are a tremor lying on the floor covered in rubble and old currency waiting for its return. All I can say is, I was once like you, the apathy, the pity, the ungrateful placement and now my home is the mouth of a shark, now my home is the barrel of a gun. I'll see you on the other side.

WARSAN SHIRE

Home

I can say it of the world,
I can say it of every country in the world,
I can say it of the sky
and of everything in this universe.
But of this windowless rented bedroom in Tehran
I can't say it, can't say home.

SABEER HAKA
translated from the Farsi by Nasrin Parvaz & Hubert Moore

I Cannot Myself

To come to this country,
my body must assemble itself

into photographs and signatures.
Among them they will search for me.

I must leave behind all uncertainties.
I cannot myself be a question.

GABEBA BADEROON

9

Empathy and conflict

As an artist, as a writer, I have to master empathy, and to do so, I must
imagine, imagine fully and imagine with discipline and commitment. If I
fail to understand, feel, convey, express what the other person is going
through, then my imagination has failed, and my art has failed. So for
me, the instinct to empathise, which is a very human and morally
critical act, existed in my relationship with these people long before I
thought of writing a poem about them. And when I came to write the
poems, I drew on the lived experience of empathy, which is an act of the
imagination [...] empathy is what allows us to see the full person – at
least in part. So seeing them as people happened before the poem.

KWAME DAWES

KWAME DAWES wrote his essay 'Back to Empathy' (2010) after being asked
how he could write about other people in *their* terms when working on a
HIV/Aids project. This is a wider question which has engaged all kind of
writers in recent decades, particularly when portraying historical events and
actual people. Poems in this section show how empathy and personal knowledge
of a community can enable poets to testify to the experience of others in an
authentic way, notably in Roger Robinson's portrayal of victims of the Grenfell
Tower fire in 2017 (472-74), and in Jay Bernard's *Surge* (470-72), their revisiting
of the 1981 New Cross fire when 13 black teenagers lost their lives. Roy
McFarlane's sequence '...they killed them' (453) from *The Healing Next Time*
(2018) takes up a challenge posed by Claudia Rankine in *Citizen* (2014).

Terrance Hayes's highly politicised Trump era *American Sonnets for My
Past and Future Assassin* (2018) were inspired by the more jazzy American
sonnets of Wanda Coleman (429). His poem 'The Golden Shovel' (427) marked
the invention of a new poetic form, named after that poem: the last words in
each line are borrowed from a poem by another writer, paying tribute in this
case to Gwendolyn Brooks, drawing on her iconic poem 'We Real Cool' (426).
Hayes does this twice in the two parts of his poem: this is called a "double
golden shovel".

Patricia Smith's 'That Chile Emmett in That Casket' (435) recalls the
aftermath of the lynching of 14-year-old Emmett Till in Mississippi in 1955.
Imtiaz Dharker's 'A Century Later' (456) is her response to the Taliban attack
on female education campaigner Malala Yousafzai in 2012.

Land Ho

I cannot speak the languages
spoken in that vessel,
cannot read the beads
promising salvation.

I know this only,
that when the green of land
appeared like light
after the horror of this crossing,

we straightened our backs
and faced the simplicity
of new days with flame.
I know I have the blood of survivors

coursing through my veins;
I know the lament of our loss
must warm us again and again
down in the belly of the whale,

here in the belly of the whale
where we are still searching for homes.
We sing laments so old, so true,
then straighten our backs again.

KWAME DAWES

A Nineteenth-century Portrait

When Mister Robert Scarlett, master
of Cambridge and Druckett plantations, stood
for his portrait, the good man made a point
of having his personal slave-boy, Oliver,
beside him, waist high, holding his game bag,

with which he'd ride to hunt wild hog
and occasional runaways. At his other side
his favourite dog. How well the boy's
dark visage serves design,
matching the dark of the trees to cast
in relief the pale, proprietorial white.

Those were the good days; they didn't last.
After the slave revolts of 1831
great houses, factories, everything was gone;
only the family tomb remained.
And what of Oliver? History has left
no afterword; a boy in a picture,
a period-piece, on which poets may stretch out a fiction.

EDWARD BAUGH

Reward

RUN AWAY from this sub-
scriber for the second time
are TWO NEGROES, viz. SMART,
an outlandish dark fellow

with his country marks
on his temples and bearing
the remarkable brand of my
name on his left breast, last

seen wearing an old ragged
negro cloth shirt and breeches
made of fearnought; also DIDO,
a likely young wench of a yellow

cast, born in cherrytime in this
parish, wearing a mixed coloured
coat with a bundle of clothes,
mostly blue, under her one good

arm. Both speak tolerable plain
English and may insist on being
called Cuffee and Khasa respect-
ively. Whoever shall deliver

the said goods to the gaoler
in Baton Rouge, or to the Sugar
House in the parish, shall receive
all reasonable charges plus

a genteel reward besides what
the law allows. In the mean
time all persons are strictly
forbid harbouring them, on pain

of being prosecuted to the utmost
rigour of the law. Ten guineas
will be paid to anyone who can
give intelligence of their being

harboured, employed, or enter-
tained by a white person upon
his sentence; five on conviction
of a black. All Masters of vessels

are warned against carrying them
out of state, as they may claim
to be free. If any of the above
Negroes return of their own

accord, they may still be for-
given by

ELIZABETH YOUNG.

KEVIN YOUNG

How We Could Have Lived or Died This Way

Not songs of loyalty alone are these,
But songs of insurrection also,
For I am the sworn poet of every dauntless rebel the world over.

WALT WHITMAN

I see the dark-skinned bodies falling in the street as their ancestors fell
before the whip and steel, the last blood pooling, the last breath
    spitting.
I see the immigrant street vendor flashing his wallet to the cops,
shot so many times there are bullet holes in the soles of his feet.
I see the deaf woodcarver and his pocketknife, crossing the street
in front of a cop who yells, then fires. I see the drug raid, the wrong
door kicked in, the minister's heart seizing up. I see the man hawking
a fistful of cigarettes, the cop's chokehold that makes his wheezing
lungs stop wheezing forever. I am in the crowd, at the window,
kneeling beside the body left on the asphalt for hours, covered in a
    sheet.

I see the suicides: the conga player handcuffed for drumming on the
    subway,
hanged in the jail cell with his hands cuffed behind him; the suspect
    leaking
blood from his chest in the back seat of the squad car; the 300-pound
    boy
said to stampede barehanded into the bullets drilling his forehead.

I see the coroner nodding, the words he types in his report burrowing
into the skin like more bullets. I see the government investigations
    stacking,
words buzzing on the page, then suffocated as bees suffocate in a jar.
    I see
the next Black man, fleeing as the fugitive slave once fled the slave-
    catcher,
shot in the back for a broken tail light. I see the cop handcuff the
    corpse.

425

I see the rebels marching, hands upraised before the riot squads,
faces in bandannas against the tear gas, and I walk beside them unseen.
I see the poets, who will write the songs of insurrection generations
    unborn
will read or hear a century from now, words that make them wonder
how we could have lived or died this way, how the descendants of slaves
still fled and the descendants of slave-catchers still shot them, how we
    awoke
every morning without the blood of the dead sweating from every pore.

MARTÍN ESPADA

We Real Cool

The Pool Players.
Seven at the Golden Shovel

We real cool. We
Left school. We

Lurk late. We
Strike straight. We

Sing sin. We
Thin gin. We

Jazz June. We
Die soon.

GWENDOLYN BROOKS

The Golden Shovel

(after Gwendolyn Brooks)

I *1981*

When I am so small Da's sock covers my arm, we
cruise at twilight until we find the place the real

men lean, bloodshot and translucent with cool.
His smile is a gold-plated incantation as we

drift by women on bar stools, with nothing left
in them but approachlessness. This is a school

I do not know yet. But the cue sticks mean we
are rubbed by light, smooth as wood, the lurk

of smoke thinned to song. We won't be out late.
Standing in the middle of the street last night we

watched the moonlit lawns and a neighbor strike
his son in the face. A shadow knocked straight

Da promised to leave me everything: the shovel we
used to bury the dog, the words he loved to sing

his rusted pistol, his squeaky Bible, his sin.
The boy's sneakers were light on the road. We

watched him run to us looking wounded and thin.
He'd been caught lying or drinking his father's gin.

He'd been defending his ma, trying to be a man. We
stood in the road, and my father talked about jazz,

how sometimes a tune is born of outrage. By June
the boy would be locked upstate. That night we

got down on our knees in my room. *If I should die
before I wake*, Da said to me, *it will be too soon.*

Into the tented city we go, we-
akened by the fire's ethereal

afterglow. Born lost and cool-
er than heartache. What we

know is what we know. The left
hand severed and school-

ed by cleverness. A plate of we-
ekdays cooking. The hour lurk-

ing in the afterglow. A late-
night chant. Into the city we

go. Close your eyes and strike
a blow. Light can be straight-

ened by its shadow. What we
break is what we hold. A sing-

ular blue note. An outcry sin-
ged exiting the throat. We

push until we thin, thin-
king we won't creep back again.

While God licks his kin, we
sing until our blood is jazz,

we swing from June to June.
We sweat to keep from we-

eping. Groomed on a die-
t of hunger, we end too soon.

TERRANCE HAYES

American Sonnet: 94

nostrum nostalgia my notes on never nada no
collect against my reluctance/forced tabulations
dey did dis, say me, and dat and dat dere
why have there been no arrests? no hearings? no justice?
(what is not offered cannot be refused)

i regress/the despoiled child, the deserted schoolyard

weeper. this is your execution
weeper. this is your groveling stone
weeper. yours is the burst & burning of a city

stunned tearless in the uselessness of limp pursuit
breathlessness besets and bring the ass earthward

rest. the answer yellows and loses its wit, its crispness
my bed to make my heart to stake my soul to take

how i committed suicide: i revealed myself to you.
i trusted you. i forgot the color of my birth

WANDA COLEMAN

American Sonnet for My Past and Future Assassin

My mother says I am beautiful inside
And out. But my lover never believed it.
My lover never believed I held her name
In my mouth. My mother calls me her silver
Bullet. Her mercy pill, the metal along her spine.
I am my mother's bewildered shadow.
My lover's bewildering shadow is mine.

I have wept listening to a terrible bewildering
Music break over & through & break down
A black woman's voice. I talk to myself
Like her sister. Assassin, you are a mystery
To me, I say to my reflection sometimes.
You are beautiful because of your sadness, but
You would be more beautiful without your fear.

TERRANCE HAYES

American Sonnet for the New Year

things got terribly ugly incredibly quickly
things got ugly embarrassingly quickly
actually things got ugly unbelievably quickly
honestly things got ugly seemingly infrequently
initially things got ugly ironically usually
awfully carefully things got ugly unsuccessfully
occasionally things got ugly mostly painstakingly
quietly seemingly things got ugly beautifully
infrequently things got ugly sadly especially
frequently unfortunately things got ugly
increasingly obviously things got ugly suddenly
embarrassingly forcefully things got really ugly
regularly truly quickly things got really incredibly
ugly things will get less ugly inevitably hopefully

TERRANCE HAYES

That Chile Emmett in That Casket

Photo, *Jet magazine*, Sept. 15, 1955

Sometimes the page was tacked, flush against plaster with a pearl hatpin,
or jammed into a dime-store frame with a glowing Jesus. In some kingly

front rooms, its place was in the shadowbox, propped on one ripped edge,
or laid curly-cornered on the coffee table, smudged and eaten sheer

with the pass-around. In the kitchen, it was blurred by stew smoke
or pot liquor – blotched until somebody got smart enough to scotch-tape

it to door of the humming fridge, and the boy without eyes kept staring.
Mamas did the slow fold before wedging it into their flowered plastic

coin purses, daddies found a sacred place in pleather wallets right next
to the thought of cash. And at least once every week, usually on Sunday

after church or when you dared think you didn't have to speak proper
to that old white lady who answered the phone at your daddy's job,

or when, as Mama said, you *showed your ass* by sassin' or backtalking,
the page would be pulled down, pulled out, unfolded, smoothed flat,

and you had to look. *Look, boy.* And they made sure you kept looking
while your daddy shook his head, mumbling *This why you got to act*

right 'round white folk, then dropped his smoke-threaded gaze to whisper
Lord, they kilt that chile more than one time. Mama held on to your eyes –

See what happen when you don't be careful? She meant white men could
turn you into a stupid reason for a suit, that your last face would be silt,

stunned in its skid and worshipped, your right eye reborn in the cave
of your mouth. *Look!* she screeched. You did. But then you remembered

there weren't any pictures of *you* in the house, pinned high on the wall,
folded up tight up against the Lord, toted like talisman in wallet or purse.

You'd searched, woe climbing like river in your chest. But there were
no pictures of you anywhere. You sparked no moral. You were alive.

PATRICIA SMITH

Travelling As We Are

They hadn't launched their briefing.
They were still cocooned in
the flame of their tongues –
Martin Luther King, Malcolm X,
James Baldwin, etcetera.

My rage unignited
I sat enclosed underground,
British among Britons, only
there, in the nearly empty London
train, going to work.

    Look, Mummy, look, a nigger. Mummy
    niggers can sit here. Mummy, look.

She didn't glance once.
She wouldn't expose a wink.
She withdrew, hooded skilfully
till her southern American voice
trailed a sigh:

    So they can, Tim.
    So they can.

I knew the flight of mind. My
demeaning stressed her excellence,
as I had known it
in her southern US town.

But this is Europe, Mummy. How come
niggers live here too?

Tim and Sally Jane, when you get home
ask your daddy. You ask your daddy.

Here loaded together we
mattered much to each other,
our tomorrow and yesterday now,
stirring each other, without
a word or glance reciprocated.

An aching hatred left the train
with me. All day suspicion
spurred me. I spoke hastily.
Retaliation wrestled me.

JAMES BERRY

In-a Brixtan markit

I walk in-a Brixtan markit,
believin I a respectable man,
you know. An wha happn?

Policeman come straight up
an search mi bag!
Man – straight to me.
Like them did a-wait fi me.
Come search mi bag, man.

Fi mi bag!
An wha them si in deh?
Two piece of yam, a dasheen,
a han a banana, a piece a pork
an mi lates Bob Marley.

Man all a suddn I feel
mi head nah fi me. This yah now
is when man kill somody, nah!

'Tony,' I sey, 'hol on. Hol on,
Tony. Dohn shove. Dohn shove.
Dohn move neidda fis, tongue
nor emotion. Battn down, Tony.
Battn down.' An, man, Tony win.

JAMES BERRY

Smile

When I see a black man smiling
like that, nodding and smiling
with both hands visible, mouthing

'Yes, Officer', across the street,
I think of my father, who taught us
the words 'cooperate', 'officer',

to memorise badge numbers,
who has seen black men shot at
from behind in the warm months north.

And I think of the fine line –
hairline, eyelash, fingernail paring –
the whisper that separates

obsequious from *safe*. Armstrong,
Johnson, Robinson, Mays.
A woman with a yellow head

of cotton candy hair stumbles out
of a bar at after-lunchtime
clutching a black man's arm as if

for her life. And the brother
smiles, and his eyes are flint
as he watches all sides of the street.

ELIZABETH ALEXANDER

10-Year-Old Shot Three Times, But She's Fine

Dumbfounded in hospital whites, you are picture-book
itty-bit, floundering in bleach and steel. Braids untwirl
and corkscrew, you squirm, the crater in your shoulder
spews a soft voltage. On a TV screwed into the wall
above your head, neon rollicks. A wide-eyed train
engine perfectly smokes, warbles a song about *forward.*

Who shot you, baby?
I don't know. I was playing.
You didn't see anyone?
I was playing with my friend Sharon.
I was on the swing,
and she was –
Are you sure you didn't –
No, I ain't seen nobody but Sharon. I heard
people yelling though, and –

Each bullet repainted you against the brick, kicked
you a little sideways, made you need air differently.
You leaked something that still goldens the boulevard.
I ain't seen nobody, I told you.
And at A. Lincoln Elementary on Washington Street,
or Jefferson Elementary on Madison Street, or Adams
Elementary just off the Eisenhower Expressway,
we gather the ingredients, if not the desire, for pathos:

an imploded homeroom, your empty seat pulsating
with drooped celebrity, the sometime counselor
underpaid and elsewhere, a harried teacher struggling
toward your full name. Anyway your grades weren't
all that good. No need to coo or encircle anything,
no call for anyone to pull their official white fingers
through your raveled hair, no reason to introduce
the wild notion of loving you loud and regardless.

Oh, and they've finally located your mama, who
will soon burst in with her cut-rate cure of stammering
Jesus' name. Beneath the bandages, your chest crawls
shut. Perky ol' Thomas winks a bold-faced lie from
his clacking track, and your heart monitor hums
a wry tune no one will admit they've already heard.

Elsewhere, 23 seconds rumble again and again through
Sharon's body. *Boom, boom*, she says to no one.

PATRICIA SMITH

Bullet Points

I will not shoot myself
In the head, and I will not shoot myself
In the back, and I will not hang myself
With a trashbag, and if I do
I promise you, I will not do it
In a police car while handcuffed
Or in the jail cell of a town
I only know the name of
Because I have to drive through it
To get home. Yes, I may be at risk,
But I promise you, I trust the maggots
Who live beneath the floorboards
Of my house to do what they must

436

To any carcass more than I trust
An officer of the law of the land
To shut my eyes like a man
Of God might, or to cover me with a sheet
So clean my mother could have used it
To tuck me in. When I kill me, I will
Do it the same way most Americans do,
I promise you: cigarette smoke
Or a piece of meat on which I choke
Or so broke I freeze
In one of these winters we keep
Calling worst. I promise that if you hear
Of me dead anywhere near
A cop, then that cop killed me. He took
Me from us and left my body, which is,
No matter what we've been taught,
Greater than the settlement
A city can pay to a mother to stop crying,
And more beautiful than the new bullet
Fished from the folds of my brain.

JERICHO BROWN

the bullet was a girl

the bullet is his whole life.
his mother named him & the bullet

was on its way. in another life
the bullet was a girl & his skin

was a boy with a sad laugh.
they say *he asked for it* –

must I define *they*? they are not
monsters, or hooded or hands black

\with cross smoke.
they teachers, *they* pay tithes

they like rap, *they* police – good folks
gather around a boy's body

to take a picture, share a prayer.
oh da horror, oh what a shame

why'd he do that to himself?
they really should stop
getting themselves killed

DANEZ SMITH

supply and demand

the more black boys you have, the more you want.
you act like we're swimming in black boys.
you can't keep black boys in your pocket.
if you had a million black boys, what would you do with them?
do you think we're made of black boys?
your black boys are all tied up in property.
black boys won't solve all your problems.
you don't just find black boys lying in the street.
it takes black boys to make black boys.
most people don't know how to save black boys.
black boys don't grow on trees.

EVIE SHOCKLEY

mi skin

my skin my cast iron skin my equator skin my cast iron
equator skin my skin my scarring skin my grey scarring
skin my grey skin my asylum seeker skin my skin my
colorblind skin my smoke skin my color smoke skin   is
burning   my burning skin my cursed skin my cursed
skin   is burning   my skin my prayer skin my prayer
marshmallow skin my cloud marshmallow skin my
burning cloud skin my skin my marshmallow   skin
is burning   my skin my unreeled skin bare my bare
unreeled skin my capitulate skin my skin my blues skin
my limpid skin my limpid blues skin my skin my blues
is burning skin & my skin   is a home   my rust
skin   my skin rusts   my rust skin   is burning

oxidises

my skin oxidises my neutral skin my black neutral skin
my pinched off black neutral skin   is burning   my
picked skin my dry skin my dry skin   is burning   my
matured skin my matured skin is laundered skin my
laundered skin is skin my becoming skin my malleable
becoming skin my language skin   is malleable   my
skin   is burning   my miracle skin my annotation
skin my annotation miracle skin my mirror skin my
splinter skin my mirror splinter skin my magic conjuring
skin my #blackboymagic skin my black skin is conjuring
skin and boys are burning

DEAN BOWEN

translated from the Dutch by the author

The N Word

I

You sly devil. Lounging in a Pinter script
or pitched from a transit van's rolled-down window;
my shadow on this unlit road, though you've been
smuggled from polite conversation. So when
a friend of a friend has you poised on his lips
you are not what he means, no call for balled fist,
since he's only signifyin(g) on the sign;
making wine from the bad blood of history.
Think of how you came into my life that day,
of leaves strewn as I had never seen them strewn,
knocking me about the head with your dark hands.

II

> Pretty little lighty but I can get dark
>
> MZ BRATT, 'Get Dark'

You came back as rubber lips, pepper grains, blik
you're so black you're blik and how the word stuck to
our tongues eclipsing – or so we thought – all fear
that any moment anyone might notice
and we'd be deemed the wrong side of a night sky.
Lately you are a *pretty little lighty* who can
get dark because, even now, dark means street
which means beast which means leave now for Benfleet.
These days I can't watch a music video
online without you trolling in the comments
dressed to kill in your new age binary clothes.

KAYO CHINGONYI

Flounder

Here, she said, *put this on your head.*
She handed me a hat.
You 'bout as white as your dad,
and you gone stay like that.

Aunt Sugar rolled her nylons down
around each bony ankle,
and I rolled down my white knee socks
letting my thin legs dangle,

circling them just above water
and silver backs of minnows
flitting here then there between
the sun spots and the shadows.

This is how you hold the pole
to cast the line out straight.
Now put that worm on your hook,
throw it out and wait.

She sat spitting tobacco juice
into a coffee cup.
Hunkered down when she felt the bite,
jerked the pole straight up

reeling and tugging hard at the fish
that wriggled and tried to fight back.
A flounder, she said, *and you can tell*
'cause one of its sides is black.

The other side is white, she said.
It landed with a thump.
I stood there watching that fish flip-flop,
switch sides with every jump.

NATASHA TRETHEWEY

441

Help, 1968

(after a photograph from The Americans *by Robert Frank)*

When I see Frank's photograph
of a white infant in the dark arms
of a woman who must be the maid,
I think of my mother and the year
we spent alone – my father at sea.

The woman stands in profile, back
against a wall, holding her charge,
their faces side by side – the look
on the child's face strangely prescient,
a tiny furrow in the space
between her brows. Neither of them
looks toward the camera; nor
do they look at each other. That year,

when my mother took me for walks,
she was mistaken again and again
for my maid. Years later she told me
she'd say I was her daughter, and each time
strangers would stare in disbelief, then
empty the change from their pockets. Now

I think of the betrayals of flesh, how
she must have tried to make of her face
an inscrutable mask and hold it there
as they made their small offerings –
pressing coins into my hands. How
like the woman in the photograph
she must have seemed, carrying me
each day – white in her arms – as if
she were a prop: a black backdrop,
the dark foil in this American story.

NATASHA TRETHEWEY

Dance Class

The best girls posed like poodles at a show
and Betty Finch, in lemon gauze and wrinkles,
swept her wooden cane along the rows
to lock our knees in place and turn our ankles.
I was a scandal in that class, big-footed
giant in lycra, joker in my tap shoes,
slapping on the off-beat while a hundred
tappers hit the wood. I missed the cues
each time. After, in the foyer, dad,
a black man, stood among the Essex mothers
clad in leopard skin. He'd shake his keys
and scan the bloom of dancers where I hid
and whispered to another ballerina
he's the cab my mother sends for me.

HANNAH LOWE

Sausages

They hang from the washing line
between the tea towels and bleached sheets.
He has pegged them in neat clusters,
dark fingers of blood and gristle
with twisted ends and oily skins.
They flame against the trees.

She smells them from the backdoor –
ginger, clove and fennel. The house is quiet.
He is hiding from her. Her mother told her
not to marry a foreigner. *You always wanted
to be different* she hissed. *Now this. He's black
and old enough to be your father.*

The sausages are Chinese dragon red,
the red of a chilli, or a shamed face.
They gather fire, drying on her line.
This is Ilford, Essex, 1965.
The neighbours eat mince and cabbage
and talk about her.

She asked him not to do it
but they taste like home to him
and he is like good food to her.
Tonight they will eat sausages together
and she will lick the oil and spice
from his hands.

HANNAH LOWE

After Reading *Mickey in the Night Kitchen* for the Third Time Before Bed

> I'm the milk and the milk's in me!... I'm Mickey!

My daughter spreads her legs
to find her vagina:
hairless, this mistaken
bit of nomenclature
is what a stranger cannot touch
without her yelling. She demands
to see mine and momentarily
we're a lopsided star
among the spilled toys,
my prodigious scallops
exposed to her neat cameo.

And yet the same glazed
tunnel, layered sequences.
She is three; that makes this

innocent. *We're pink!*
she shrieks, and bounds off.

Every month she wants
to know where it hurts
and what the wrinkled string means
between my legs. *This is good blood*
I say, but that's wrong, too.
How to tell her that it's what makes us –
black mother, cream child.
That we're in the pink
and the pink's in us.

RITA DOVE

Jamaican British
(after Aaron Samuels)

Some people would deny that I'm Jamaican British.
Anglo nose. Hair straight. No way I can be Jamaican British.

They think I say I'm black when I say Jamaican British
but the English boys at school made me choose: Jamaican, British?

Half-caste, half mule, house slave – Jamaican British.
Light skin, straight male, privileged – Jamaican British.

Eat callaloo, plantain, jerk chicken – I'm Jamaican.
British don't know how to serve our dishes; they enslaved us.

In school I fought a boy in the lunch hall – Jamaican.
At home, told Dad, *I hate dem, all dem Jamaicans* – I'm British.

He laughed, said, *you cannot love sugar and hate your sweetness,*
took me straight to Jamaica – passport: British.

Cousins in Kingston called me Jah-English,
proud to have someone in their family – British.

Plantation lineage, World War service, how do I serve Jamaican British?
When knowing how to war is Jamaican British.

RAYMOND ANTROBUS

Cause

& to the burning I say
   worry is a whole country.

I've been myself longer
than my undoing –
       heavy trunk of silverware
museum glass polish
     portraiture
of bent flags.

I'm here as my grandparents were
     only with a moving mouth.

   During empire
my people were subjects first
citizens later   once the vigilantes
managed to zip up their coats

    flames lambent

my grandmother died with umbrellas
outstretched in her gut my grandmother
    died

    to be British
is to be everywhere.

<pre>
                Some roots
have been in the earth
        for so long
they know only to call themselves   earth.

A worm's pink nipple bleeds into snow.

        My birth
my mothers brown skin   I'd already
filled half myself   with Britannia's
air   it took them a month to find my name.
</pre>

ANTHONY ANAXAGOROU

Departure Lounge Twenty Seventeen

<pre>
Before Trump marshalled January
to do winter's work to breach fruit

        children peppered oceans
        like ends of warm bread

before Harvey Weinstein Tarana Burke
spoke smoke into a litany of nuns

        before functionaries filled death ledgers
        with names they mispronounced

before Theresa May triggered Article 50
crouched on a wet rooftop in Lisbon

        the departure lounge was heavy
        with pilots who no longer trusted the sky

& my grandmother is making her way
into a forest barefoot

before floral tributes crown
a Mancunian grief
</pre>

before *Celotex* expressed sympathies
for the seventy-two it turned into moons

& my grandmother is making her way
into a forest barefoot

before oceans reversed slowly into cages
like blue meat in a slaughterhouse

before the Pope prayed in apology
for the drift of the refugee crunching roaches

underfoot before Darren Osborne sat in a room
full of his mood watching *Three Girls* too loud

I wished to god
I could keep my wishing for my son

but before I turn I need to leave
the rubbish where it can be seen:

a mountain has abandoned snow
freezing hands to warn my heart

& no matter how many times I try forgetting
I still hear

my grandmother's name yelled into a forest
its bodies taking on water

chainsaws stressing honey at the root
I'm calling

but January keeps my voice for itself
dumping it where only wilderness breeds

lifting memory   spilling into cloud
before washing her feet   before clipping her nails
before watching her turn to face the gone

ANTHONY ANAXAGOROU

You and your partner go to see the film *The House We Live In*. You ask your friend to pick up your child from school. On your way home your phone rings. Your neighbor tells you he is standing at his window watching a menacing black guy casing both your homes. The guy is walking back and forth talking to himself and seems disturbed.

You tell your neighbor that your friend, whom he has met, is babysitting. He says, no, it's not him. He's met your friend and this isn't that nice young man. Anyway, he wants you to know, he's called the police.

Your partner calls your friend and asks him if there's a guy walking back and forth in front of your home. Your friend says that if anyone were outside he would see him because he is standing out-side. You hear the sirens through the speakerphone.

Your friend is speaking to your neighbor when you arrive home. The four police cars are gone. Your neighbor has apologised to your friend and is now apologising to you. Feeling somewhat responsible for the actions of your neighbor, you clumsily tell your friend that the next time he wants to talk on the phone he should just go in the backyard. He looks at you a long minute before saying he can speak on the phone wherever he wants. Yes, of course, you say. Yes, of course.

*

The new therapist specialises in trauma counseling. You have only ever spoken on the phone. Her house has a side gate that leads to a back entrance she uses for patients. You walk down a path bordered on both sides with deer grass and rosemary to the gate, which turns out to be locked.

At the front door the bell is a small round disc that you press firmly. When the door finally opens, the woman standing there yells, at the top of her lungs, Get away from my house. What are you doing in my yard?

It's as if a wounded Doberman pinscher or a German shepherd has gained the power of speech. And though you back up a few steps, you manage to tell her you have an appointment. You have an appointment? she spits back. Then she pauses. Everything pauses. Oh, she says, followed by, oh, yes, that's right. I am sorry.

I am so sorry, so, so sorry.

*

In line at the drugstore it's finally your turn, and then it's not as he walks in front of you and puts his things on the counter. The cashier says, Sir, she was next. When he turns to you he is truly surprised.

Oh my God, I didn't see you.

You must be in a hurry, you offer.

No, no, no, I really didn't see you.

CLAUDIA RANKINE

August 4, 2011 / In Memory of Mark Duggan

Though this house in London has been remodeled, the stairs, despite being carpeted, creak. What was imagined as a silent retreat from the party seems to sound through the house. By the fifth step you decide to sit down and on the wall next to you is a torn passport photo of half a woman's face blown up and framed as art. Where did you imagine you were going? you say aloud to her.

'The purpose of art,' James Baldwin wrote, 'is to lay bare the questions hidden by the answers.' He might have been channeling Dostoyevsky's statement that 'we have all the answers. It is the questions we do not know.'

Where can I imagine you have been?

A man, a novelist with the face of the English sky – full of weather, always in response, constantly shifting, clouding over only to clear briefly – stands before you, his head leaning against the same wall as the torn-up girl. You begin discussing the recent riots in Hackney. Despite what is being said you get lost in his face, his responsiveness bringing what reads as intimacy to his eyes. He says the riots were similar to the Rodney King–LA riots; however, he feels the UK media handled them very differently from the US media.

The Hackney riots began at the end of the summer of 2011 when Mark Duggan, a black man, a husband, a father, and a suspected drug dealer, was shot dead by officers from Scotland Yard's Operation Trident (a special operations unit addressing gun crime in black communities). As the rioting and looting continued, government officials labeled the violent outbreak 'opportunism' and 'sheer criminality', and the media picked up this language. Whatever the reason for the riots, images of the looters' continued rampage eventually displaced the fact that an unarmed man was shot to death.

In the United States, Rodney King's beating, caught on video, trumped all other images. If there had been a video of Duggan being executed, there might be less ambiguity around what started the riots, you hazard to say.

Will you write about Duggan? the man wants to know. Why don't you? you ask. Me? he asks, looking slightly irritated.

How difficult is it for one body to feel the injustice wheeled at another? Are the tensions, the recognitions, the disappointments, and the failures that exploded in the riots too foreign?

A similar accumulation and release drove many Americans to respond to the Rodney King beating. Before it happened, it had happened and happened. As a black body in the States, your response was necessary if you were to hold on to the fiction that this was an event 'wrongfully ordinary', therefore a snafu within the ordinary.

Though the moment had occurred and occurred again with the deaths, beatings, and imprisonment of other random, unarmed black men, Rodney King's beating somehow cut off the air supply in the US body politic by virtue of the excessive, blatant barrage of racism and compromised justice that followed on the heels of his beating. And though in this man's body, the man made of English sky, grief exists for Duggan as a black man gunned down, there is not the urgency brought on by an overflow of compromises, deaths, and tempers specific to a profile woke to and gone to sleep to each day.

Arguably, there is no simultaneity between the English sky and the body being ordered to rest in peace. This difference, which has to do with 'the war (the black body's) presence has occasioned', to quote Baldwin, makes all the difference. One could become acquainted with the inflammation that existed around Duggan's body and it would be uncomfortable. Grief comes out of relationships to subjects over time and not to any subject in theory, you tell the English sky, to give him an out. The distance between you and him is thrown into relief: bodies moving through the same life differently. With your eyes wide open you consider what this man and you, two middle-aged artists, in a house worth more than a million pounds, share with Duggan. Mark Duggan, you are part of the misery. Apparently your new friend won't write about Mark Duggan or the London riots; still you continue searching his face because there is something to find, an answer to question.

CLAUDIA RANKINE

from ...they killed them

Will you write about Duggan? the man wants to know. Why don't you?
CLAUDIA RANKINE

Jean Charles de Menezes, 2005

Kratos will be born out of fear and anxiety
coming alive in the midst of London bombings

inheriting the traits of Nike and Bia and Zelus
chasing after fugitives on the run looking dark like us

Zelus will ignore confirmation of said suspect
and will run with Bia from Scotia Road

with the determination of Nike and the need to protect
blindly following the man with 'Mongolian eyes'

Escaping the farms of Brazil the violence of the favellas
an electrician who came to the city of Big Ben
where opportunities ring out for hard-working men
he leaves home in the fervour of a summer day
from bus to closed station from bus to open station
he buys a newspaper walks through a ticket barrier
runs to catch the tube sitting breathless
as strangers advance towards him

And bind him by his arms on a train
And shoot him nine times in the head

Operation Kratos guidelines allowed officers to shoot without warning, since
issuing a warning could allow a potential suicide bomber to detonate a device.

Mark Duggan, 2011

> He wasn't an angel, but if you are brought up in a place like
> the Broadwater Farm estate, you better not be an angel because
> you won't survive.
>
> STAFFORD SCOTT, veteran community activist
> (Hugh Muir: Tottenham riots: *The Guardian*)

Murdered   Survived
    Because there *are very few angels on Broadwater Farm*
        Planning an attack   Just transporting
           In possession of a firearm
One of Britain's most violent gangsters   a son, father, brother &
                                      multiple partners
      being followed, tyres screeching, officers shouting
He's reaching, he's reaching   He's raising his hands holding a phone
  two shots in the arm & chest   a plume of feathers filling the air
                He was no angel
holding a gun, throwing it away not holding a gun, hands held high
    a gun was found on the green   nobody saw the gun fly away
             the gun in the black sock
        There are no angels to be found
    in the shadows of the death of PC Blakelock.

ROY McFARLANE

dinosaurs in the hood

let's make a movie called *Dinosaurs in the Hood*.
Jurassic Park meets *Friday* meets *The Pursuit of Happyness*.
there should be a scene where a little black boy is playing
with a toy dinosaur on the bus, then looks out the window
& sees the *T. rex*, because there has to be a *T. rex*.

don't let Tarantino direct this. in his version, the boy plays
with a gun, the metaphor: black boys toy with their own lives,
the foreshadow to his end, the spitting image of his father.
nah, the kid has a plastic brontosaurus or triceratops
& this is his proof of magic or God or Santa. i want a scene

where a cop car gets pooped on by a pterodactyl, a scene
where the corner store turns into a battleground. don't let
the Wayans brothers in this movie. i don't want any racist shit
about Asian people or overused Latino stereotypes.
this movie is about a neighborhood of royal folks —

children of slaves & immigrants & addicts & exile — saving their town
from real ass dinosaurs. i don't want some cheesy, yet progressive
Hmong sexy hot dude hero with a funny, yet strong, commanding
Black girl buddy-cop film. this is not a vehicle for Will Smith
& Sofia Vergara. i want grandmas on the front porch taking out raptors

with guns they hid in walls & under mattresses. I want those little spitty,
screamy dinosaurs. i want Cicely Tyson to make a speech, maybe two.
i want Viola Davis to save the city in the last scene with a black fist afro pick
through the last dinosaur's long, cold-blood neck. but this can't be
a black movie. this can't be a black movie. this movie can't be dismissed

because of its cast or its audience. this movie can't be a metaphor
for black people & extinction. this movie can't be about race.
this movie can't be about black pain or cause black people pain.
this movie can't be about a long history of having a long history with hurt.
this movie can't be about race. nobody can say nigga in this movie

who can't say it to my face in public. no chicken jokes in this movie.
no bullets in the heroes. & no one kills the black boy. & no one kills
the black boy. & no one kills the black boy. besides, the only reason
i want to make this is for that first scene anyway: the little black boy
on the bus with a toy dinosaur, his eyes wide & endless

> his dreams possible, pulsing, & right there.

DANEZ SMITH

Slow Food

I would like to feed this child who is dying with slow food,
So that time might stand still for him, so that a grandfather
Clock might not fall apart in his arms. All of the laziness of air

In our warm temperate climate, all the anxious hands
Of young barristers at this morning's Farmers' Market,
All of this complete snobbery of the gut, might bear down

Upon one dying child. Here is my Euro, child. Here is
The olive oil and the stuffed artichoke. Here is the conscience
And the conscience money. They stole my land too,

They took my small cottage apart, stone by stone.
They surveyed all of us and we nearly died. I am sending, child,
Very fast Irish food from my evicted great grandmother.

THOMAS McCARTHY

A Century Later

The school-bell is a call to battle,
every step to class, a step into the firing-line.
Here is the target, fine skin at the temple,
cheek still rounded from being fifteen.

Surrendered, surrounded, she
takes the bullet in the head

and walks on. The missile cuts
a pathway in her mind, to an orchard
in full bloom, a field humming under the sun,
its lap open and full of poppies.

This girl has won
the right to be ordinary,

wear bangles to a wedding, paint her fingernails,
go to school. *Bullet*, she says, *you are stupid.*
You have failed. You cannot kill a book
or the buzzing in it.

A murmur, a swarm. Behind her, one by one,
the schoolgirls are standing up
to take their places on the front line.

IMTIAZ DHARKER

Poetry

The day before yesterday there was war
yesterday was the same
and it's still war in my time
time that's not just mine

money prowls around the world
and finances itself with war

war may not speak its name
it's called defence

poetry is the brushwood
in which I'll hide
when the soldiers come
in their screaming tanks

REMCO CAMPERT
translated from the Dutch by Donald Gardner

Safe House

When they were beginning to build a country
some of the men came to hide in a house
where there was a family, and a child upstairs,
listening. They told him what to say if anyone

ever asked. Say they were never there.
Say there was only a family in that house.
And during the night the boy went to the room
where their bags and belongings were hidden.

He felt along the canvases, the mouldy wet
and sag of the straps. His fingers touched on
papers and coins, and lifted out the revolver,
its coolness and the weight of it in his hands.

Then he felt nothing. His blood crept slowly
and dark along the floorboards, underneath them,
and the room shook, and stood still,
and seemed to hang for a moment in that night.

When they found him they cleaned him,
his face, gently and quickly, and his mother
wrapped him in a blanket and took him
out to a corner of the farm and buried him.

Back in the house they gathered his things,
and built up a fire again in the kitchen,
burning his clothes, his shoes, all the signs
and small, clumsy turnings of a child.

And afterwards, in the freezing dark, the father
went out to find the doctor and the parish priest
to tell them what had happened, and what they
should say if anyone ever asked.

Tell them there was never a child.
Say they were never there.
There was never a home
or the found, easy measures of a family.

There was never a map that could lead back to
or out of that place, foreknown or imagined,
where the furze, the dark-rooted vetch, turned
over and over with the old ground and disappeared.

LEANNE O'SULLIVAN

We Lived Happily during the War

And when they bombed other people's houses, we

protested
but not enough, we opposed them but not

enough. I was
in my bed, around my bed America

was falling: invisible house by invisible house by invisible house.

I took a chair outside and watched the sun.

In the sixth month
of a disastrous reign in the house of money

in the street of money in the city of money in the country of money,
our great country of money, we (forgive us)

lived happily during the war.

ILYA KAMINSKY

In a Time of Peace

Inhabitant of earth for forty-something years
I once found myself in a peaceful country. I watch the neighbors open
        their phones

to watch a cop demanding a man's driver's license and
when the man reaches for his wallet, the cop
shoots. Into the car window. Shoots.

It is a peaceful country.

We pocket our phones and go.
To the dentist,
to buy shampoo,
pick up the children from school,
get basil.

Ours is a country in which a boy shot by police lies on the pavement
for hours.
We see in his open mouth
the nakedness
of the whole nation.

We watch. Watch
others watch.
The body of a boy lies on the pavement exactly like the body of a boy.

It is a peaceful country.

And it clips our citizens' bodies
effortlessly, the way the president's wife trims her toenails.

All of us
still have to do the hard work of dentist appointments,
of remembering to make
a summer salad: basil, tomatoes, it is a joy, tomatoes, add a little salt.

This is a time of peace.

I do not hear gunshots,
but watch birds splash over the backyards of the suburbs. How
    bright is the sky
as the avenue spins on its axis.
How bright is the sky (forgive me) how bright.

ILYA KAMINSKY

Breathing

Like the pith around a piece of fruit
or the bound parcels of the clouds,
memory breathes like an invisible world.

From the outside it doesn't exist, or is only silence.

From the inside it is a going forth of bulldozers,
of charged cells, of ant soldiers
shifting in disarray.

LUIS MUÑOZ
translated from the Spanish by Curtis Bauer

If They Come for Us

these are my people & I find
them on the street & shadow
through any wild all wild
my people my people
a dance of strangers in my blood
the old woman's sari dissolving to wind
bindi a new moon on her forehead
I claim her my kin & sew

the star of her to my breast
the toddler dangling from stroller
hair a fountain of dandelion seed
at the bakery I claim them too
the Sikh uncle at the airport
who apologises for the pat
down the Muslim man who abandons
his car at the traffic light drops
to his knees at the call of the Azan
& the Muslim man who drinks
good whiskey at the start of maghrib
the lone khala at the park
pairing her kurta with crocs
my people my people I can't be lost
when I see you my compass
is brown & gold & blood
my compass a Muslim teenager
snapback & high-tops gracing
the subway platform
Mashallah I claim them all
my country is made
in my people's image
if they come for you they
come for me too in the dead
of winter a flock of
aunties step out on the sand
their dupattas turn to ocean
a colony of uncles grind their palms
& a thousand jasmines bell the air
my people I follow you like constellations
we hear the glass smashing the street
& the nights opening dark
our names this country's wood
for the fire my people my people
the long years we've survived the long
years yet to come I see you map
my sky the light your lantern long
ahead & I follow I follow

FATIMAH ASGHAR

Look

It matters what you call a thing: *Exquisite* a lover called me. *Exquisite.*

Whereas *Well, if I were from your culture, living in this country*, said the man outside the 2004 Republican National Convention, *I would put up with that for this country;*

Whereas I felt the need to clarify: *You would put up with* TORTURE, *you mean* and he proclaimed: *Yes;*

Whereas what is your life;

Whereas years after they LOOK down from their jets and declare my mother's Abadan block PROBABLY DESTROYED, we walked by the villas, the faces of buildings torn off into dioramas, and recorded it on a handheld camcorder;

Whereas it could take as long as 16 seconds between the trigger pulled in Las Vegas and the Hellfire missile landing in Mazar-e-Sharif, after which they will ask *Did we hit a child? No. A dog.* they will answer themselves;

Whereas the federal judge at the sentencing hearing said *I want to make sure I pronounce the defendant's name correctly;*

Whereas this lover would pronounce my name and call me *Exquisite* and lay the floor lamp across the floor, softening even the light;

Whereas the lover made my heat rise, rise so that if heat sensors were trained on me, they could read my THERMAL SHADOW through the roof and through the wardrobe;

Whereas *you know we ran into like groups like mass executions. w/ hands tied behind their backs. and everybody shot in the head side by side. it's not like seeing a dead body walking to the grocery store here. it's not like that. it's iraq you know it's iraq. it's kinda like acceptable to see that there and not—it was kinda like seeing a dead dog or a dead cat lying—;*

463

Whereas I thought if he would LOOK at my exquisite face or my father's, he would reconsider;

Whereas *You mean I should be disappeared because of my family name?* and he answered *Yes. That's exactly what I mean*, adding that his wife helped draft the PATRIOT Act;

Whereas the federal judge wanted to be sure he was pronouncing the defendant's name correctly and said he had read all the exhibits, which included the letter I wrote to cast the defendant in a loving light;

Whereas today we celebrate things like his transfer to a detention center closer to home;

Whereas his son has moved across the country;

Whereas I made nothing happen;

Whereas *ye know not what shall be on the morrow. For what is your life?* It is even a THERMAL SHADOW, it appears so little, and then vanishes from the screen;

Whereas I cannot control my own heat and it can take as long as 16 seconds between the trigger, the Hellfire missile, and *A dog.* they will answer themselves;

Whereas *A dog.* they will say: Now, therefore,

Let it matter what we call a thing.

Let it be the exquisite face for at least 16 seconds.

Let me LOOK at you.

Let me LOOK at you in a light that takes years to get here.

SOLMAZ SHARIF

Thursday

I'm trying to get to work earlier and make the
short walk from Fenchurch Street Station to
the tube at Tower Hill where a guard is pulling
across the gate and commuters are being evacuated
through the gap and he says it might be closed for
ten minutes half an hour and I think typical walk
back the way I came and on towards Monument
where it's closed again and this guard says power
failure so I walk towards Bank posting a birthday
card to my sister's boyfriend and at the entrance
to Bank it's the same so I phone my mum who I
know will have the radio on but she says there's
nothing on the travel news you should get a bus
to Victoria so I locate a bus going to Victoria and
follow it to the bus stop and join the crowd that's
formed to wait for the next one and finally it comes
but it's jammed and I watch with admiration as
people with more balls than I'll ever have leap on
through the exit doors until the driver gets wise
and shuts them so I go and find another bus stop
and settle for a bus to Waterloo with a seat and tell
myself I'm not late yet I'm getting a different view
of the city and then I hear the man behind say
explosion and coming down the stairs a text arrives
from my friend at work asking if I'm ok and so I
phone her and tell her I'm fine and ask her which is
the best bus to catch to Pimlico and then I try my
mum but now she's engaged and I'm standing opposite
the Shell building where my grandma worked hoping
for a 507 and my mum rings and says it's bad but all
my family members are safe in their offices and I'm
not to get on any more buses so I start walking through
the sirens aiming for the building where my desk is
waiting exactly the way I left it yesterday evening.

LORRAINE MARINER

The Burning of the Houses

Tottenham is on fire and I work in an arts centre
where the sky is blue and I can hear birdsong
from a sound installation of birds
cooing outside my office window.
This is London. Hackney is on fire now
and Jamie is looking up from his desk.
He stops working. He tweets that he can see
people smashing up a bus. He says there is a car
being soaked in petrol. He asks if there is someone
in that car. He tells us that car has been set alight.
This is London. Croydon is on fire now
and Anna is Facebooking furiously from Manchester
calling everyone bastards for doing this.
I am watching the BBC and reading Twitter
flicking between #LondonRiot and my friends.
Sometimes you can be proud of your friends.
I remember when Bianca came to stay
and we got tickets to watch *The Night
James Brown Saved Boston* in the QEH.
People are getting hurt. Television isn't going
to save us. But it's okay now, some of my friends
are linking to videos of kittens which must mean
everything is fine. This is London. It is on fire.
I go to bed while it is burning. I wake up
and parts of it are still burning.

CHRISSY WILLIAMS

The Garden

The streetlights shed pearls that night,
stray dogs ran but did not bark at the strange
shadows; the Minister of All could not sleep,

mosquitoes swarmed around his net,
his portrait and his pitcher and drinking glass;
the flags stiffened on the embassy building but
did not fall when the machine guns
flared and reminded that stars were inside
the decrepit towns, in shanty-zinc holes,
staring at the fixed constellation; another
asthmatic whirl of pistons passed,
the chandelier fell, the carpet sparkled,
flames burst into the lantana bushes, the stone
horse whinnied by the bank's marble entrance,
three large cranes with searchlights lit
the poincianas, a quiet flamboyance, struck
with the fever of children's laughter;
then, all at once, the cabbage palms
and the bull-hoof trees shut their fans,
the harbour grew empty and heavy,
the sea was sick and exhausted, the royal
palms did not salute when the jeeps roamed
up the driveway and circled the fountain,
the blue mahoe did not bow and the lignum
vitae shed purple bugles but did not
surrender, the homeless did not run, but the dead
flew in a silver stream that night, their silk
hair thundered and their heels crushed
the bissy nuts and ceramic roofs;
the night had the scent of cut grass
sprayed with poison, the night smelled
of bullets, the moon did not hide,
the prisoners prayed in their bunkers,
the baby drank milk while its mother slept,
and by the window its father
could not part the curtains.

ISHION HUTCHINSON

Selling Out
(for Mat Johnson)

Off from a double at McDonald's,
no autumnal piñata, no dying
leaves crumbling to bits of colored
paper on the sidewalks only yesterday,
just each breath bursting to explosive fog
in a dead-end alley near Fifth, where on
my knees, with my fingers laced on my head
and a square barrel prodding a temple,
I thought of me in the afterlife.
Moments ago, Chris Wilder and I
jogged down Girard, lost in the promise
of two girls who winked past pitched
lanes of burgers and square chips
of fish, at us, reigning over grills and vats.
Moments ago, a barrage of beepers
and timers smeared the lengths of our chests.
A swarm of hard-hatted dayworkers
coated in white dust, mothers on relief,
the minimum-waged poor from the fast-
food joints lining Broad, inched us closer
to a check-cashing line towards the window
of our dreams,—all of us anxious to enact
the power of our riches: me in the afterlife.
What did it matter, Chris and I still
in our polyester uniforms caked
with day-old batter, setting out
for an evening of passion marks?
We wore Gazelles, matching sheepskins
and the ushanka, miles from Leningrad.
Chris said, *Let's first cop some blow* despite
my schoolboy jitters. A loose spread
of dealers preserved corners. Then a kid,
large for the chrome Huffy he pedaled,
said he had the white stuff and led us
to an alley fronted by an iron gate on

a gentrified street edging Northern Liberties.
I turned to tell Chris how the night
air dissolved like soil, how jangling
keys made my neck itch, how maybe
this wasn't so good an idea, when
the cold opening of gun-barrel
steel poked my head, and Chris's eyes
widened like two water spills before
he bound away into a future of headphones
and release parties. Me? The afterlife?
Had I ever welcomed back the old
neighborhood? Might a longing
persistent as the seedcorn maggot
tunnel through me? All I know:
a single dog barked his own vapor,
an emptiness echoed through blasted
shells of rowhomes rising above,
and I heard deliverance in the bare
branches fingering a series of powerlines
in silhouette to the moon's hushed
excursion across the battered fields
of our lives, that endless night
of ricocheting fear and shame.
No one survives, no one unclasps
his few strands of gold chains
or hums 'Amazing Grace' or pours
all his measly bills and coins into the trembling,
free hand of his brother and survives.
No one is forced facedown and waits
forty minutes to rise and begin again
his march, past the ice-crusted dirt,
without friendship or love, who barely knew
why the cry of the earth set him running,
even from the season's string of lights,
flashing its pathetic shot at cheer—to arrive
here, where the page is blank, an afterlife.

MAJOR JACKSON

from **Surge**

Clearing

He takes my head and places it in a plastic bag

downstairs, two officers stamp their feet
blow into their hands

the windows are cups of water filled with winter

he holds the bag open, searching
for a gaze to meet

cold
thirsts at the bones

he doesn't see me standing there
he doesn't hear me speak

an officer circles the front yard leaning
back to see the smoke

         or is it steam

is it fire or water that can bring a child back

elide that which is heavy in his hand
and that which watches from the corner of the room

this house is a gas lamp
soot frosts its glasswhite gut

the officer closes his eyes
two blank pennies in a fount

from the bag I watch his face turn away
from the corner his body bending towards mine

+

the officer said – oh, it's very common for culprits to go missing –
I said my son isn't a culprit, and how dare he imply it – and one
of the officers stood up by the window and looked out – he didn't
want to look us full in the eye – he made it clear, he made it clear
– from the moment he set foot in the house – the moment he set
foot – what he thought of us – and when they come back a few
days later – I think the Tuesday, I think the Tuesday – they said
what were you wearing on the night of the fire? – I said probably
– probably – your new trousers – and he said was you wearing a
yellow shirt? – I said yes – Brown shoes? – I said yes – and he
took out the items from a plastic bag – he took your things from a
plastic bag – and he says does this look like it? Does this look like
it belongs to you? – I says yes – and he says do you recognise this
key? – I said why don't we try it – and we struggled – and it fit –
I'm sorry, I'm so sorry, I'm so sorry – so I said what are you sorry
for? I want to see my son – stammer, stammer, they say they don't
think it is a good idea – I said, I am your father – I said, I said, I
am your father – your father – I want to see you –

                    – they led us down to a room – and on the
table there you was – no face, nothing to speak of – I said – I said
– this is the body where you found the clothes? – nod, nod – So I
said, it must be you – this must be my son

-

You came, dad –

        – I had been lying there all night – and I couldn't move.
I opened my eyes and I was in the house and everything was black,
dad – I had been at the party a few hours and I didn't know any-
thing about what happened, dad – and I felt someone touch me,
but I was stiff, dad – I never been so stiff before – I tried to say
it's me, it's me – but they were looking at me so strangely, dad –
like he couldn't stand to look at me – couldn't stand the sight of

me – Police always looked at me like that – and he turned me over
– and he took the shirt from under me, and they wrapped me in a
blanket and drove me here – and I was lying there waiting for you,
dad – across the table, there were bodies, dad – Twisted, dad – no
heads – like screaming branches of a tree, dad – loads of them, loads
of them, I swear – and I heard them say – they were saying –

And then you came and I was calling out to you, dad
– and I know you heard me because here we are, dad – come back
– don't bury me – I can't stand it – I can barely stand it when the
lights go off – and I'm here – and spend the whole night listening
for you dad – I want to crawl between mum and you – in your
bed, in your sheets, dad – that's the only kind of burying I want –

JAY BERNARD

Doppelgänger

A week after the building burned
I saw my dead wife; she smiled at me.

Right now it's hard for me
to tell the living from the dead.

My wedding ring is sinking
into my swollen finger.

There is pressure building there;
but I do not want to use soap to slide it off.

Even though she is dead
I am still married to her.

I see children playing
who look like my wife when she was young.

I knew my wife when she was young.
I wanted to talk to her, this woman

who looked liked my wife;
I wanted to hold her

but what I really wanted was my wife,
who is dead.

As I trace my thumb
over the silver ring.

ROGER ROBINSON

The Portrait Museum

The morning after, the streets filled with portraits
of missing people – brothers with bushy beards,

olive-skinned, wrinkle-faced grandmothers,
pig-tailed daughters with red ribbons, smiling –

stuck on tree trunks, walls and fence boards,
the neon red MISSING floating above their heads.

In a minute of pure clairvoyance we understand
that many of these pictures are the faces of the dead,

some looking like they were saying the word goodbye
as the picture was shot at a family gathering.

Without sleep, some struggle to keep their posters
straight, stop the sellotape sticking to itself.

These were the flimsy paper faces of hope for the living;
those not taped well are blown away on the breeze.

Many with posters refuse this first day of mourning;
as days went on, the wind blew most of them away.

ROGER ROBINSON

The Father

This twelve-year-old girl, doing an interview on the TV about her father being missing after the fire, is becoming her father. She is already head and shoulders above her mother who stands behind her, red-rimmed eyes darting with worry. Note when the interviewer asks how she feels, the daughter starts becoming her father. She concentrates her answer on the actions she must take, the things that are directly within her control. Days later she will fill in the forms necessary for them to get new housing. She will wake up her mother, weak with grief, and bring to her bed fattet hummus and makdous with olive oil and za'tar. She will make her mother have a shower in the morning and comb her mother's hair and lay her clothes on the bed. She has taken to reading several newspapers while drinking strong cardamom-flavoured coffee while Umm Kulthum is singing about her heart on the radio.

ROGER ROBINSON

The Boundary

The boundary between my life and another's death
passes through the sofa in front of the TV,
a pious shoreline where we receive
our daily bread of horror.
Faced with the sublime injustice
that has dragged us ashore to let us
contemplate the shipwreck, to be just
represents the minimum coin
of decency we can bestow on ourselves,
beggars of sense,
and on the god who with impunity
has made us comfortable on dry land,
on the right side of the screen.

VALERIO MAGRELLI
translated from the Italian by Jamie McKendrick

Bellwether

At first it was nothing – a thought, a cough in a gale
then just a voice, then another, till none could be heard
but all spoke as one. And some called it chatter
and some called it rumour. And soon came a leader

who cut through the babble to what we were saying,
told us why and to who, and now we were more
than the sum of ourselves. Some called it bigotry,
others theology. On you led till nothing could

touch us, till each glance we caught looked away
and no challenge came. Loyal to a fault we pressed on
in your wake. To some a messiah, to the rest a base liar,
we were all on a bandwagon now and – hazard or bluff,

right to the brink – some called it hate, some called it love.

ANDRÉ MANGEOT

Eating Thistles

We ate thistles, and spoke a language
as sharp and barbed as the wire on their walls.

We slept on stone, bathed in snow,
made combs from thorns, clothes from nettles.

Words froze on our tongues
and fell in frozen lumps on barren land.

In their cities and in their towns
they gloried in victory, a nation once again.

We heard their pipes and their drums,
gunshot, fireworks, songs of celebration.

Maddened by power, powered by madness,
they closed their borders, then turned against their own.

Better to sleep on stone, however hard,
better to eat thistles, though we choke,

better our frozen silence than their fiery rhetoric,
better thorns and nettles than pomp and glory,

better to die in a barren wilderness
than to survive in a nation born of vanity.

DEBORAH MOFFATT

Dispute Over a Mass Grave

The one you have finished examining
is my son. That is the milky coloured Kurdish
suit his father tailored for him, the blue shirt
his uncle gave to him. Your findings prove
that it is him – he was a tall fifteen year old,
was left handed, had broken a rib.

I know she too has been looking for her son
but you have to tell her that this is not him.
Yes the two of them were playmates and fought
the year before. But it was my son who broke
a rib, hers only feigned to escape trouble.

That one is mine! Please give him back to me.
I will bury him on the verge of my garden –
the mulberry tree will offer him its shadow,
the flowers will earnestly guard his grave,
the hens will peck on his gravestone,
the beehive will hum above his head.

CHOMAN HARDI

A Day for Love

This is the day for love, the day not to think
of wars, to tell violence: 'we have had enough,
stand in the corner on one foot', give poverty
a loaf of bread so that it can snooze, warn oppression
to be careful: 'An oppressor is on the way.'

This is the day to remember
our first kiss, the first whisper,
the smell of your hands in the lavender garden,
the youthful rain, lush behind you and your oblivion
as you drenched yourself in the colour of my eyes.

We have this day for gratitude
so that I can thank you, thank God that you
are mine. Thanks for all the mornings when we
enclose our daughter like closed brackets
and I want to cry.

Please don't steal the day from us. Don't
tell us about the girl who was murdered in her sleep.
Don't show images of the foetus, shot dead inside
her mother. Don't tell us about the stupidity of leaders,
the folly of politicians, the brutality of humans.

We want to hold on to this moment today,
to think about love's voice, colour and taste.
Please leave this day to us. And don't worry,
tomorrow we will roll up our sleeves once again,
we will listen out. We will be here

to write another letter against oppression,
to sign another petition against injustice.
But today, let us be, to consider our love.

CHOMAN HARDI
translated from the Kurdish by the author

Chorus from The Cure at Troy

Human beings suffer.
They torture one another.
They get hurt and get hard.
No poem or play or song
Can fully right a wrong
Inflicted and endured.

History says, Don't hope
On the side of the grave,
But then, once in a lifetime
The longed-for tidal wave
Of justice can rise up
And hope and history rhyme.

So hope for a great sea-change
On the far side of revenge.
Believe that a farther shore
Is reachable from here.
Believe in miracles.
And cures and healing wells.

Call miracle self-healing,
The utter self-revealing
Double-take of feeling.
If there's fire on the mountain
And lightning and storm
And a god speaks from the sky

That means someone is hearing
The outcry and the birth-cry
Of new life at its term.
It means once in a lifetime
That justice can rise up
And hope and history rhyme.

SEAMUS HEANEY

10

The future?

The vast majority of scientists agree that global warming is real, it's already happening and that it is the result of our activities and not a natural occurrence. The evidence is overwhelming and undeniable. We're already seeing changes. Glaciers are melting, plants and animals are being forced from their habitats, and the number of severe storms and droughts is increasing.

AL GORE (2006)

The poems in this section extend the territory covered in my Bloodaxe anthology *Earth Shattering: ecopoems* (2007) whose particular focus is ecological balance and environmental destruction. Ecopoetry goes beyond traditional nature poetry to take on distinctly contemporary issues, recognising the interdependence of all life on earth, the wildness and otherness of nature, and the irresponsibility of our attempts to tame and plunder nature.

These concerns are encapsulated in the final poem of *Staying Human*, Nick Drake's 'The Future' (498), a later version of a section from *The Farewell Glacier* (2012), a book of poems which grew out of a journey he made to the High Arctic in 2010 with Cape Farewell, the arts climate change organisation. Sailing close to the vast glaciers that dominate the archipelago of Svalbad north of Norway, they saw clear evidence of the effects of climate change on the ecosystem including polar bear prints on pieces of pack ice floating in the water.

This anthology is published in the year of the coronavirus pandemic, and I have extended this section to include a number of poems written in response to this global crisis. Many more are being written and will be written, but these ten in particular struck me as especially relevant to this book's concerns and likely to have continuing resonance in what they record. Peter Sirr's 'Ode' (492) celebrates the power of music to bring people together, describing how Italians trapped at home gave spontaneous musical performances from their balconies. Gerda Stevenson's 'Hands' (493) is about taking part in the weekly national applause for National Health Service workers, in rural Scotland. David Tait's two poems draw on his experience as someone who lives and works in China; Ruth Padel gives a global view from London, while Imtiaz Dharker switches from London to India; Amit Majmudar and Joshua Bennett add an American perspective. Seven of the poems were among the first to be published on the *WRITE where we are NOW* project website set up by Carol Ann Duffy at Manchester Writing School to bring together responses to the pandemic from poets around the world.

Lockdowns and travel restrictions imposed by governments across the world have caused a temporary reduction in global pollution. The main cause of environmental destruction – globalisation – is now itself threatened by environmental forces, in the form of a global plague. How that interaction will play out in years to come will be the subject of ecopoetry of the future.

Stranger Thing

(The Whitechapel fatberg, c/o the Museum of London)

Chip fat, cold shits, dead paints, hate mail, grease,
used wet-wipes, condoms, nappies, cotton buds,
paracetamol, toenail-crescents, needles, hair –

the dregs, swill, scum, muck, slop we flush away
are harvest festival for the moony monster
who rules the empire of the upside down

beneath the illusion of floorboards, parks and streets;
stranger thing, behemoth, lonely ogre, shy
Caliban created by our multitudes,

dreaming where the sewers slowly flow
through whispering galleries and gargoyle crypts,
bringing offerings to the awful sanctuary.

We sent our heroes down in hazmat suits
to besiege it; now these abominable lumps
festering in sealed and chilled vitrines

on live-feed for the curiosity of the world
are all that's left. The glass holds our reflections,
the beautiful ones who love to scare ourselves,

taking selfies with the alien bogey-beast,
our nightmare mirror image even now
regenerating in the dark beneath our feet.

NICK DRAKE

A fatberg is a huge, congealed lump of oil, rubbish and waste which blocks the sewers beneath a city. The largest fatberg recorded was under Whitechapel. It is estimated to have weighed 130 tonnes – two jumbo jets – and was 250 metres long. The Museum of London conserved and displayed samples of it in *Fatberg!* (2018). Vyki Sparkes, the curator, noted: *It's grand, magnificent, fascinating and disgusting. The perfect museum object!* [ND]

The Great Pacific Garbage Patch

All century trash floated round the gyre
of the Pacific: bright and shiny, shoes
baked themselves open, grew weedy gills,
shoals of rolling bottles nudged each other,
blister packs burst delicately –
the scent of rubber wove itself round
chair legs like a cat.
     There were swirls of wilted condoms,
ribbed and stippled, a shining dummy teat,
slowly turning tyres: the stuff of shucked
and cast-off lives, cresting rills of milky foam,
breeding in long nests of hair.
     Worst of all in the warm clutter
were the shopping bags of every shade,
plaited by the waves' regular hand
or domed, translucent as a bloom of medusae,
ripped membranes flickering like something precious.
     One day when the sky hung heavy,
I gunned the outboard motor, ducked the boom
to take a closer look. The brine was thick,
sounding a thin high note like a bell.
     Mass jostled for attention,
each piece sliding and mounting the other
as if silence pushed it out of the sea,
back into my hands, offering it up.

SARAH WESTCOTT

Still Life with Sea Pinks and High Tide

Thrift grows tenacious at the tide's reach.
What is that reach when the water
is rising, rising?

Our melting, shifting, liquid world won't wait
for manifesto or mandate, each
warning a reckoning.

Ice in our gin or vodka chirrups and squeaks
dissolving in the hot, still air
of talking, talking.

MAURA DOOLEY

Colony Collapse Disorder

When I lived in the city I knew where I was,
what being there was. I knew I breathed
under a film of constant light,
that electricity was life. It moved
in my body, which I knew was an atom of the city,
and kept us twitching in unity. I felt
information bloom in my blood. It sang
in my cells as though it had always been there.
I knew without it I had no structure.

To leave the city was to leave one's memory.
Outside was a garden gone wild. Stars
were night-flowers in a mossy dome, opening
their dazzling mouths to amaze, spreading
exponentially the further from the city I went.
I knew nothing. What nothing meant. I feared
the dark and the space between things: space
needs filling. I'd cry for the city, its order.
To be let back in was to regain the future.

Now I live elsewhere the system is reversed.
The city is a picture from a book I once read
and nothing to do with me. Life is a movement
between dirt and sky. I see this clearly.

The stars are generators. Without them we'd fail.
Going back to the city is to speed myself up
to a drawn out buzz that I know is killing me.
Going anywhere other than elsewhere is rehearsing
this end: the shut-down of travelling energy.

All those years living inside weakened me.
Taken away from elsewhere I dim.
Friends visit and tell me that elsewhere is death
and the sky cannot feed me. Not indefinitely.
Their eyes are blown bulbs. They rattle. I smell
honey on their skin and know how it is.
When they move I hear humming like a swarm at a distance.
When they speak I hear their voices, and under
the city quietly droning.

POLLY ATKIN

Exodus

They waited until the houses were emptied out
to pick them up and stuff them into their luggage.
They took down the clouds, the moon, the stars,
the telephone wires with their pigeons,
the pots, the birds and the antennas.
They rolled up the landscape of the tropics
as if it were a canvas and packed it all up
like a circus they could carry to another city,
something they could re-inflate,
lift up and drive into the dirt
of a vacant lot
in New York or Barcelona.

FRANK BÁEZ

translated from the Spanish by Scott Cunningham

What Is It Worth?

Those masters of barbarity tell us:
I'll give you a millionaire's bank account,
in exchange for your blue sky,
I'll build you a nice supermarket
in exchange for your mountains.
One million dollars
for your children's smiles
as they run in the rain.
We Mokayas laugh at their ignorance,
even the smallest children
know that money turns to manure
when you pass over to Tzuan.
We Mokayas ask you,
the masters of decay.
Is a millionaire's bank account
enough to bring back
the laughter of our dead?
How much money is enough
to cleanse sadness from the soul?

MIKEAS SÁNCHEZ
translated by Wendy Call from the author's Spanish version
of her bilingual Zoque-Spanish poem

Tzuan: one of the levels of the inner world, according to Zoque cosmology.

Dominion

Dear God, if you can imagine us, Man,
Without a chainsaw in our hands or the gun
Or looking away from the prices on the screen
For half a minute, even then in that
Even by you perhaps unimaginable state

The truth is we're not good enough, never were,
Never will be, we're not fit, we don't fit in,
Nothing will live with us except the viruses
And dogs and lice, nothing likes us down here,
Everything else is subtler, finer, fitter than us.

Take a coral reef: we come visiting
It gives up the ghost, it's a boneyard by morning,
Spectral groves. And that's us all over,
The ashes, the fallout, whatever we come near
Even in white, with a gauze over the gob,

We're the kiss of death. Dear God, that day
In Eden when you made Adam boss
What a catastrophe, even you must see it by now,
Anything would have been better than us,
A dodo, for example, a booby, a diplodocus.

DAVID CONSTANTINE

The Body's New Weather

In waves it came. But waves so small at first
nobody noticed
the leaves dropping all summer
or the landscape's frayed
yellow edges or the days we went
without wind. Then winter
packed up and didn't come back. Then, again —
the glaciers burnt dry and the bears
suddenly without their soft
houses of snow. Then somebody
shot them and we thanked God for our climate's
new harvest. But then we felt in
our own bodies this new food rotting —
strange heat in the lungs, cancer

ripening where the right meat
should have been and we named them
our own illnesses, maladies of the body
not of the earth the body
builds itself from. But then the earth
turned on us, each new season collapsing
until there was only high summer
and we felt then how the land must —
aching and empty and still we reached
into ourselves pulling up nothing. Or rather
not nothing but another new desert,
another woodland cut free of song.
Only then did our bodies turn themselves on
to protest like sirens in a city
that has already been bombed.

DOM BURY

Two Hundred Million Animals

Imagine the two hundred million animals we kill for sport
each year. Imagine them piled in a heap – skulls,
beaks, horns, tusks, fangs, feathers, furs, scales, wattles,
coxcombs, paws, talons, flippers, bristles, tails.
Imagine their markings put asunder, their innards gauzed
by flies, their gassy sighs. Imagine them stuffed,
mounted, shrined. Ululate, then, the names we coin
to catch their beauty – we, who alone of all the creatures
have need of names, of categories, maybe
even of beauty, who laud their looks, the ways by which
they move, their temperament, their playfulness,
stealth and mystery – inspirations of art, music, poetry –
as though we would throw the earth open
before them, assert their inheritance the equal of our own.

PATRICK DEELEY

The End of the World

They've nothing in common, the young girl knocked
from her bicycle and dying on a roadside
in Harold's Cross, and the tribesman of Sumatra
being interviewed on television, shaking
his head at the levelled forest, cut and burn stretching
for miles behind him; they've nothing in common

except, as the man says, the end of the world
is happening. And the sight of a green snake flicking
its tongue at a chainsaw that keeps cutting;
and the sight of a rainbow flourished above the city
after we look up from the crumpled shape
of the girl, both haunt us, being more than props

for pathos, more than backdrops to the uselessness
even of beauty in face of greed or misfortune.
The end of the world is happening, and grief that stands
sudden tears in our staring eyes might wish them
closed as soon, with no desire to open again –
but this, too, is the world, and somehow a beginning.

PATRICK DEELEY

Alpha Step

A change to my usual sleeping position,
earth holding me close
like I'm something that it loves.
I feel a murmur through the hedgerow,
old gods thawing from the permafrost.
Only a matter of time
before an Empire falls
into the hands of an idiot
and there are more ways of saying things

than things worth saying;
only a matter of love to steer the wind,
which batters us daily, this only life
that climbs beyond unfashionable
beginnings, leaving us leaving it,
breathless software, a bite taken out
of the grand old narrative,
while our ghosts refuel midair.
Deep time. Lovely time.
The human print will not survive.
I mean like, woo, there it was.

JACK UNDERWOOD

Birdsong

We strained all the fish from the waters
of the world, both fresh and salt, and ate them.

Pried the last of the secretive, pallid squid

from their crevices and ate them,
sucked snails from their shells.

Next the birds, because birdsong
won't keep other animals alive.

Mammals stopped breeding. We ate them all.
Reptiles lay starving in the sun until we

scaled them and ate their cold-blooded meat.

Most amphibians vanished on their own.
Drifts of feathers buried the shells and bones.

Now the insects outnumber us
two hundred million to one.

The worms, billions to one.

Earth without animals comes before
earth without humans. We starve last.

The trees are dropping sickened leaves,

too few to cover us when we lie down
at life's end, after the insects and worms.

CHASE TWICHELL

Herds of Humans

Look in the eye of the dolphin,
the eye of the rat. The animals know
what we decline to know.

Herds of displaced humans
arm themselves against as many
kinds of death as they can imagine.

Cloud death.
Death of the trees.
Death of all the laws.

The four winds wince when they pass
too close to a blade, too close
to a fragment of bone or glass.

Here comes a feral dog, drawn by
the fat in the fire, a little taste of it,
a lick of it, a scrap, a bone.

CHASE TWICHELL

By Degrees

The security guard puts the gun to my head
then clicks. He turns it to show me: 36 degrees

and waves me in, his expression hidden
behind his mask, his eyes vacant.

I walk around the almost empty supermarket.
No eggs, no veg, the milk sold out, less pasta

than three days ago. Chinese New Year music
still plays on the store's radio, its merriness

like a slap. People queue up rather than use self-service,
nervous to touch what others have touched.

Heading back I see my apartment is sealed off
I must walk round the back, to the other entrance

guarded now by five policemen with temperature guns.
I go in and they scan me again: 37 degrees.

Other cities don't have it like this.
Going out like this is a privilege.

Shanghai, China: 2 February 2020

DAVID TAIT

The Virus at My Window

The street below me us is still firmly shut
apart from the realtor's, for some reason,
and the fruit shop, with its oranges and dragon-fruit.

Everyone going past is wearing masks
and walking slowly, as though on tiptoe,
as though having nowhere to go.

It's quiet too. The winter smog drifts like a sinister mist,
and the woman next door plays her new piano,
bought in a moment of quarantined boredom.

She gives it up and we hear the birds: pigeons
and sparrows – rare to hear them – and then
the distant mewling of an ambulance siren.

It's heading this way, and everyone on the street
stops to watch it pass. It's passing but it isn't slowing down.
The people on the street sigh, then keep walking.

Shanghai, China: 7 February 2020

DAVID TAIT

Cranes Lean In

Cranes lean in, waiting for an all-clear
that will not come.

Forehead pressed to glass,
phone at my ear, I learn

to sail on your voice
over a sadness of building sites,

past King's Cross, St Pancras,
to the place where you are.

You say nothing
is too far, mothers

will find their daughters,
strangers will be neighbours,

even saviours
will have names.

You are all flame
in a red dress.

Petals brush my face.
You say at last

the cherry blossom
has arrived

as if that is what
we were really waiting for.

The Barbican, London: 22 March 2020

IMTIAZ DHARKER

Ode

The streets are empty
but a crowd has gathered in the air.
Trombones and cellos on the balconies,
a song gradually taking hold.
The music invents a square
where all of us slowly appear,
a plainclothes orchestra surprising ourselves
like the flashmob we watched together:
first the lone double bass like a statue coming alive
then the bassoon and violins,
the rushing brass like firemen looking for a fire,
the shoppers dropping their bags and pumping the ode.

The man in the T-shirt turns to us, his hands in the air.
We're the city now and the square,
leaping from our strange disguises
to sing to each other across the darkness.

17 March 2020

PETER SIRR

Hands

(to all our NHS staff)

Two minutes to eight. We wrap up,
step out and wait; no moon or stars to light
this lampless pinpoint on the planet's map –
night hushed, happed in mist.
Across the field, behind the hill,
invisible hands are poised;
we listen, uncertain who will lead:
out there, through the dark,
the first palms give their little strike,
and we offer ours; more follow,
ghostly applause tapping the damp air –
flesh we've washed and washed, rough
with trying to keep the killer at bay –
neighbours giving thanks
to all those anonymous hands
holding onto life for us.

Scottish Borders: 29 March 2020

GERDA STEVENSON

An American Nurse Foresees Her Death

I stepped out of a killzone shaped like a bedroom
then went home to sleep in my garage.
This hand that sponged the fever off a body
waves at my kids through the living room window.
I text my husband through a weeping wall.
The scrubs go in a Mommy hamper
I warn my kids away from
with a Crayola skull and crossbones.
The face on the laptop doesn't let on
how the knuckles sanitised raw bleed in blue gloves
and "lunch" is an apple between codes.
When the shift ends, if it ever ends,
I ghost the perimeter of my own life
and set the alarm for four thirty in the morning.
The virus doesn't want me working.
The virus wants to grant me days of rest,
a bed of my own
in a killzone shaped like a break room.
Nurses I know are nursing nurses
through the neverending fevers
ending them. That will be me soon,
one or the other, or one then the other.
At sign out last Friday,
we didn't say bed numbers. We said first names.

AMIT MAJMUDAR

Seen from a Drone, Delhi

People standing in windows,

sauntering out of houses
loaded with bags and boxes, laptops,
iPads, Kindles and chargers, hairdryers,

olives, chocolates, children, skeleton
staff, one maid and driver,
wending their way up vacant roads
to the place in the hills, the nearest
neighbour far over the valley,
out in the orchards, under the awnings
and yellow umbrellas. There they are
waving, there they are yawning.

Here are the rats behind tinted windows,
leaving in convoys, consulting watches
and phones, all flashing lights, bullish
horns, outriders in sunglasses powering
through, scattering these people who never
will learn to keep their distance, who never
hear the warnings, herd together like cattle,
these jostlers, these fruit-sellers, vendors,
dress-makers, cobblers, tea-boys and hawkers,
these cleaners, day-labourers, fetchers
and carriers, these unskilled workers.

These people, these people, ants
in an anthill, down there running
this way and that, carrying bundles of rags,
bundles of bundles that cry like babies,
swarming on buses and trains. Stopped.
The drone is recording: grandmothers,
mothers and fathers, daughters and sons
heaving burdens, holding each other
up, holding each other, illegally touching
gathering thronging clustering clutching
starting the long walk home.

The eye of the drone watches their going.

Gone.

IMTIAZ DHARKER

Seen from a Drone, Mumbai

On Day 5, look how our city is beautified
by the absence of these people. Clarified
totally, hushed. No chaos now or crowds.
Witness this historic moment, sights
you would never have thought to see
in your lifetime. Here is a bird's-eye
view of the unburdened flyover, cricket-
less stadium, unpeopled shore.
By Permission of the Authorities, we
are empowered to bring, direct
to your smartphone, these unprecedented
scenic Scenes from a Drone. Feast
your eyes on the Throne of Power,
the House of State Government,
Office of Police Commissioner, this
place of worship, its saffron flag. See
the sea-link snaking over sea, trains
like maggots feeding on the carcass
of a station. So much silence, deafening.
Our sound track is fitting, one
long drone broken only by birds,
disturbed, rising on a spiral
to the camera. Then birdsong.
Even in Lockdown there is a Moral
to be found. Nature Triumphs.
This is what the tweets are saying.
Dolphins in Venice went viral,
no matter it was a hoax,
fish were revealed in the canal
and in Llandudno the goats
ran wild and joyful in the streets.
This is truly happening
all over Twitter, all over
the whole world.

IMTIAZ DHARKER

Still life with a map of the world outside the window

Each soul is its own planet. The skies are still.
Look one way, the wild is back.
Smell the blossom, hear more
birdsong than we heard for a century.
Look inside. Home in. Video, zoom,
the family locked in and afraid.
Look the other way, a shy intern
is ringing wives
who can't be with their husband as he dies
to say they've gone. The student
who signed up as a volunteer
is loading the dead in body bags, surprised
they are still warm. Your friend, your dear
friend, three months overtime
on a Covid ward and her face, her skin,
girth-sore from the visor,
her sleep filled with dying eyes
behind a mask. Look on TV. Politicians
who don't care we don't believe them
spilling lives like snow. Look on the streets,
forgotten holiness, deniers
who refuse to keep the distance that keeps safe,
cough in the face of a young
key worker at check-out. But look across the road,
your neighbours shopping for the old, the ill,
ringing round for food runs, waving, all of us,
at the door on Thursday night. Clap for the invisible
carers, risking their lives. Beat the tom-tom
for a world we'll try to make again,
make better, now the only things to keep you sane
are the mobile phone and labyrinth
of your own backyard. If you have one.

Kentish Town, London, 28 May 2020

RUTH PADEL

Dad Poem

No visitors allowed
is what the masked woman behind
the desk says only seconds
after me and your mother
arrive for the ultrasound. *But I'm the father*,
I explain, like it means something
defensible. She looks at me as if
I've just confessed to being a minotaur
in human disguise. Repeats the line. Caught
in the space between astonishment
& rage, we hold hands a minute
or so more, imagining you a final time
before our rushed goodbye,
your mother vanishing
down the corridor
to call forth a veiled vision
of you through glowing white
machines. One she will bring
to me later on, printed and slight
-ly wrinkled at its edges,
this secondhand sight
of you almost unbearable
both for its beauty and
necessary deferral.
What can I be to you now,
smallest one, across the expanse
of category & world catastrophe,
what love persists
in a time without touch

JOSHUA BENNETT

498

The Future

Dear mortals,
I know you are busy with your colourful lives;
you grow quickly bored
and detest moralising.
I have no wish to waste the little time that remains
on arguments and heated debates.
I wish I could entertain you
with some magnificent propositions
and glorious jokes;
but the best I can do is this:
I haven't happened yet; but I will.
I am the future, but before I appear
please
close the scrolls of information,
let the laptop sleep,
sit still and shut your eyes.
Listen –
things are going to change –
don't open your eyes, not yet! –
I'm not trying to frighten you.
Think of me not as a wish or a nightmare
but as a story you have to tell yourselves
not with an ending
in which everyone lives happily ever after,
or a B-movie apocalypse,
but maybe starting with the line
'to be continued...'
and see what happens next.
Remember this;
I am not written in stone
but in time
so please don't shrug and say
what can we do,
it's too late, etc, etc, etc...

Dear mortals,
you are such strange creatures
with your greed and your kindness,
and your hearts like broken toys.
You carry fear with you everywhere
like a tiny god
in its box of shadows.
You love shopping and festivals
and good food.
You love to dance
in the enchantment of time
like angels in a forest of mirrors.
Your lives are held
in the beautiful devices
familiar in your hands.
And perhaps you lie to yourselves
because you're afraid of me.
But always remember
we are in this together,
face to face and eye to eye.
I hold you in my hands
as I am held in yours.
We are made for each other.
Now – open your eyes
and tell me what you see.

NICK DRAKE

ACKNOWLEDGEMENTS

The poems in this anthology are reprinted from the following books, all by permission of the publishers listed unless stated otherwise. Thanks are due to all the copyright holders cited below for their kind permission:

Aria Aber: 'Asylum' from *Hard Damage* (University of Nebraska Press, 2019). **Fleur Adcock:** 'Happy Ending' from *Poems 1960-2000* (Bloodaxe Books, 2000). **Tatamkhulu Afrika:** 'The Woman at the Till' first published in *Nine Lives* (Carrefour/Hippogriff, 1991), copyright © 1991 Tatamkhulu Afrika, reprinted by permission of the Estate of Tatamkhulu Afrika. **John Agard:** 'Checking Out Me History' from *Half-caste and other poems* (Hodder, 2004, 2006), by permission of Caroline Sheldon Ltd. **Kaveh Akbar:** 'What Use Is Knowing Anything If No One Is Around' from *Calling a Wolf a Wolf* (Alice James Books, USA, 2017; Penguin Books, UK, 2018). **Ellery Akers:** 'The Word That Is a Prayer' from *Practicing to Tell the Truth* (Autumn House Press, 2015), by permission of The Permissions Company, LLC on behalf of Autumn House Press. **Elizabeth Alexander:** 'Smile' from *American Blue: Selected Poems* (Bloodaxe Books, 2006), by permission of Bloodaxe Books Ltd. **Moniza Alvi:** 'And if' and 'Flight' from *Split World: Poems 1990-2005* (Bloodaxe Books, 2008). **Anthony Anaxagorou:** 'Cause' and 'Departure Lounge Twenty Seventeen' from *After the Formalities* (Penned in the Margins, 2019). **Linda Anderson:** 'Sanctuary' from *The Station Before* (Pavilion Poets/Liverpool University Press, 2020). **Raymond Antrobus:** 'Jamaican British' from *The Perseverance* (Penned in the Margins, 2018). **Simon Armitage:** 'Poem' from *Zoom!* (Bloodaxe Books, 1989). **Craig Arnold:** 'Meditation on a Grapefruit', from *Poetry* (October 2009), by permission of the literary estate of Craig Arnold. **Mona Arshi:** 'Delivery Room' from *Dear Big Gods* (Pavilion Poets/Liverpool University Press, 2019). **Fatimah Asghar:** 'If They Come for Us' from *If They Come for Us* (One World, a division of Penguin Random House LLC, New York, 2018). Epigraph on page 367, https://msmagazine.com/2017/05/17/five-female-poets-identity-migration/ **Werner Aspenström:** 'You and I and the World' from *The Star by My Head: Poets from Sweden*, ed. & tr. Malena Mörling & Jonas Ellerström (Milkweed Editions/The Poetry Foundation, 2013). **Polly Atkin:** 'Colony Collapse Disorder' from *Basic Nest Architecture* (Seren Books, 2017). **Zohar Atkins:** 'Song of Myself (Apocryphal)' from *Ninevah* (Carcanet Press, 2019). **Annemarie Austin:** extract from 'Country' and 'What My Double Will', from *Very: New & Selected Poems* (Bloodaxe Books, 2008). **Janet Ayachi:** 'Spooning Stars' from *Hand Over Mouth Music* (Pavilion Poets: Liverpool University Press, 2019). **Gennady Aygi:** 'People' from *Into the Snow: Selected Poems of Gennady Aygi*, tr. Sarah Valentine (Wave Books, 2011), copyright © 2011 Estate of Gennady Aygi, translation © 2011 Sarah Valentine by permission of the publisher and translator.

Ken Babstock: 'As Marginalia in John Clare's *The Rural Muse*' from *Methodist Matchet* (House of Anansi Press, Inc, Toronto, 2011), by permission of the publisher. **Gabeba Baderoon:** 'I Cannot Myself' from *The Dream of the Next Body* (Kwela Books, Roggebaai, South Africa, 2005), by permission of Blake Friedmann Ltd. **Frank Báez:** 'Exodus', from *Anoche soñé que era un DJ* (Libros Jai-Alai, Miami, 2014), translation by Scott Cunningham first published on the *Poetry International* website, 2019, by permission of the author and translator. **Stanisław Barańczak:** 'If China', tr. Magnus J. Krynski from *Selected Poems: The Weight of the Body* (Northwestern University Press, 1989), originally published in *Triquarterly*, an imprint of Northwestern University Press, by permission of the author's estate. **Justyna Bargielska:** 'Different rose' from *The Great Plan B*, tr. Maria Jastrzębska (Smokestack Books, 2018). **Maria Barnas:** 'Why I Am Not a Painter', tr. Donald Gardner, from *The Enchanting Verses Literary Review*, XXVI (December 2017), original Dutch poem from *Jaja de oerknal* (De Arbeiderspers, Amsterdam, 2013), by permission of the publisher and translator. **John Barr:** 'Bonsai Master' from *Dante in China* (Red Hen Press, 2018), by permission of the author and The Permissions Company, LLC on behalf of Red Hen Press. **Ellen Bass:** 'Gate C22', from *The Human Line* (Copper Canyon Press, 2007), copyright © 2007 by Ellen Bass, by permission of The Permissions Company, LLC on behalf of Copper Canyon Press, www.coppercanyonpress.org; 'Any Common Desolation', first published on *Poem-a-Day* on 18 November 2016, by the Academy of American Poets, © Ellen Bass 2016, by permission of the author. **Edward Baugh:** 'A Nineteenth-century Portrait' from *Black Sand: New and Selected Poems* (Peepal Tree Press, 2013). **Zeina Hashem Beck:** 'You Fixed It' from *Louder than Hearts* (Bauhan Publishing, Peterborough, NH, USA, 2017), by permission of the author. **Joshua Bennett:** 'Dad Poem', first published in *Wall Street Journal*, by permission of the author. **Connie Bensley:** 'Cookery' from *Finding a Leg to Stand On: New & Selected Poems* (Bloodaxe Books, 2012). **Dzifa Benson:** 'Self Portrait as a Creature of Numbers' from www.dzifabenson.com, first published in *Brand*, issue 6, by permission of the author. **Fiona Benson:** 'Sheep' from *Bright Travellers* (Jonathan Cape, 2014); 'Ruins' and 'Hide and Seek' from *Vertigo & Ghost* (Jonathan Cape, 2019), by permission of the Random House Group Ltd. **Tara Bergin:** 'Wedding Cake Decorations' from *The Tragic Death of Eleanor Marx* (Carcanet Press, 2017). **Jay Bernard:** 'Clearing ', '+' and '-' from *Surge* (Chatto & Windus, 2019), by permission of the Random House Group Ltd. **Emily Berry:** 'The photo that is most troubling is the one I don't want to show you', from *Stranger, Baby* (Faber & Faber, 2017). **James Berry:** 'Travelling As We Are' and 'In-a Brixton Markit' from *A Story I Am In: Selected Poems* (Bloodaxe Books, 2001). **Liz Berry:** 'The Republic of Motherhood' from *The Republic of Motherhood* (Chatto & Windus, 2018), by permission of the Random House Group Ltd. **Sujata Bhatt:** 'A Different History' from *Collected Poems* (Carcanet Press, 2013). **Caroline Bird:** 'Marriage of Equals' from *The Hat-Stand Union* (Carcanet Press, 2013); 'A Surreal Joke' and 'The End of the Bed' from *In These Days of Prohibition* (Carcanet Press, 2017). **Jacqueline Bishop:** 'Snakes' from *Fauna* (Peepal Tree Press, 2006). **Rachael Boast:** 'Desperate Meetings of Hermaphrodites' from *Pilgrim's Flower* (Picador, 2013), by permission of Macmillan Publishers Ltd. **Nina Bogin:** 'Initiation, II' from *In the North* (Graywolf Press, 1989), by permission of The Permissions Company, LLC on behalf of Graywolf Press, www.graywolfpress.org. **Eavan Boland:** 'Lines for a Thirtieth Wedding Anniversary' and 'Nocturne' from *New Collected Poems* (Carcanet Press, 2005). **Malika Booker:** 'Cement' and 'Erasure' from *Pepper Seed* (Peepal Tree Press, 2013). **Dean Bowen:** 'mi skin', first published in Dutch in *Tirade* #472 (2018), (https://www.vanoorschot.nl/oorshop/tirade-472/). **Alison Brackenbury:** 'All' and 'So' from *Gallop: Selected Poems* (Carcanet Press, 2019). **Deirdre Brennan:** 'Born Dead' ('Marghghin'), from *Ag mealladh réalta* (Coiscéim, 2000), tr. Biddy Jenkinson from *Leabhar na hAthghabhála: Poems of Repossession*, ed. Louis de Paor (Bloodaxe Books/Cló Iar-Chonnacht, 2016), by permission of the author and translator. **Zoë Brigley:** 'Star / Sun / Snow' and 'The Hole in the Glass' from *Hand & Skull* (Bloodaxe Books, 2019). **Lucie Brock-Boido:** 'Soul Keeping Company' from *Soul Keeping Company* (Carcanet Press, 2010). **Gwendolyn Brooks:** 'We Real Cool' and 'a song in the front yard' from *Selected Poems* (Harper & Row, 1963), copyright © 1963 by Gwendolyn Brooks, by permission of the Estate of Gwendolyn Brooks, c/o Brooks Permissions, PO Box 19355, Chicago, IL 60619, USA. **Jericho Brown:** 'Prayer of the Backhanded' from *Please* (New Issues Poetry & Prose, Western Michigan University, 2008), by permission of the author; 'Colosseum' from *The New Testament* (Copper Canyon Press, USA, 2014; Picador, UK, 2018); 'As a Human Being', 'Bullet Points' and 'Of My Fury' from *The Tradition* (Copper Canyon Press, USA, 2019; Picador, UK, 2019), by permission of Macmillan Publishers Ltd. **Colette Bryce:** 'Belfast Waking, 6 a.m.' from *Self-Portrait in the Dark* (Picador, 2008); 'Helicopters' from *The Whole & Rain-domed Universe* (Picador, 2014), by permission of Macmillan Publishers Ltd. **Elizabeth Burns:** 'Listening to Bach's B Minor Mass in the Kitchen' from *Lightkeepers* (Wayleave Press, 2016), by kind permission of the author's estate. **John Burnside:** 'The Day Etta Died' from *All One Breath* (Jonathan Cape, 2014), by permission of the Random House Group Ltd. **Dom Bury:** 'The Body's New Weather' from *Rites of Passage* (Bloodaxe Books, 2021). **Paddy Bushe:** 'The Rolling Wave' from *On a Turning Wing* (Dedalus Press, 2016). **David Butler:** 'And Then The Sun Broke Through' from *All the Barbaric Glass* (Doire Press, 2017). **Mairéad Byrne:** 'Facing the Music' from *You Have to Laugh: New and Selected Poems* (Barrow Street, 2013), by permission of the author.

Niall Campbell: 'Night Watch' and 'February Morning' from *Noctuary* (Bloodaxe Books, 2019). **Remco Campert:** 'Poetry', tr. Donald Gardner, from *In Those Days* (Shoestring Press, 2014), by permission of the publisher and translator. **Moya Cannon:** 'Introductions' and 'Milk' from *Carrying the Songs* (Carcanet Press, 2007). **Vahni Capildeo:** 'III. Going Nowhere, Getting Somewhere' (from 'Five Measures of Expatriation'), from *Measures of Expatriation* (Carcanet Press, 2016). **Patrizia Cavalli:** 'Here I am, I do my bit...', 'I'm pretty clear, I'm dying...' and 'Very simple love that believes in words...' from *My Poems Won't Change the World: Selected Poems*, ed. Gina Alhadeff (Penguin Books, 2018). **John Challis:** 'The Love' from *The Resurrectionists* (Bloodaxe Books, 2021). **Mary Jean Chan:** '//' from *Flèche* (Faber & Faber, 2019). **Amarjit Chandan:** 'In This Country', tr. the author & Julia Casterton, from *Modern Poetry in Translation*, 2016 no.1, and *The Parrot The Horse & The Man* (Arc Publications, 2017), by permission of the author. **Chen Chen:** 'Poem in Noisy Mouthfuls' from *When I Grow Up I Want to Be a List of Further Possibilities* (BOA Editions, USA, 2017; Bloodaxe Books, 2019), by permission of Bloodaxe Books Ltd. **Kayo Chingonyi:** 'The N Word' from *Kumukanda* (Chatto & Windus, 2017), by permission of the Random House Group Ltd. **Gillian Clarke:** 'Honesty' and 'Snow' from *Ice* (Carcanet Press, 2012). **Jane Clarke:** 'Vows' and 'Who owns the field?' from *The River* (Bloodaxe Books, 2015); 'Hers' and 'The trouble' from *When the Tree Falls* (Bloodaxe Books, 2019). **John Cooper Clarke:** 'Bed Blocker Blues' from *The Luckiest Guy Alive* (Picador, 2018), by permission of Macmillan Publishers Ltd. **Lucille Clifton:** 'daughters ' from *The Collected Poems of Lucille Clifton 1965-2010*, ed. Kevin Young & Michael S. Glaser (BOA Editions, USA, 2015), by permission of The Permissions Company, LLC on behalf of BOA Editions, www.boaeditions.org. **Elisabeth Sennitt Clough:** 'Potato Season' first published in *Glass* (Paper Swans Press, 2016) and later in *Sightings* (Pindrop Press, 2016), by permission of the author. **Catriona Clutterbuck:** 'Her Body' from *The Magpie and the Child: Threnodies for Emily*, forthcoming from Wake University Press, by permission of the author. **Wanda Coleman:** 'American Sonnet: 94' from *Mercurochrome* (Black Sparrow Press, 2001). **Billy Collins:** 'Helium' from *The Rain in Portugal* (Picador, 2017), by permission of Penguin Random House, Inc. **Jane Commane:** 'Midlands kids' from *Assembly Lines* (Bloodaxe Books, 2018). **Stewart Conn:** 'Conundrum' from *The Touch of Time: New & Selected Poems* (Bloodaxe Books, 2014). **David Constantine:** 'Dominion' from *Collected Poems* (Bloodaxe Books, 2004); 'Pity' from *Nine Fathom Deep* (Bloodaxe Books, 2009). **Jasmine Ann Cooray:** 'Call Centre Blues' from *The Rialto*, 86 (Summer 2016), by permission of the author. **Wendy Cope:** 'To My Husband' and 'One Day' from *Anecdotal Evidence* (Faber & Faber, 2018). **Ellen Cranitch:** 'Blasket Sound' from *The Immortalist* (Templar Poetry, 2017), by permission of the publisher and author.

David Dabydeen: 'Catching Crabs' from *Turner: New & Selected Poems* (Peepal Tree Press, 2002). **Fred D'Aguiar:** 'Excise' from *The Rose of Toulouse* (Carcanet Press, 2013). **Ailbhe Darcy:** 'After my son was born' from *Insistence* (Bloodaxe Books, 2018). **Keki Daruwalla:** 'Migrations' from *Collected Poems 1970-*

2005 (Penguin Books India, 2006), by permission of the author. **Amir Darwish:** 'Where I come from' from *Dear Refugee* (Smokestack Books, 2019), by permission of the author. **Dick Davis:** 'Uxor Vivamus…' and 'Making a Meal of It' from *Love in Another Language: Collected Poems and Selected Translations* (Carcanet Press, 2017). **Kwame Dawes:** 'Land Ho' from *Requiem* (Peepal Tree Press, 1996). Extract from 'Back to Empathy' from https://www.poetryfoundation.org/harriet/2010/04/back-to-empathy **Carlos Drummond de Andrade:** 'Absence' and 'The House of Lost Time' from *Multitudinous Heart: Selected Poems*, tr. Richard Zenith (Farrar, Straus & Giroux, Inc., 2015), by permission of Penguin Random House UK. **Louis de Paor:** 'Marmalade' from *The Brindled Cat and the Nightingale's Tongue* (Bloodaxe Books/Cló Iar-Chonnacht, 2014) by permission of the author. **Eunice de Souza:** 'Advice to Women' from Women in Dutch Painting (Praxis, Mumbai, 1988), by permission of Melanie Silgardo. **John F. Deane:** 'The Red Gate' from *Snow Falling on Chestnut Hill: New and Selected Poems* (Carcanet Press, 2012); 'The World is Charged' from *Dear Pilgrims* (Carcanet Press, 2018). **Aleš Debeljak:** 'A Letter Home', tr. Andrew Zawacki, from *Without Anesthesia: New and Selected Poems*, ed. Andrew Zawacki (W.W. Norton & Company, 2011), by permission of the translator. **Patrick Deeley:** 'The End of the World' and 'Two Hundred Million Animals' from *The End of the World* (Dedalus Press, 2019). **Imtiaz Dharker:** 'Minority' from *Postcards from god* (1997); 'Carving' from *The terrorist at my table* (2006); 'Passport photo', 'Screen-saver', 'Say His Name' and 'A Century Later' from *Over the Moon* (2014); 'Chaudhri Sher Mobarik looks at the loch' and 'Flight Radar' from *Luck is the Hook* (2018), all published by Bloodaxe Books; 'Cranes Lean In' (first published in *The Guardian* on 20 April 2020), 'Scenes from a Drone, Mumbai' and 'Scenes from a Drone, Delhi', from *WRITE where we are NOW* (Manchester Metropolitan University, https://www2.mmu.ac.uk/write/ 2020), by permission of the author. **Natalie Diaz:** 'The Beauty of a Busted Fruit' from *When My Brother Was an Aztec* (Copper Canyon Press, 2012), by permission of The Permissions Company, LLC on behalf of Copper Canyon Press, www.coppercanyonpress.org. **Matthew Dickman:** 'The World is Too Huge to Grasp' from *All-American Poem* (The American Poetry Review, 2008), by permission of the publisher. **Alex Dimitrov:** 'Some New Thing' from *Together and by Ourselves* (Copper Canyon Press, 2017), by permission of The Permissions Company, LLC on behalf of Copper Canyon Press, www.coppercanyonpress.org. **Katie Donovan:** 'Off Duty' from *Off Duty* (Bloodaxe Books, 2015). **Maura Dooley:** 'Dancing at Oakmead Road' from *Sound Barrier: Poems 1982-2002* (Bloodaxe Books, 2002); 'Still Life with Sea Pinks and High Tide' from *The Silvering* (Bloodaxe Books, 2016). **Tishani Doshi:** 'Girls Are Coming Out of the Woods' from *Girls Are Coming Out of the Woods* (Bloodaxe Books, 2018), by permission of the author and publisher. **Mark Doty:** 'Michael's Dream' from *Atlantis* (Jonathan Cape, 1995), by permission of the Random House Group Ltd. **Rita Dove:** 'Canary' and 'After Reading *Mickey in the Night Kitchen* for the Third Time Before Bed' from *Grace Notes* (W.W. Norton & Company, 1989). **Finuala Dowling:** 'At eighty-five, my mother's mind', 'Widowhood in the dementia ward' and 'Birthday in the dementia ward' from *Pretend You Don't Know Me: New & Selected Poems* (Bloodaxe Books, 2018). **Nick Drake:** 'Stranger Thing' and 'The Future' (here published in a later version) from *Out of Range* (Bloodaxe Books, 2018). **Carol Ann Duffy:** 'Empty Nest' from *Sincerity* (Picador, 2018), by permission of Rogers, Coleridge & White Ltd; epigraph on page 111, BBC Radio 4, August 1997. **Sasha Dugdale:** 'Asylum' and 'Perhaps Akhmatova was right' from *Red House* (Carcanet Press, 2011). **Beata Duncan:** 'The Notebook', from *Berlin Blues* (Green Bottle Press, 2017), by permission of the literary estate of Beata Duncan. **Helen Dunmore:** 'My life's stem was cut' and 'Hold out your arms' from *Counting Backwards: Poems 1975-2017* (Bloodaxe Books, 2019). **G.F. Dutton:** 'The Miraculous Issue' from *The Bare Abundance: Selected Poems 1975-2001* (Bloodaxe Books, 2002).

Lauris Edmond: 'Late song' from *Night burns with a white fire: the essential Lauris Edmond*, ed. Frances Edmond & Sue Fitchett (Steele Roberts Aotearoa Publishers, Wellington, New Zealand, 2017), by permission of the Lauris Edmond Literary Estate. **Inua Ellams:** 'Swallow Twice' from *The Wire-Headed Heathen* (Akashic Books, 2015), by permission of the author and publisher. **Anna Enquist:** 'All at Once', tr. David Colmer, from *The Enchanting Verses Literary Review*, XXVI (online 2017, print 2018), original poem 'Ineens' from *Alle gedichten* (De Arbeiderspers, Amsterdam, 2005), by permission of the translator, author and publisher. **Martín Espada:** 'How We Could Have Lived or Died This Way' from *Vivas to Those Who Have Failed* (W.W. Norton & Company, 2016); 'Rednecks' from *Imagine the Angels of Bread* (W.W. Norton & Company, 1996). **Martina Evans:** 'I Want to Be like Frank O'Hara' from *The Windows of Graceland: New & Selected Poems* (Carcanet Press, 2016).

Ruth Fainlight: 'Oxygen Mask' and 'Somewhere Else Entirely' from *Somewhere Else Entirely* (Bloodaxe Books, 2018). **Gerard Fanning:** 'That Note' from *Hombre: New and Selected Poems* (Dedalus Press, 2011). **U.A. Fanthorpe:** 'A Minor Role' from *Queuing in the Sun* (2003), from *New & Collected Poems* (Enitharmon Press, 2010), by permission of the estate of U.A. Fanthorpe. **Paul Farley:** 'Hole in the Wall' from *The Mizzy* (Picador, 2019), by permission of Macmillan Publishers Ltd. **Vicki Feaver:** 'You Are Not' from *I Want! I Want!* (Jonathan Cape, 2019), by permission of the author. **Elaine Feinstein:** 'A Visit' and 'Beds' from *Talking to the Dead* (Carcanet Press, 2007); 'Long Life' from *Cities* (Carcanet Press, 2010). **James Fenton:** 'For Andrew Wood' from *Yellow Tulips: Poems 1968-2011* (Faber & Faber, 2012). **David Ferry:** 'Lake Water' from *Bewilderment: New Poems and Translations* (University of Chicago Press, 2012). **Janet Fisher:** 'Life and Other Terms' from *Life and Other Terms* (Shoestring Press, 2015). **Nick Flynn:** 'The Day Lou Reed Died' from *My Feelings*, copyright © 2015 by Nick Flynn, reprinted with the permission of The Permissions Company, LLC on behalf of Graywolf Press, Minneapolis, Minnesota, www.graywolfpress.org.

Carolyn Forché: 'The Boatman' from *In the Lateness of the World* (Bloodaxe Books, 2020). **Tom French:** 'The Last Light' from *The Last Straw* (The Gallery Press, 2018), by permission of The Gallery Press, Loughcrew, Oldcastle, Co. Meath, Ireland. **David Friedland:** 'Blind man', from *After Image* (Snailpress/Quartz Press, Cape Town, South Africa, 2002), by permission of the author.

Tess Gallagher: 'I Stop Writing the Poem' and 'With Stars' from *Midnight Lantern: New & Selected Poems* (Graywolf Press, USA, 2011; Bloodaxe Books, UK, 2012), by permission of The Permissions Company, LLC on behalf of Graywolf Press, www.graywolfpress.org. **Azita Ghahreman:** 'The Boat That Brought Me', tr. Maura Dooley & Elhum Shakerifar, from *Negative of a Group Photograph* (Bloodaxe Books/Poetry Translation Centre, 2018), by permission of the Poetry Translation Centre. **Jack Gilbert:** 'Failing and Flying' from *Transgressions: Selected Poems* (Bloodaxe Books, 2006), by permission of Alfred A. Knopf, Inc. **Marjorie Lotfi Gill:** 'Gift' from Refuge (Tapsalteerie, 2018) by permission of the author. **Aracelis Girmay:** 'Ars Poetica' from *Kingdom Animalia*, copyright © 2011 by Aracelis Girmay, by permission of The Permissions Company, LLC on behalf of BOA Editions, www.boaeditions.org. **Louise Glück:** extract from 'Averno' from *Averno* (Carcanet Press, 2006). **Lorna Goodison:** 'My Mother's Sea Chanty' from *Collected Poems* (Carcanet Press, 2018). **Al Gore:** epigraph on page 479 from *An Inconvenient Truth* (2006). **Mina Gorji:** 'Exit' from *Art of Escape* (Carcanet Press, 2020). **Rebecca Goss:** 'The Lights', 'My Animal' and 'Last Poem' from *Her Birth* (Northern House/Carcanet Press, 2013). **Ann Gray:** 'I wish I had more mothers' from *I Wish I Had More Mothers* (smith|doorstop, 2018). **Linda Gregerson:** extract from 'Sleeping Bear', copyright © 2016 by Linda Gregerson, poem commissioned by the Academy of American Poets and funded by a National Endowment for the Arts Imagine Your Parks grant and published on https://www.poets.org. **Linda Gregg:** 'Let Birds', from *All of It Singing: New and Selected Poems* (Graywolf Press, 2008), by permission of The Permissions Company, LLC on behalf of Graywolf Press, www.graywolfpress.org. **Vona Groarke:** 'Ghost Poem' from *X* (The Gallery Press, 2014), by permission of The Gallery Press, Loughcrew, Oldcastle, Co. Meath, Ireland. **Philip Gross:** 'The Displaced Persons Camp' from *Changes of Address: Poems 1980-1998* (Bloodaxe Books, 2001). **Lars Gustafsson:** 'The silence of the world before Bach' from *Selected Poems*, tr. John Irons (Bloodaxe Books, 2015).

Sabeer Haka: 'Mulberries', 'Politics' and 'Home', tr. Nasrin Parvaz & Hubert Moore, from *Modern Poetry in Translation*, 2015 no.1. **Kimiko Hahn:** 'After being asked if I write "the occasional poem"' from *Foreign Bodies* (W.W. Norton & Company, 2020), first published in *The New Yorker*, 15 September 2019, by permission of W.W. Norton & Company Inc. **Choman Hardi:** 'Dispute Over a Mass Grave' and 'A Day for Love' from *Considering the Women* (Bloodaxe Books, 2015). **Kerry Hardie:** 'Ship of Death' from *A Furious Place* (The Gallery Press, 1996); 'After My Father Died' from *The Sky Didn't Fall* (The Gallery Press, 2003); both included in *Selected Poems* (The Gallery Press/Bloodaxe Books, 2011), by permission of The Gallery Press, Loughcrew, Oldcastle, Co. Meath, Ireland. **Anjum Hasan:** 'The Day No One Died' from *World Literature Today* (November 2010), by permission of the author. **Robert Hass:** 'A Story About the Body' from *The Apple Trees at Olema: New & Selected Poems* (Bloodaxe Books, 2011). **Geoff Hattersley:** 'Frank O'Hara Five, Geoffrey Chaucer Nil' from *Don't Worry* (Bloodaxe Books, 1994), by permission of the author. **Terrance Hayes:** 'The Golden Shovel' from *Lighthead* (Penguin Books, 2010); 'American Sonnet for My Past and Future Assassin' ('My mother says I am beautiful inside...'), from *American Sonnets for My Past and Future Assassin* (Penguin Books, 2018); 'American Sonnet for the New Year', from *The New Yorker*, 14 January 2019, by permission of the author. **Anne Haverty:** 'Objecting to Everything Today', from *A Break in the Journey* (New Island Books, 2018), by permission of the author. **Dermot Healy:** 'As You Get Older' from *The Travels of Sorrow* (The Gallery Press, 2015), by permission of The Gallery Press, Loughcrew, Oldcastle, Co. Meath, Ireland. **Seamus Heaney:** 'Scaffolding' from *Death of a Naturalist* (Faber & Faber, 1966); 'A Drink of Water', 'The Given Note', 'Song' and Chorus from *The Cure at Troy* from *Opened Ground: Poems 1966-1996* (Faber & Faber, 1998). **John Hegley:** 'A Declaration of Need' from *New & Selected Potatoes* (Bloodaxe Books, 2013) and *Beyond Our Kennel* (Methuen, 1998) by permission of Methuen. **Nicki Heinen:** 'The Ward' from *Itch* (Eyewear Publishing, 2017), by permission of the author. **W.N. Herbert:** 'Breakfrost' from *The Laurelude* (Bloodaxe Books, 1998). **Tracey Herd:** 'Happy Birthday' from *Not in This World* (Bloodaxe Books, 2015). **Judith Herzberg:** 'Old Age' and 'The Way' from *But What: Selected Poems*, tr. Shirley Kaufman with Judith Herzberg (Oberlin College Press, 1988), by permission of Uitgeverij De Harmonie, Herengracht 555, 1017 BW Amsterdam, Netherlands. **Xidu Heshang:** 'Fictionalising Her', tr. Liang Yujing, from *Modern Poetry in Translation*, 2014 no.2. **Selima Hill:** six poems from *Grunter* from *Fruitcake* (Bloodaxe Books, 2009); ten poems from *Sunday Afternoons at the Gravel-pits* from *Jutland* (Bloodaxe Books, 2015). **Jane Hirshfield:** 'Even the Vanishing Housed' from *Each Happiness Ringed by Lions: Selected Poems* (Bloodaxe Books, 2005). **Tony Hoagland:** 'Personal' from *Unincorporated Persons in the Late Honda Dynasty* (Graywolf Press, USA & Bloodaxe Books, UK, 2010), by permission of The Permissions Company, LLC on behalf of Graywolf Press, www.graywolfpress.org. **Vladmír Holan:** 'Snow' from *Mirroring: Selected Poems of Vladimír Holan*, tr. C.G. Hanzlicek & Dana Hábová (Wesleyan University Press, 1985). **Vincenza Holland:** 'Excuse Me' from *Mrs Turnbull's Tree* (The Mote Press, 1990), by permission of the author's estate. **Sarah Holland-Batt:** 'No End to Images', from *The Hazards* (University of Queensland Press, 2015). **Wayne Holloway-Smith:** 'the posh mums are boxing in the square...' from *Love Minus Love* (Bloodaxe Books, 2020). **Jeong Ho-seung:** 'Death of a Cellphone' from *A Letter Not Sent* (Seoul Selection USA Inc, 2016), tr. Brother Anthony of Taizé & Susan Hwang, by permission of the translators.

Ranjit Hoskoté: 'Couple' from *Central Time* (New Delhi: Viking/Penguin, India, 2014) © Ranjit Hoskoté, by permission of the author. **Marie Howe:** 'Magdalene Afterwards' and 'One Day' from *Magdalene* (W.W. Norton & Company, 2017). **Sarah Howe:** 'On a line by Xu Lizhi', a poem commissioned by the Magdalene College Festival of Sound in 2015, by permission of the author. **Cynthia Huntington:** 'For Love' from *Poets of the New Century*, ed. Roger Weingarten & Richard Higgerson (David R. Godine, Boston, 2001), by permission of the author. **Ishion Hutchinson:** 'The Garden', from *House of Lords and Commons* (Farrar, Straus and Giroux, USA, 2016; Faber & Faber, UK, 2017).

Teresa Samuel Ibrahim: 'Longing' and 'The last train across Ariat Bridge', as told to Patricia Schonstein, from *Africa! My Africa! an anthology of poems*, ed. Patricia Schonstein (African Sun Press, Cape Town, South Africa, 2012), by permission of Patricia Schonstein.

Major Jackson: 'Selling Out' from *Hoops* (W.W. Norton & Company, 2006), by permission of the author. **Darío Jaramillo:** 'Impossible Loves' (2 & 4) and 'Mozart on the Motorway' from *Impossible Loves*, tr. Richard Gwyn (Carcanet Press, 2019). **Randall Jarrell:** 'Well Water' from *The Complete Poems* by Randall Jarrell, published by Farrar, Straus & Giroux, Inc; copyright © 1969, 1996 by Mrs Randall Jarrell; used with permission. **Nadine Aisha Jassat:** 'The Years' and 'Let Me Tell You' from *Let Me Tell You This* (404 Ink, 2019). **Louis Jenkins:** 'Fish Out of Water' from *Nice Fish: New and Selected Prose Poems* (Holy Cow! Press, 711 Woodland Ave, Duluth, MN 55812, USA, 1995). **Adil Jussawalla:** 'Mother's Ninety-fourth Birthday' from *Trying to Say Goodbye* (Almost Island Books, Mumabi, 2011), by permission of the author.

Ilya Kaminsky: 'We Lived Happily during the War' and 'In a Time of Peace' from *Deaf Republic* (Faber & Faber, 2019). **Kirun Kapur:** 'Anthem' from *Visiting Indira Gandhi's Palmist* (Elixir Press, Denver, Colorado, 2015). **Karin Karakaşlı:** 'History-Geography', tr. Sarah Howe & Canan Marasligil, from *History-Geography* (Poetry Translation Centre, 2017). **Jackie Kay:** 'High Land' from *Darling: New & Selected Poems* (Bloodaxe Books, 2007). **Mimi Khalvati:** 'Smiles' and 'The Brag' from *Afterwardness* (Carcanet Press, 2019). **Katharine Kilalea:** 'You were a bird' from *One Eye'd Leigh* (Carcanet Press, 2009). **Suji Kwock Kim:** 'Monologue for an Onion' from *Notes from the North* (The Poetry Business, 2020), by permission of the author. **Galway Kinnell:** 'Wait' from *Selected Poems* (Bloodaxe Books, 2001). **Thomas Kinsella:** 'Mirror in February' from *Collected Poems* (Carcanet Press, 2001). **Hester Knibbe:** 'Yes', from *Hungerpots: New & Selected Poems*, tr. Jacqueline Pope (Eyewear Publishing, 2015). **Jennifer L. Knox:** 'Drones' from *Days of Shame & Failure* (Bloof Books, 2015). **Ron Koertge:** 'Lily' from *Vampire Planet: New & Selected Poems* (Red Hen Press, 2016). **Zaffar Kunial:** 'Prayer' from *Us* (Faber & Faber, 2018), by permission of the author. **Ilyse Kusnetz:** 'Harbinger' and epigraph on page 271 ('I've been thinking about poetry's ability to help us grieve') from *Angel Bones* (Alice James Books. 2019).

Danusha Laméris: 'Small Kindnesses' and 'Insha'Allah' from *The Moons of August* (Autumn House Press, 2014), by permission the author. **Joan Larkin:** 'Want' from *My Body* (Hanging Loose Press, 2017). **Dorothea Lasky:** 'The Miscarriage' from *Milk* (Wave Books, 2018), copyright © 2018 by Dorothy Lasky, by permission of the author and Wave Books. **Tom Leonard:** 'Being a Human Being', from *Outside the Narrative: Selected Work 1965-2009*. (Etruscan Books and Word Power Books 2011), by permission of the author's estate. **Melissa Lee-Houghton:** 'Love-Smitten Heart' from *Sunshine* (Penned in the Margins, 2016). **Denise Levertov:** 'The Fountain' from *The Collected Poems of Denise Levertov* (New Directions, 2013). **Tim Liardet:** 'Self-Portrait with Aquarium Octopus Flashing a Mirror' from *Arcimboldo's Bulldog: New and Selected Poems* (Carcanet Press, 2018). **Sarah Lindsay:** 'The Arms of a Marvelous Squid' and 'If God Made Jam' from *Debt to the Bone-Eating Snotflower* (Copper Canyon Press, 2013), by permission of The Permissions Company, LLC on behalf of Copper Canyon Press, www.coppercanyonpress.org. **Pippa Little:** 'Against Hate' from *Twist* (Arc Publications, 2017). **Theresa Lola:** 'Tailoring Grief', from *In Search of Equilibrium* (Nine Arches Press, 2019). **Michael Longley:** 'Ceilidh' from *Snow Water* (2004), from *Collected Poems* (Jonathan Cape, 2006); 'Age' from *Angel Hill* (Jonathan Cape 2017); by permission of the Random House Group Ltd. **Audre Lorde:** 'Diaspora' and 'Litany of Survival' from *The Collected Poems of Audre Lorde* (W.W. Norton & Company, 1997), by permission of Abner Stein. **Hannah Lowe:** 'Sausages' and 'Dance Class' from *Chick* (Bloodaxe Books, 2013). **Thomas Lux:** 'Refrigerator, 1957' from *Selected Poems* (Bloodaxe Books, 2014). **Aoife Lyall:** 'Sounds of that day', first published in *New Writing Scotland* 38 (2020), and 'Ubi Sunt', both from *Mother, Nature* (Bloodaxe Books, 2021). **Thomas Lynch:** 'Refusing at Fifty-two to Write Sonnets' from *Walking Papers* (Jonathan Cape, 2010), by permission of the Random House Group Ltd. **Noelle Lynskey:** 'Stillborn', first published in *The Irish Times*, 8 September 2018, by permission of the author.

Olivia McCannon: 'New Road', first published in Issue 10 of the *Aldeburgh Poetry Festival Poetry Paper*, by permission of the author. **Thomas McCarthy:** 'Slow Food' from *Pandemonium* (Carcanet Press, 2016). **Roy McFarlane:** extracts from '...and they killed them' ('Jean Charles de Menezes, 2005' and 'Mark Duggan, 2011') from *The Healing Next Time* (Nine Arches Press, 2018). **Roger McGough:** 'The Wrong Beds' from *That Awkward Age* (Viking, 2009), by permission of Peter, Fraser & Dunlop. **Ciara MacLaverty:** '"That's Quite a Trick If You Can Pull It Off"' from *Past Love in the Museum of Transport* (Tapsalteerie, 2018), by permission of the author. **Ian McMillan:** 'The Evening of the Day Pavarotti Died' from *To Fold the Evening Star: New and Selected Poems* (Carcanet Press, 2016). **Hollie McNish:** 'Embarrassed' from *Nobody Told Me: Poetry and Parenthood* (Blackfriars, 2016), by permission of the author.

Nikola Madzirov: 'When Someone Goes Away Everything That's Been Done Comes Back' from

Remnants of Another Age, tr. Peggy Reid, Graham W. Reid, Magdalena Horvat and Adam Reed (BOA Editions, USA, 2011; Bloodaxe Books, UK, 2013), by permission of The Permissions Company, LLC on behalf of BOA Editions, www.boaeditions.org. **Valerio Magrelli:** 'Vanishing Point', 'The Embrace' and 'The Boundary' from *The Embrace: Selected Poems*, tr. Jamie McKendrick (Faber & Faber, 2010). **Mir Mahfuz Ali:** 'My Son Waits by the Door' from *Midnight, Dhaka* (Seren Books, 2014). **Derek Mahon:** 'Rising Late' from *Against the Clock* (The Gallery Press, 2018); 'Insomnia' from *Life on Earth* (The Gallery Press, 2008); 'Aran' from *New Collected Poems* (The Gallery Press, 2011); by permission of The Gallery Press, Loughcrew, Oldcastle, Co. Meath, Ireland. **Amit Majmudar:** 'An American Nurse Foresees her Death', first published on *Poets Respond* (www.rattle.com), by permission of the author. **André Mangeot:** 'Bellwether' from *Blood Rain* (Seren, 2020), by permission of the author. **Joan Margarit:** 'Love is a place' from *Love is a place*, tr. Anna Crowe (Bloodaxe Books, 2016). **Lorraine Mariner:** 'Thursday' from *Furniture* (Picador, 2009), by permission of Macmillan Publishers Ltd. **Gretchen Marquette:** 'Want' from *May Day* (Graywolf Press, 2016), by permission of The Permissions Company, LLC on behalf of Graywolf Press, www.graywolfpress.org. **Lieke Marsman:** 'The Following Scan Will Last Less Than a Minute', 'The Following Scan Will Last One Minute' and 'The Following Scan Will Last Five Minutes' from *The Following Scan Will Last Five Minutes*, tr. Sophie Collins (Pavilion Poets: Liverpool University Press, 2019). **Steven Matthews:** 'Last Christmas Cracker' from *On Magnetism* (Two Rivers Press, 2017), by permission of the author. **Bejan Matur:** 'The Moon Sucks up Our Grief' and 'Night Spent in the Temple of a Patient God' from *In the Temple of a Patient God*, tr. Ruth Christie (Arc Publications, 2004). **Hanny Michaelis:** 'It's terrible', tr. Judith Wilkinson, from *The Enchanting Verses Literary Review*, XXVI (December 2017); 'Over the years', tr. Judith Wilkinson, from *Poetry International* website, 2009 (earlier version published on www. languageandculture.net); by permission of the translator, *Poetry International* and G.A. van Oorschot; Dutch original poems from *Verzamelde gedichten* (Van Oorschot, Amsterdam, 1996). **Anne Michaels:** three extracts from *Correspondences: a poem*, with portraits by Bernice Eisenstein (Bloomsbury, 2013). **Kei Miller:** 'Epilogue' from 'A Short History of Beds We Have Slept In Together' from *A Light Song of Light* (Carcanet Press, 2010). **Czesław Miłosz:** epigraph on page 67, *The Paris Review*, Winter 1994/1995. **Geraldine Mitchell:** 'How the Body Remembers' and 'Sneak' from *Mountains for Breakfast* (Arlen House, 2017). **Deborah Moffatt:** 'Eating Thistles' from *Eating Thistles* (Smokestack Books, 2019). **Reza Mohammadi:** 'Illegal Immigrant', tr. Nick Laird & Hamid Kabir, from *My Voice: A Decade of Poems from the Poetry Translation Centre*, ed. Sarah Maguire (Bloodaxe Books/Poetry Translation Centre, 2015). **John Montague:** epigraph on page 217, *Irish University Review*, Spring 1989. **Jessica Mookherjee:** 'Ursa Minor' from *Tigress* (Nine Arches Press, 2019). **Esther Morgan:** 'Latch' from *The Wound Register* (Bloodaxe Books, 2018). **Blake Morrison:** 'Happiness' from *Shingle Street* (Chatto & Windus, 2015), by permission of the Random House Group Ltd. **Sinéad Morrissey:** 'Fairground Music' from *Through the Square Window* (Carcanet Press, 2010). **Lisel Mueller:** 'In Passing' from *Alive Together* (Baton Rouge: Louisiana State University Press, 1996); copyright © 1996 by Lisel Mueller. **Luis Muñoz:** 'Leave Poetry', 'The Foreigner' and 'Breathing' from *From Behind What Landscape: New and Selected Poems*, tr. Curtis Bauer (Vaso Roto Ediciones, Madrid, 2015), by permission of the author. **Theresa Muñoz:** 'Be the first to like this' from *Gutter* 08 (August 2013), by permission of the author.

André Naffis-Sahely: 'An Island of Strangers' and 'Vanishing Act' from *The Promised Land: Poems from Itinerant Life* (Penguin Books, 2017). **Daljit Nagra:** 'Our Town with the Whole of India' from *Look We Have Coming to Dover!* (Faber & Faber, 2007). **Miriam Nash:** 'Love Song for a Keeper' from *All the Prayers in the House* (Bloodaxe Books, 2017). **Eiléan Ní Chuilleanáin:** 'The Morandi Bridge' from *The Mother House* (The Gallery Press, 2019), by permission of The Gallery Press, Loughcrew, Oldcastle, Co. Meath, Ireland. **Doireann Ní Ghríofa:** 'Inventory: Recovery Room', 'Tooth' and 'On Patrick Street' from *Clasp* (Dedalus Press, 2013); 'Jigsaw Puzzle' ('Mireanna Mearaí'), tr. Eiléan Ni Chuilleanáin, from *Calling Cards*, ed. Peter Fallon & Aifric Mac Aodha (The Gallery Press/Poetry Ireland, 2018), by permission of The Gallery Press, Loughcrew, Oldcastle, Co. Meath, Ireland. **Caitlín Nic Íomhair:** 'Praise the Young' ('Mol an Oige'), tr. Colette Bryce, from *Calling Cards*, ed. Peter Fallon & Aifric Mac Aodha (The Gallery Press/Poetry Ireland, 2018), by permission of The Gallery Press, Loughcrew, Oldcastle, Co. Meath, Ireland. **Stephanie Norgate:** 'Miracle' from *The Conversation* (Bloodaxe Books, 2021). **Boris A. Novak:** 'Decisions: 11' from *The Master of Insomnia: Selected Poems* (Dalkey Archive Press, 2012). **Selina Nwulu:** 'We have everything we need' from *9 Original Poems on Climate Change* (RSA, 2015). **Naomi Shihab Nye:** 'Shoulders' and 'Gate A-4' from *Tender Spot: Selected Poems* (Bloodaxe Books, second edition, 2015); 'Mediterranean Blue' from *The Tiny Journalist* (BOA Editions, 2019); all by permission of The Permissions Company, LLC on behalf of BOA Editions, www.boaeditions.org; 'Supple Cord' from *A Maze Me: Poems for Girls* (Greenwillow Books, 2005; HarperCollins, 2014), by permission of HarperCollins Publishers.

Conor O'Callaghan: 'Kingdom Come' from *The Sun King* (The Gallery Press, 2013), by permission of The Gallery Press, Loughcrew, Oldcastle, Co. Meath, Ireland. **Julie O'Callaghan:** 'No Can Do' from *Tell Me This Is Normal: New & Selected Poems* (Bloodaxe Books, 2008); 'Beyond' and 'Cyber You' from *Magnum Mysterium* (Bloodaxe Books, 2020). **Bernard O'Donoghue:** 'Ter Conatus' from *Selected Poems* (Faber & Faber, 2008). **Dennis O'Driscoll:** 'Nocturne' and 'Then' from *Collected Poems* (Carcanet Press, 2017). **Lani O'Hanlon:** 'Going to the Well' first published in *Mslexia*, by permission of the author. **Frank O'Hara:** 'Why I Am Not a Painter' from *Why I Am Not a Painter and other poems* (Carcanet Press, 2003);

'The Day Lady Died' and 'Autobiographia Literaria' from *Selected Poems*, ed. Donald Allen (Carcanet Press, 2005). **Michael O'Loughlin:** 'In This Life' from *Poems 1980-2015* (New Island Books, 2017). **Mary O'Malley:** 'A Lift' from *Playing the Octopus* (Carcanet Press, 2016). **Musa Okwonga:** 'Hundreds of cockroaches drowned today', © Musa Okwonga 2015, first published on www.okwonga.com, by permission of the author. **Sharon Olds:** 'To Our Miscarried One, Age Thirty Now' from *Stag's Leap* (Jonathan Cape, 2012), by permission of the Random House Group Ltd; 'In the Temple Basement', from *Paris Review*, issue 226, Fall 2018, and 'I Cannot Say I Did Not', first published in *The New Yorker*, 9 September 2019, both from *Arias* (Jonathan Cape, 2019), by permission of *The New Yorker* and the Random House Group Ltd. **Gregory Orr:** 'To Be Alive' from *Concerning the Book That Is the Body of the Beloved* (Copper Canyon Press, 2005), by permission of The Permissions Company, LLC on behalf of Copper Canyon Press, www.coppercanyonpress.org. **Derry O'Sullivan:** 'Stillborn 1943: Calling Limbo', tr. from the Irish by Kaarina Hollo of 'Marbhghin 1943: Glaoch ar Liombó', from *Cá bhfuil do Iúdás?* (Coiscéim, 1987), by permission of the author and translator. **Leanne O'Sullivan:** 'My Father Asks Me Why' and 'The Cord' from *Waiting for My Clothes* (Bloodaxe Books, 2004); 'Safe House' and 'A Healing' from *The Mining Road* (Bloodaxe Books, 2013); 'Leaving Early' and 'Note' from *A Quarter of an Hour* (Bloodaxe Books, 2018). **Michelle O'Sullivan:** 'Lines' from *The Flower and the Frozen Sea* (The Gallery Press, 2015); 'What Was Mistook' from *This One High Field* (The Gallery Press, 2018); by permission of The Gallery Press, Loughcrew, Oldcastle, Co. Meath, Ireland. **Alice Oswald:** 'A Short History of Falling' from *Falling Awake* (Jonathan Cape, 2016), by permission of United Agents.

Ruth Padel: 'Still life with a map of the world outside the window' from *WRITE where we are NOW* (Manchester Metropolitan University, https://www2.mmu.ac.uk/write/ 2020), by permission of the author. **Bobby Parker:** 'Working Class Voodoo' from *Working Class Voodoo* (Offord Road Books, 2018). **Sandeep Parmar:** 'An uncommon language' and extracts from 'Essay: An uncommon language' from *The Poetry Review*, 108:3 (Autumn 2018) and *Poetry*, 214 no.1 (April 2019) by permission of the author. **Abigail Parry:** 'The Quilt' from *Jinx* (Bloodaxe Books, 2018). **Elise Partridge:** extract from 'The Book of Steve' and 'Last Days' from *The If Borderlands: Collected Poems* (New York Review Books, 2017). **Linda Pastan:** 'Imaginary Conversation', from *Insomnia* (W.W. Norton & Company, 2015) by permission of Linda Pastan in care of the Jean V. Naggar Literary Agency, Inc. **Vera Pavlova:** 'If there is something to desire…' from *If There Is Something to Desire*, tr. Steven Seymour (Alfred A. Knopf, 2010), by permission of Alfred A. Knopf, Inc. **Rebecca Perry:** 'Windows' from *Beauty/Beauty* (Bloodaxe Books, 2015). **Fernando Pessoa:** 'They Spoke to Me of People, and of Humanity' from *Fernando Pessoa & Co.: Selected Poems*, tr. Richard Zenith (New York: Grove Press, 1998). **Pascale Petit:** 'My Mother's Love', 'Her Harpy Eagle Claws' and 'My Wolverine' from *Mama Amazonica* (Bloodaxe Books, 2017). **Robert Pinsky:** 'Samurai Song' from *Jersey Rain* (Farrar, Straus & Giroux, 2000). **Clare Pollard:** 'The Day Amy Died' from *Incarnation* (Bloodaxe Books, 2017). **Shivanee Ramlochan:** two extracts from 'The Red Thread Cycle', from *Everyone Knows I am a Haunting* (Peepal Tree Press, 2017).

Claudia Rankine: four extracts from *Citizen* and 'August 4, 2011 / In Memory of Mark Duggan' also from *Citizen* (Graywolf Press, USA, 2014; Penguin Books, UK, 2015), by permission of The Permissions Company, LLC on behalf of Graywolf Press, www.graywolfpress.org. **Vidyan Ravinthiran:** 'Aubade', 'Ceylon' and 'My Sri Lankan Family' from *The Million-petalled Flower of Being Here* (Bloodaxe Books, 2019). **Deryn Rees-Jones:** 'Meteor' from *Burying the Wren* (Seren, 2010), by permission of the publisher; 'Home' from *Home on the Move: Two poems go on a journey*, ed. Manuela Perteghella & Ricarda Vidal (Parthian Books, 2019), by permission of the author. **Roger Reeves:** 'Someday I'll Love Roger Reeves' from *King Me* (Copper Canyon Press, 2014), by permission of The Permissions Company, LLC on behalf of Copper Canyon Press, www.coppercanyonpress.org. **Denise Riley:** 'Listening for Lost People', from *Say Something Back* (Picador, 2016), by permission of Macmillan Publishers Ltd. **Alberto Ríos:** 'We Are of a Tribe' from *Goodbye Mexico: Poems of Remembrance*, ed. Sarah Cortez (Texas Review Press, 2014), by permission of the author. **Ana Ristović:** 'The Body' from *Directions for Use*, tr. Steven & Maja Teref (Zephyr Press, 2017), by permission of The Permissions Company, LLC on behalf of Zephyr Press. **Max Ritvo:** 'Poem to My Litter' and 'Heaven Is Us Being a Flower Together' from *Four Reincarnations* (Milkweed Editions, 2016); 'Cachexia' from *The Final Voicemails*, ed. Louise Glück (Milkweed Editions, 2018). **Roger Robinson:** 'To His Homeland' from *The Butterfly Hotel* (Peepal Tree Press, 2013); 'The Portrait Museum', 'The Father' and 'Doppelgänger' from *A Portable Paradise* (Peepal Tree Press, 2019). **Pattiann Rogers:** epigraph on page 67 from *The Dream of the Marsh Wren* (Milkweed Editions, 1999). **Valérie Rouzeau:** extract from 'Vrouz' from *Talking Vrouz*, tr. Susan Wicks (Arc Publications, 2013). **Tuvia Ruebner:** 'Wonder' from *In the Illuminated Dark: Selected Poems of Tuvia Ruebner*, tr. Rachel Tzvia Back. (Hebrew Union College Press and the University of Pittsburgh Press, 2015). **Mary Ruefle:** 'Timberland' and 'Trust Me' from *Apparition Hill*, copyright © 2002 by Mary Ruefle, by permission of The Permissions Company, LLC on behalf of CavanKerry Press, cavankerrypress.org.

Jacob Saenz: 'Sweeping the States', from *Throwing the Crown* (Copper Canyon Press, 2018), by permission of The Permissions Company, LLC on behalf of Copper Canyon Press, www.coppercanyonpress.org. **Lawrence Sail:** 'Recognition' from *Guises* (Bloodaxe Books, 2020). **Jacob Sam-La Rose:** 'Never' and 'The Other End of the Line' from *Breaking Silence* (Bloodaxe Books, 2011). **Mikeas Sánchez:** 'What Is it Worth?', tr. Wendy Call, from *Modern Poetry in Translation*, 2019 no.3. **Peter Sansom:** 'Mini Van' from

Careful What You Wish For (Carcanet Press, 2015). **Mikiro Sasaki:** 'Sentiments', from *Sky Navigation Homeward: New & Selected Poems*, tr. Mitsuko Ohno, Beverley Curran & Nobuaki Tochigi (Dedalus Press, 2019). **Vijay Seshadri:** 'Bright Copper Kettles' from *3 Sections* (Graywolf Press, 2013), by permission of The Permissions Company, LLC on behalf of Graywolf Press, www.graywolfpress.org. **Jo Shapcott:** 'Of Mutability' from *Of Mutability* (Faber & Faber, 2010). **Solmaz Sharif:** 'Look' from *Look* (Graywolf Press, 2016), by permission of The Permissions Company, LLC on behalf of Graywolf Press, www.graywolfpress. org. **Ruth Sharman:** 'Fragments' and 'Hilltop' from *Scarlet Tiger* (Templar Poetry, 2016), by permission of the author. **Brenda Shaughnessy:** 'I Wish I Had More Sisters' from *Our Andromeda* (Graywolf Press, 2012), by permission of The Permissions Company, LLC on behalf of Graywolf Press, www.graywolfpress. org. **Natalie Shaw:** 'Like when we went to the cinema that time' from *Oh be quiet* (Against the Grain Poetry Press, 2020), by permission of the author. **Warsan Shire:** 'Conversations about home (at the deportation centre)', from *teaching my mother how to give birth* (flipped eye publishing, 2011), by permission of the author and flipped eye publishing limited; 'for women who are difficult to love' © 2016 by Rocking Chair Books Ltd, by permission of Rocking Chair Books Limited. **Evie Shockley:** 'supply and demand' from *semiautomatic* (Wesleyan University Press, 2017). **Penelope Shuttle:** 'Outgrown' from *Unsent: New & Selected Poems* (Bloodaxe Books, 2012), by permission of David Higham Associates. **Ribka Sibhatu:** 'In Lampedusa', tr. André Naffis-Sahely, from *Modern Poetry in Translation*, 2016 No.1.), by permission of the translator. **Richard Siken:** 'Landscape with Fruit Rot and Millipede' from *War of the Foxes* (Copper Canyon Press, 2015), by permission of The Permissions Company, LLC on behalf of Copper Canyon Press, www.coppercanyonpress.org. **Charles Simic:** 'Mirrors at 4 A.M.' from *New and Selected Poems 1962-2012* (Houghton Mifflin Harcourt, 2013). **Safiya Sinclair:** 'Autobiography' and 'Family Portrait' from *Cannibal* (University of Nebraska Press, 2016). **Jasvir Singh:** epigraph on page 217, 'Thought for the Day', *Today programme*, BBC Radio 4, 20 February 2020. **Peter Sirr:** four extracts from '1. Continual Visit' from 'The Rooms', from *The Rooms* (The Gallery Press, 2014), by permission of The Gallery Press, Loughcrew, Oldcastle, Co. Meath, Ireland; 'Ode' by permission of the author. **Danez Smith:** 'dinosaurs in the hood' from *Don't Call Us Dead* (Graywolf Press, USA, 2017; Chatto & Windus, UK, 2018), by permission of The Permissions Company, LLC on behalf of Graywolf Press, www.graywolfpress.org; 'the bullet was a girl', © 2015 by Danez Smith, originally published in *Poem-a-Day* on 3 September 2015 by the Academy of American Poets. **Patricia Smith:** 'That Chile Emmett in the Casket' and '10-Year-Old Shot Three Times, but She's Fine' from *Incendiary Art* (Triquarterly Books/Northwestern University Press, USA, 2017; Bloodaxe Books, UK, 2019), by permission of Northwestern University Press. **Tracy K. Smith:** 'The World Is Your Beautiful Younger Sister' and 'Nanluoxiang Alley' (from 'Eternity') from *Wade in the Water* (Penguin Books, 2018). **Göran Sonnevi:** 'Whose life, you asked...' from *A Child Is Not a Knife: Selected Poems*, ed. & tr. Rika Lesser (Princeton University Press, 1993). **Fadwa Souliman:** 'For Lana Sadiq', tr. Marilyn Hacker, first published in *Modern Poetry in Translation*, 2017 no.2, from *Blazons: New and Selected Poems 2000-2018* by Marilyn Hacker (Carcanet Press, 2019). **Jean Sprackland:** 'CCTV' from *Sleeping Keys* (Cape, 2013), by permission of the Random House Group Ltd. **William Stafford:** 'You Reading This, Be Ready' from *The Way It Is: New & Selected Poems* (Graywolf Press, 1998), by permission of The Permissions Company, LLC on behalf of Graywolf Press, www.graywolfpress.org. **A.E. Stallings:** 'Olives' from *Olives* (TriQuarterly Books/Northwestern University Press, 2012); 'Like, the Sestina' from *Like* (Farrar, Straus & Giroux, 2018). **Aleš Šteger:** 'Egg' and 'Chocolate' from *The Book of Things*, tr. Brian Henry (BOA Editions, 2010), by permission of The Permissions Company, LLC on behalf of BOA Editions, www.boaeditions.org. **Anne Stevenson:** 'Anaethesia' from *Completing the Circle* (Bloodaxe Books, 2020). **Gerda Stevenson:** 'Hands' from *WRITE where we are NOW* (Manchester Metropolitan University, https://www2.mmu.ac.uk/write/ 2020), by permission of the author. **Ruth Stone:** 'The Excuse' and 'Wanting' from *What Love Comes To: New & Selected Poems* (Copper Canyon Press, USA, 2008; Bloodaxe Books, UK, 2009), by permission of Bloodaxe Books Ltd. **Mark Strand:** 'Lines for Winter' from *Selected Poems* by Mark Strand, copyright © 1979, 1980 Mark Strand, by permission of Alfred A. Knopf, an imprint of the Knopf Doubleday Publishing Group, a division of Penguin Random House LLC, all rights reserved. **Phoebe Stuckes:** 'Kiss me quick', 'Gold Hoop Earrings' and 'Attempt' from Platinum Blonde (Bloodaxe Books, 2020). **Arundhathi Subramaniam:** 'Home' from *Where I Live: New & Selected Poems* (Bloodaxe Books, 2009). **Hannah Sullivan:** extract from 'The Sandpit after Rain' from *Three Poems* (Faber & Faber, 2018). **Matthew Sweeney:** 'My Life as a Painter' from *My Life as a Painter* (Bloodaxe Books, 2018); 'The Tube' from *Shadow of the Owl* (Bloodaxe Books, 2020). **Anna Swir:** 'My Body Effervesces' and 'The Same Inside' from *Talking to My Body*, tr. Czeslaw Miłosz & Leonard Nathan (Copper Canyon Press, USA, 1996), translation copyright © 1996 Czeslaw Milosz & Leonard Nathan, by permission of The Permissions Company, LLC on behalf of Copper Canyon Press, www.coppercanyonpress.org. **George Szirtes:** 'Water', from 'Three Poems for Sebastião Salgado', from *New & Collected Poems* (Bloodaxe Books, 2008). **Wisława Szymborska:** 'Some People', 'The Day After – Without Us', 'Cat in an Empty Apartment' and 'A Contribution to Statistics', tr. Stanisław Barańczak & Clare Cavanagh, from *Map: Collected and Last Poems* (Houghton Mifflin Harcourt, 2015).

David Tait: 'By Degrees' and 'The Virus at My Window' from *WRITE where we are NOW* (Manchester Metropolitan University, https://www2.mmu.ac.uk/write/ 2020), by permission of the author. **R.S. Thomas:** epigraph on page 343, BBC Radio 3, November 1991. **Sara Berkeley Tolchin:** 'Burrow

Beach' from *What Just Happened* (The Gallery Press, 2015), by permission of The Gallery Press, Loughcrew, Oldcastle, Co. Meath, Ireland. **Tomas Tranströmer**: 'Allegro', 'The Half-Finished Heaven' and 'Schubertiana' from *New Collected Poems*, tr. Robin Fulton (Bloodaxe Books, 2011). **Jessica Traynor**: 'In Praise of Fixer Women' from *The Quick* (Dedalus Press, 2018), by permission of Dedalus Press. **Natasha Trethewey**: 'Flounder' from *Domestic Work* (Graywolf Press, 2000), by permission of The Permissions Company, LLC on behalf of Graywolf Press, www.graywolfpress.org; 'Help, 1968' from *Thrall* (Houghton Mifflin, 2012). **Katharine Towers**: 'Childhood' from *The Remedies* (Picador, 2016), by permission of Macmillan Publishers Ltd. **Hama Tuma**: 'Just a Nobody', tr. the author, from *Modern Poetry in Translation*, 2016 No.1. **Tim Turnbull**: 'Ode on a Grayson Perry Urn' from *Caligula on Ice* (Donut Press, 2009), by permission of the author. **Chase Twichell**: 'Herd of Humans' and 'Birdsong' from *Things as It Is* (Copper Canyon Press, 2018), by permission of The Permissions Company, LLC on behalf of Copper Canyon Press, www.coppercanyonpress.org.

Jack Underwood: 'Happiness' and 'William' from *Happiness* (Faber & Faber, 2015); 'Alpha Step' from *Poetry*, 215 no 3 (February 2020), by permission of the author.

M. Vasalis: 'The IJsselmeer Dam', tr. David Colmer, first published online by the David Reid Poetry Translation Prize (winning entry) 2011, original poem 'Afsluitdijk' from *Verzamelde Gedichten* (Van Oorschot, Amsterdam, 2002), by permission of the translator and publisher. **Jan Erik Vold**: 'The Fact That No Birds Sing' from *En som het Abel Ek* (Gyldendal, Oslo, 1988), translation by Jan Erik Vold first published on *Poetry International*, 2012, by permission of the author. **Ocean Vuong**: 'Someday I'll Love Ocean Vuong' from *Night Sky with Exit Wounds* (Jonathan Cape, 2017), by permission of the Random House Group Ltd.

Jan Wagner: 'quince jelly', tr. Iain Galbraith from *Self-Portrait with a Swarm of Bees: Selected Poems* (Arc Publications, 2015). **Sarah Westcott**: 'The Great Pacific Garbage Patch' from *Slant Light* (Pavilion Poets/Liverpool University Press, 2016). **Jay Whittaker**: 'The call' and 'Bedfellow' from *Wristwatch* (Cinnamon Press, 2017). **Menno Wigman**: 'Everyone Is Beautiful Today', tr. David Colmer, from *Window-Cleaner Sees Paintings* (Arc Publications, 2016); 'Body, my body', tr. Sean O'Brien, Karlien van den Beukel & Menno Wigman (Poettrio, 2017), also published in *Poem: International English Language Quarterly*, 6 (3), 2018, ed. Fiona Sampson, by permission of Newcastle University. **Chrissy Williams**: 'The Burning of the Houses' from *Bear* (Bloodaxe Books, 2017). **Robert Wrigley**: 'A Lock of Her Hair' from *The Church of Omnivorous Light: Selected Poems* (Bloodaxe Books, 2013).

Dean Young: 'Street of Sailmakers' from *Bender: New & Selected Poems* (Copper Canyon Press, 2012), by permission of The Permissions Company, LLC on behalf of Copper Canyon Press, www.coppercanyonpress.org. **Kevin Young**: 'Reward' from *Most Way Home* (Zoland Books, 2000), copyright © 2000 by Kevin Young, with the permission of Zoland Books/Steerforth Press.

Adam Zagajewski: 'Refugees' and 'The Three Kings' from *Selected Poems* (Faber & Faber, 2004); 'Music Heard with You' and 'Describing Paintings' from *Eternal Enemies* (Farrar, Straus & Giroux, 2008); 'Chaconne' from *Asymmetry: Poems* (Farrar, Straus & Giroux, 2018). **Zhang Zao**: 'Mirror', tr. Fiona Sze-Lorrain, from *Modern Poetry in Translation* ('Strange Tracks'), 2013 no.1, and forthcoming in *Mirror: Poems* by Zhang Zao, tr. Fiona Sze-Lorrain (Zephyr Press).

Every effort has been made to trace copyright holders of the poems published in this book. The editor and publisher apologise if any material has been included without permission or without the appropriate acknowledgement, and would be glad to be told of anyone who has not been consulted.

INDEX OF WRITERS

INDEX OF TITLES & FIRST LINES